Learning Puppet

Build intelligent software stacks with the Puppet
configuration management suite

Jussi Heinonen

BIRMINGHAM - MUMBAI

Learning Puppet

First published: August 2015

Production reference: 1270815

Published by Packt Publishing Ltd.
Livery Place
35 Livery Street
Birmingham B3 2PB, UK.

ISBN 978-1-78439-983-2

www.packtpub.com

Credits

Author
Jussi Heinonen

Reviewers
Vlastimil Holer
Ashish Jaiswal
Amar Krishna
Eric Stonfer

Commissioning Editor
Kartikey Pandey

Acquisition Editor
Nikhil Karkal

Content Development Editor
Anish Sukumaran

Technical Editors
Dhiraj Chandanshive
Pramod Kumavat

Copy Editors
Janbal Dharmaraj
Rashmi Sawant

Project Coordinator
Izzat Contractor

Proofreader
Safis Editing

Indexer
Hemangini Bari

Graphics
Sheetal Aute

Production Coordinator
Shantanu N. Zagade

Cover Work
Shantanu N. Zagade

About the Author

Jussi Heinonen is a seasoned systems developer and an open source enthusiast who lives in Cambridge, UK. He has been working for various software businesses in the media and telecommunications sectors since 1998. During this period, he acquired a few Linux certifications, and more recently, in 2014 and 2015, he passed the Puppet Certified Professional exam. He currently works at the Financial Times as a senior integration engineer. His role revolves around building and designing software delivery pipelines that enable developers to create high-quality software quickly and frequently. In his spare time, he likes to spend time with his family and loves to watch games at Arsenal Football Club.

There are many people who have contributed to this book, and I'd like to take this opportunity to say thanks to them.

First and foremost, a big thank you to the folks at Packt Publishing, especially Nikhil and Anish, for giving me the opportunity to write this book. Your support and guidance throughout the writing process has been invaluable.

Secondly, a huge credit to the reviewers, in particular, Vlastimil Holer, who have helped me streamline the content of this book and improve the reading experience.

Thirdly, I'd like to thank my lovely wife, Thury, and my children, Markus, Jakob, and Elisa, for allowing me to take occasional breaks from daddy duties to concentrate on writing this book.

Finally, I would like to thank my colleagues at the Financial Times, namely the members of the Integration Engineering team and Team CMS. In the past years, I've been working with them in various projects involving Puppet. This has enabled me to hone my Puppet skills and learn how to use this tool to solve specific business problems.

About the Reviewers

Vlastimil Holer is a systems engineer who focuses on automation. He has worked with Unix-like systems for more than a decade, and he first used Puppet in 2008 while preparing and managing the growing deployment of the GoodData cloud BI on Amazon EC2. Currently, he is working on the CERIT Scientific Cloud project at Masaryk University, where he manages and automates the computing, cloud, and storage infrastructures.

Ashish Kumar Jaiswal has been working for the past 4 and a half years and has worked on Puppet for almost 4 years. Puppet was the root cause for the growth of his technical career.

He is currently working on a project called obmondo.com—an "Operations as a service" project—using Puppet to automate server configuration and management. This project sets up the whole Puppet infrastructure without a Puppet server, and it's just far off to click on the profile you want your server to have.

I would like to thank Corey Ralph, an Aussie guy who was my manager at my previous organization, and my wife, Dhara Jaiswal. She is just too kind at heart. I would also like to thank my beautiful family, which includes my mom, dad, and two sisters.

Amar Krishna is a DevOps professional and loves to automate everything that comes his way. He has used Puppet and scripting for automation. He started his career with Linux and PHP and moved on to high-performance computing, where he worked with one of the largest clusters in India. Then, he moved on to the cloud computing world, where he worked on tools such as CloudStack and OpenStack. He was involved in one of the biggest cloud projects in India. Currently, he is working at Reliance Jio Infocomm.

This was his first book as a reviewer and he loved it. He would like to review more books in the future.

I would really like to thank all my colleagues for helping me.

www.PacktPub.com

Support files, eBooks, discount offers, and more

For support files and downloads related to your book, please visit www.PacktPub.com.

Did you know that Packt offers eBook versions of every book published, with PDF and ePub files available? You can upgrade to the eBook version at www.PacktPub.com and as a print book customer, you are entitled to a discount on the eBook copy. Get in touch with us at service@packtpub.com for more details.

At www.PacktPub.com, you can also read a collection of free technical articles, sign up for a range of free newsletters and receive exclusive discounts and offers on Packt books and eBooks.

https://www2.packtpub.com/books/subscription/packtlib

Do you need instant solutions to your IT questions? PacktLib is Packt's online digital book library. Here, you can search, access, and read Packt's entire library of books.

Why subscribe?

- Fully searchable across every book published by Packt
- Copy and paste, print, and bookmark content
- On demand and accessible via a web browser

Free access for Packt account holders

If you have an account with Packt at www.PacktPub.com, you can use this to access PacktLib today and view 9 entirely free books. Simply use your login credentials for immediate access.

Table of Contents

Preface

This book is a step-by-step guide to get started with Puppet development, and use Puppet modules as the building blocks to deploy production-ready application clusters in the virtual environment.

The journey begins with the installation of the development environment on the VirtualBox hypervisor and the installation of the Puppet Learning VM that will be used platforms to test and develop Puppet modules.

You will learn how to manage virtual machines and snapshots effectively and enhance the developer's experience with advanced VirtualBox features.

Once the development environment is up and running, this book will focus on Puppet module development in detail. You will be guided through the process of how to utilize the existing modules that are available in the public module repository, write your own modules, and use modules to deploy a real-world web application that includes features such as monitoring and load balancing. When an application cluster is deployed, the focus shifts to how to scale the environment and turn the static configuration into a dynamic one through stored configurations and PuppetDB. The latter part of the book will provide you with practical advice on Puppet troubleshooting, and how to manage your environment with a wealth of features provided by the Puppet Enterprise Console. Starting from the basics, this step-by-step guide will walk you through the process of becoming the master of your own Puppets.

What this book covers

Chapter 1, Puppet Development in Isolation, teaches you how to set up the local Puppet development environment quickly and start experimenting with Puppet on the command line in a matter of minutes.

Chapter 2, Managing Packages in Puppet, shows you how to restore the virtual machine snapshot and set up shared folders and host-only networking to enhance the developer's experience. You can also learn how to purge a software package using Puppet.

Chapter 3, My First Puppet Module, explains the concept of Puppet modules. You will learn how to install third-party Puppet modules from Puppet Forge and how to create and use your own modules.

Chapter 4, Monitoring Your Web Server, teaches you how to use Puppet to install the Nagios monitoring server and how to add a web server to monitor using Puppet.

Chapter 5, Load Balancing the Cluster, introduces you to parameterized classes and defined types and teaches you to use these to configure load balancing in the cluster.

Chapter 6, Scaling Up the Puppet Environment, introduces you to the Puppet Master, which enables you to centrally manage a large number of Puppet Agent nodes. You will learn how to sign Puppet Agent certificates and join agents to the Puppet environment.

Chapter 7, Making the Configuration Dynamic, teaches you how to use Puppet's Exported Resources to pass Puppet resources between nodes. This chapter also introduces you to the PuppetDB queries that are used to discover services in the cluster.

Chapter 8, Extending Puppet, teaches you how to extend Puppet beyond its built-in functionality. This chapter introduces you to custom facts and functions.

Chapter 9, The Puppet Enterprise Console, explores the Puppet Enterprise Console, which is a web-based management console that runs on the Puppet Master node. In this chapter, we will learn about Role-based Access Control and how to classify nodes using the External Node Classifier.

Chapter 10, Troubleshooting Puppet, teaches you how to identify the most common issues in Puppet and how to tackle them. This chapter provides you with basic troubleshooting skills.

What you need for this book

A computer that runs a Windows, Mac, or Linux operating system. The computer should have a minimum of 4 GB of memory and 10 GB of free hard drive space.

Who this book is for

This book is aimed at people who are new to configuration management and IT automation processes. You may have a background in software development, and you may have set yourself a goal of learning how to take full control of the software deployment process; or perhaps, you are more experienced in the system administration field, and are looking for better ways to manage system configuration changes at scale. Although previous experience in IT is helpful, it is not a requirement. This book will get you up to speed with Puppet development quickly and effortlessly.

Conventions

In this book, you will find a number of styles of text that distinguish between different kinds of information. Here are some examples of these styles, and an explanation of their meaning.

Code words in text, database table names, folder names, filenames, file extensions, pathnames, dummy URLs, user input, and Twitter handles are shown as follows: "Experiment with the Puppet command-line commands `puppet describe`, `puppet resource`, and `puppet apply`."

A block of code is set as follows:

```
file {
  '/etc/sysconfig/network-scripts/ifcfg-eth1':
    content =>
'DEVICE="eth1"
BOOTPROTO="dhcp"
ONBOOT="yes"',
}
```

Any command-line input or output is written as follows:

```
puppet describe --list | less
```

New terms and **important words** are shown in bold. Words that you see on the screen, in menus or dialog boxes for example, appear in the text like this: "Start the Oracle VM VirtualBox Manager and select **Import Appliance** from the **File** menu."

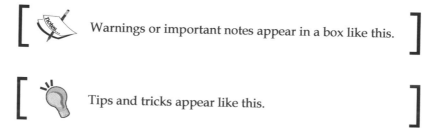

> Warnings or important notes appear in a box like this.

> Tips and tricks appear like this.

Reader feedback

Feedback from our readers is always welcome. Let us know what you think about this book—what you liked or may have disliked. Reader feedback is important for us to develop titles that you really get the most out of.

To send us general feedback, simply send an e-mail to feedback@packtpub.com, and mention the book title via the subject of your message.

If there is a topic that you have expertise in and you are interested in either writing or contributing to a book, see our author guide at www.packtpub.com/authors.

Customer support

Now that you are the proud owner of a Packt book, we have a number of things to help you to get the most from your purchase.

Downloading the example code

You can download the example code files from your account at http://www.packtpub.com for all the Packt Publishing books you have purchased. If you purchased this book elsewhere, you can visit http://www.packtpub.com/support and register to have the files e-mailed directly to you.

Errata

Although we have taken every care to ensure the accuracy of our content, mistakes do happen. If you find a mistake in one of our books—maybe a mistake in the text or the code—we would be grateful if you could report this to us. By doing so, you can save other readers from frustration and help us improve subsequent versions of this book. If you find any errata, please report them by visiting `http://www.packtpub.com/submit-errata`, selecting your book, clicking on the **Errata Submission Form** link, and entering the details of your errata. Once your errata are verified, your submission will be accepted and the errata will be uploaded to our website or added to any list of existing errata under the Errata section of that title.

To view the previously submitted errata, go to `https://www.packtpub.com/books/content/support` and enter the name of the book in the search field. The required information will appear under the **Errata** section.

Piracy

Piracy of copyrighted material on the Internet is an ongoing problem across all media. At Packt, we take the protection of our copyright and licenses very seriously. If you come across any illegal copies of our works in any form on the Internet, please provide us with the location address or website name immediately so that we can pursue a remedy.

Please contact us at `copyright@packtpub.com` with a link to the suspected pirated material.

We appreciate your help in protecting our authors and our ability to bring you valuable content.

Questions

If you have a problem with any aspect of this book, you can contact us at `questions@packtpub.com`, and we will do our best to address the problem.

1
Puppet Development in Isolation

Welcome dear reader. You have arrived at the starting point of the journey to learn Puppet. Whether you have a background in software development, IT infrastructure, or somewhere in between or there about, I believe you have heard people talking about Puppet, and how Puppet can help you automate the configuration management and software deployment processes. I've been using Puppet on a daily basis for the past 4 years, and I feel that it has improved my quality of life at work a lot. I have a background in system administration, and I build software stacks from a set of packages, configuration files, and other types of resources. Prior to Puppet, I used to use various self-written scripts to automate the deployment processes in order to make the process repeatable, but I'm doing much less of that since I discovered Puppet. The problem with scripts, as I see it, is that they are hard to transfer across and to hand over, as scripts are often complex and difficult to read by people who are unfamiliar with the language in which the scripts are written.

Puppet can help you overcome this issue in a two-fold solution:

- Puppet manages resources, such as files, users, and services out of the box. Instead of writing custom Shell scripts to manage resources, we write the Puppet script, which we call the manifest.

- Puppet has its own language called Puppet DSL that is easy to understand by the developers as well as the people involved in the infrastructure.

The moment I start feeling bored with the project I'm working on, because I'm not learning new skills any more, I start to wrap things up, finalize the documentation, and tidy up all the loose ends. The handover process for the project used to involve several days of training followed by a period of several weeks of questions about how the scripts work, and how to change the logic in them. The questions often were as simple as "How do you do this thing in Bash?".

Now the logic has been moved away from the custom scripts to Puppet manifests that are written in Puppet DSL. When I get a question such as "How do I do this in Puppet?", I can reply by saying "Here is a book about Puppet called Learning Puppet. By the end of this chapter, you'll already know how to manage your systems with Puppet". There are dozens of books written on Puppet. This one aims to be a little bit different from those by taking a slightly more practical approach to Puppet development. We will perform the following tasks here:

- Download the Puppet Learning VM
- Take a snapshot of the Learning VM to enable an easy rollback to the original system state
- Start the Learning VM
- Experiment with the Puppet command-line commands: `puppet describe`, `puppet resource`, and `puppet apply`

Puppet Manifests

Before we get our hands dirty with Puppet, I'd like to expand the topic a little bit.

As you may already know, Puppet is a configuration management tool that enables you to build application stacks from a set of files that the Puppet community refers to as the manifests.

Manifests are a set of instructions that describes how operating systems and application resources are managed by Puppet and how the system configuration should look like after the manifest has been applied to the system.

Manifests are written in a language called Puppet DSL, where DSL stands for Domain Specific Language. DSL is a commonly used term for programming languages that are not general-purpose languages.

When I write Puppet manifests, I consider it a development process. I call it a development process because the process consists of multiple rounds of iterations during which the manifest evolves.

Here is a simplified overview of the Puppet manifest development process:

For iteration 1, follow the given steps:

Begin by writing the initial manifest that installs a software package > Apply the manifest > Ensure that package is installed.

For iteration 2, follow the given steps:

Extend the manifest to apply the configuration for the package > Apply the manifest > Ensure that the configuration was correctly applied.

For iteration 3, follow the next steps:

Add the logic to start up the service > Apply the manifest > Ensure that the service started > Finish.

In this example, the development processes had three rounds of iterations, each of them containing a task called Apply the manifest.

 The manifest develops from the initial version, which does very little to the version of the manifest that manages the whole stack.

Imagine a situation where we write a manifest that creates a Linux user account with a root level access but no password. An account with a root level access is equivalent to a local administrator account on a Windows computer. When you apply the manifest on your computer, Puppet will create a user account on your computer without a password, which makes your computer vulnerable to attacks.

In contrast, if you apply the manifest in an isolated development environment, the configuration change is easy to undo as you can quickly tear down the environment and rebuild it from scratch.

Another reason for developing manifests in isolation is consistency. My choice of operating system is Ubuntu Linux and I run it on MacBook Pro hardware. You may run Mac OS X on the Mac mini, and a friend of mine just downgraded to Windows 7 as she was unhappy with the functionality offered by Windows 8.1.

Each of these operating system flavors will behave slightly differently, although all of them do share similar capabilities such as running a virtualization software.

To ensure that the examples and exercises covered in this book produce consistent results for you and me, we will start our journey by installing the VirtualBox virtualization software package, which enables us to run a set of virtual machines that forms our isolated development environment.

Downloading Oracle VirtualBox

 To complete this task, you will need an Internet connection and a web browser such as Mozilla Firefox.

If you prefer to use an alternative virtualization technology, you are free to do so as long as the software supports the following functionalities, and you know how to configure the software to enable the following functionalities:

- The ability to run multiple virtual machines concurrently
- Virtual machine snapshots
- Support for shared folders
- Support for host-only networking
- Support for the Open Virtualization Format (.ovf) and Virtual Machine Disk (.vmdk) file formats

This book is based on Oracle VirtualBox Version 4.3. To ensure that the configuration examples this book provides work well, I'd recommend that you download VirtualBox Version 4.3.

VirtualBox 4.3 can be downloaded for free from the VirtualBox website at https://www.virtualbox.org/wiki/Download_Old_Builds_4_3 (Google: virtualbox download 4.3).

On the download page, you should see a category for the VirtualBox platform packages. Select the download option that is most suitable for your operating system:

- Windows users should download VirtualBox for the Windows hosts
- If your computer runs Apple software, choose VirtualBox for OS X hosts
- If you are a Linux user, you can either download the VirtualBox for Linux hosts or alternatively, you may check the software repositories configured on your system and see whether VirtualBox is made available for your Linux distribution

When you have downloaded the VirtualBox installation package, it is time to install it. Double-click on the installation package that you downloaded, and you will see the installation wizard pop up on the screen.

Install VirtualBox with the default options, and we will take a look at how to configure VirtualBox to optimize it for our development environment.

Downloading the Puppet Learning VM

You now should have VirtualBox installed, which can run virtual machines for our isolated development environment.

We will be using the Puppet Learning VM Version 3.7.1, which I've uploaded to an Amazon S3 bucket.

The Puppet Learning VM is a virtual machine image that comes with preinstalled Puppet software. Installing Puppet is not a difficult or too time-consuming task, but it will save us all a little bit of our valuable time if we use the Puppet Learning VM, so we can start experimenting with Puppet quicker.

Follow these steps to complete the download process:

1. To download the Puppet Learning VM Version 3.7.1, go to `http://learning-puppet-packt.s3-website-eu-west-1.amazonaws.com`, and click on the link that says *To download Puppet Learning VM v.3.7.1 click here*.

2. Once the download is finished, you should find a file called `learn_puppet_centos-6.5-pe-3.7.1-ptb-ovf.zip` in the download folder of your web browser.

3. Double-click on the `learn_puppet_centos-6.5-pe-3.7.1-ptb-ovf.zip` file to open the Zip file archive manager and extract the files to the filesystem.

4. At this stage, I'd recommend that you create a dedicated directory under your home directory that acts as a repository for virtual machine files as well as the Puppet manifest files that we will create later in this book.

5. Once the zip archive has been extracted to the directory, you should find the `learn_puppet_centos-6.5.ovf` and `learn_puppet_centos-6.5-disk1.vmdk` files on the disk.

Next, we will import the virtual machine to the VirtualBox, take a snapshot of it, and then we should be ready to start experimenting with Puppet.

Importing the Puppet Learning VM into VirtualBox

The extracted virtual machine image file has to be imported to VirtualBox before we can launch it. Here are the steps to import the image to VirtualBox:

1. Start the Oracle VM VirtualBox Manager and select **Import Appliance** from the **File** menu. This will start the **Import Virtual Appliance** wizard:

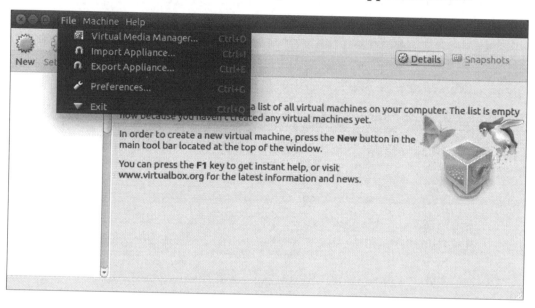

2. Click on the browser button that says **Choose a virtual appliance file to import** when you hover the mouse pointer over the button. Now you can navigate to the directory where the VirtualBox files were extracted to. On my computer, I extracted the files to the `/home/jussi/learning/vm` directory, so I'll go to this location and select the file called `learn_puppet_centos-6.5.ovf`. OVF is a virtual machine template file that is an open standard XML file:

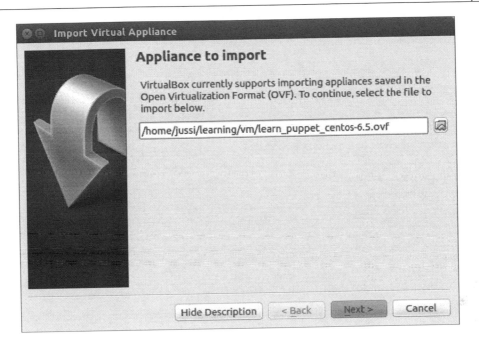

3. Once the file is selected, click on **Open**, then click on **Next**, and you should now be in the **Appliance settings** view:

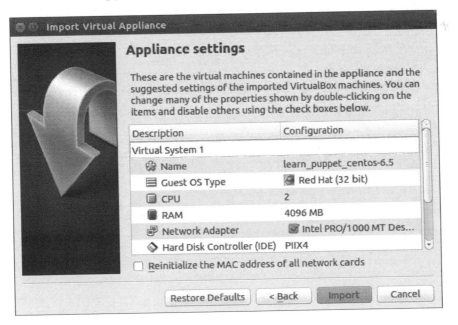

Here, we can configure the virtual machine settings, such as increasing the amount of memory or adding more processor cores.

We don't need to change the default settings, so let's just click on the **Import** button to start the import process:

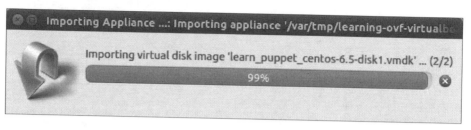

Virtual machine snapshots

While the virtual machine appliance is importing, I'll give you a quick introduction to virtual machine snapshots and how we can use them.

A virtual machine snapshot stores the state of the virtual machine at a particular point of time. We can have multiple snapshots of a virtual machine, and we can easily switch between them.

The example I've just given may give you impression that snapshots are backups. They are not!

Snapshots only contain the data that has changed since the previous snapshot, and therefore, an individual snapshot cannot be used to reconstruct the whole virtual machine. To reconstruct the virtual machine from the snapshot, VirtualBox will need the virtual disk file (`learn_puppet_centos-6.5-disk1.vmdk`), all prior snapshots plus the snapshot you want to restore the state to.

When you create a snapshot of the virtual machine, which we will do shortly, you will tell VirtualBox to start writing changes to a snapshot file instead of the virtual machine disk file.

Every time you create a snapshot, VirtualBox creates a new snapshot file and starts writing changes to it.

The snapshots are laid out in the following type of tree structure:

If a virtual machine has only one snapshot and we delete it, then VirtualBox writes changes in the snapshot file onto the disk. If a virtual machine contains more than one snapshot and you delete one, then VirtualBox merges two consecutive snapshots.

Having many snapshots may have an impact on the disk's performance, because the disk operations have to traverse through many snapshots to find the file to make the changes. For disk performance reasons it is recommended that you delete older snapshots when they are no longer needed.

Snapshot of the virtual machine

Before we start the virtual machine, we should take a snapshot of it so that we can quickly revert to the point of time where we started.

To take a snapshot of the virtual machine and name it, follow the given steps:

1. First, select the virtual machine, then click on the **Snapshots** button at the top right-hand corner of the Oracle VM VirtualBox Manager window:

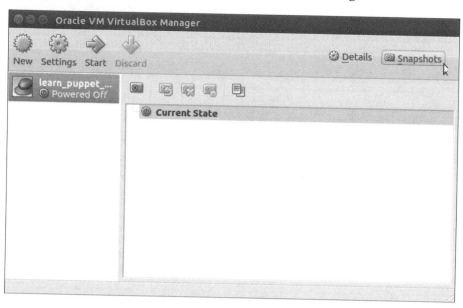

2. In the **Snapshots** view, click on the **Take snapshot** button:

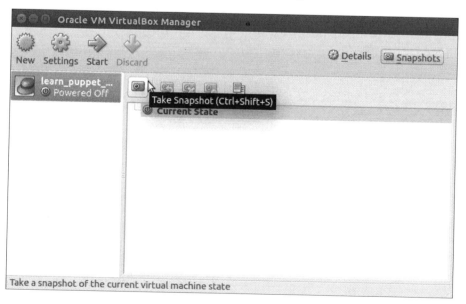

3. Provide a name for the snapshot, I have named it `Base image`. Then, click on **OK**:

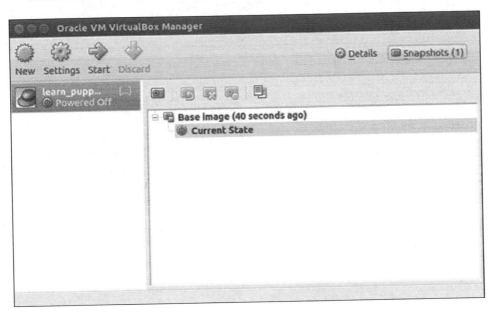

Now, we have a snapshot that enables us to go back to the previous state of the VM as we make changes to the system configuration.

Puppet on command line

Now it is the right time to start the real Puppet work:

1. Select the virtual machine from the list, and click on the **Start** button at the top of the window.

2. Once the virtual machine has booted up, you should see a login prompt:

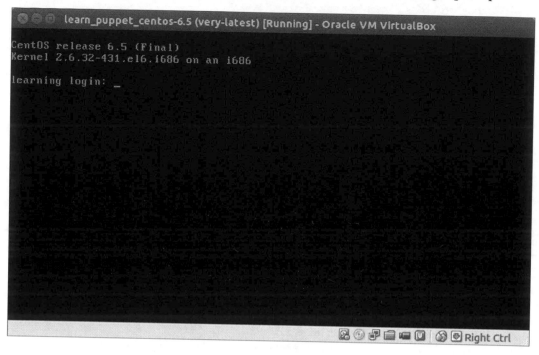

3. At the login prompt, type in the user name `root` and hit *Enter*. Then, type in password `puppet` and hit *Enter* again.

4. You have now entered the development environment, where we can start familiarizing with the Puppet commands and manage our system. You are free to play around and change the configuration as much as you like.

5. If you happen to break the environment, you can easily restore the original configuration from the snapshot as we did in the earlier paragraph.

Puppet version

The Puppet executable can be run from the command line. Let's begin with confirming which version of Puppet we are running. We can check the version by running the following command:

```
puppet --version
```

At the time of writing, the command run on the Learning VM, it shows the Version as 3.7.3 (Puppet Enterprise 3.7.1.).

The first Version number 3.7.3 is for the open source version of Puppet that we are using. The second Version number 3.7.1 is for the Puppet Enterprise version number.

What is the difference between these two versions? The difference between them is how these products are packaged, distributed, and supported.

The open source Puppet

The open source Puppet is the community-driven version of Puppet that is developed by the open source community and maintained by Puppet Labs. It can be used and distributed freely.

The Puppet Enterprise edition

The Puppet Enterprise edition is a distribution that is developed, maintained, and supported by Puppet Labs, which is the commercial arm behind Puppet.

Companies can purchase the Puppet Enterprise license from Puppet Labs, and in return, Puppet Labs provides support services and software updates for the Puppet Enterprise software bundle that enables companies to get up and running with Puppet quickly.

The Puppet Enterprise edition is free to use in environments that consist of 10 or less Puppet managed hosts.

The environment that we will be building throughout the course of this book will consist of four hosts only, which makes Puppet Enterprise a perfect fit for our goal of learning Puppet.

Puppet resources

So now we know how to extract the version using the Puppet command-line utility. Let's shift our focus to the resources next.

Resources in Puppet are known as types. Types are operating system resources such as a file, a user, or a package. There are tens of built-in types in Puppet, and in addition to these, you can create your own custom types to manage resources.

We will learn more about custom types later in *Chapter 5, Load Balancing the Cluster*, but for now we will take a look at the built-in types and see how to use them.

A complete list of available built-in types is available on the Puppet Labs website at http://docs.puppetlabs.com/references/latest/type.html.

Run the `puppet describe --list` command in the Learning VM to list all the built-in types known to Puppet.

The output will contain about 60 resources and their descriptions. To paginate the output, you can extend the command by adding `|` `less` to the end of it.

Here is the command to view the output page by page:

```
puppet describe --list | less
```

You should now be able to scroll the output up and down using the arrow keys, and you can exit the view by pressing *Q* on the keyboard.

All the Puppet types have attributes that are used to describe the characteristics of the resources we want Puppet to manage.

For example, the type user has attributes such as a name for the user name and a password for the user account password.

To list the available attributes for a specific type of resource, you can use the `puppet describe <type>` command. For example, to list the available attributes of a type user, you can run the `puppet describe user`, or `puppet describe user | less` command to paginate the output.

If you scroll down the list of attributes, you can find a password attribute that is used to set a password for the user account. Another attribute that you can find on the list is called `ensure`, which defines the state of the user account. The attribute can have three values:

- `present`: This ensures that an account is created unless it already exists
- `absent`: This ensures that the account is removed if it exists
- `role`: This is a specific user attribute of the Unix operating system, such as Oracle Solaris, and therefore it has has no meaning when running Puppet on Linux like we are doing

Managing resources from the command line

We can manage Puppet resources from the command line using the following syntax: `puppet resource <type> <name> <attribute1>=<value> <attribute2>=<value>`.

Let's create a user called `Elisa` on the system using Puppet. In the Learning VM terminal, type in the following command and and hit the *Enter* key:

```
puppet resource user Elisa ensure=present
```

When the command is executed successfully, it produces the following output:

The first line of the output displays a notice confirming that the user account `Elisa` was created by Puppet. Lines 2-4 show the syntax that we will be using when we declare resources in the Puppet manifest files. The manifest files will be explained more in detail later.

Let's take a look at the syntax line by line:

- Line 1: `Notice: /User[Elisa]/ensure: created`

  This displays a confirmation of an action that Puppet has created a user called `Elisa`.

- Line 2: `user { 'Elisa':`

  This declares a resource for a type user, which follows the opening curly brace (`{`), that indicates that the user resource name and optional attributes are to follow. The name `'Elisa':` at the end of the line sets the Puppet resource name, which will become the name of the user account. The Puppet resource name must contain a colon at the end.

- Line 3: `ensure => 'present'`

  This attribute means that a user account must be created unless it already exists.

- Line 4: `}`

  The closing curly brace indicates the end of the resource statement.

The name `Elisa` on line 2 has two use cases. Firstly, it declares the name of the Puppet resource. Each Puppet resource must have a unique name, otherwise Puppet reports an error.

Secondly, the name `Elisa` is used as the name of the user account that was created. If the user statement contains a name attribute (alongside the ensure attribute), then the value of the name attribute would become the name of the user account and the name `Elisa` would only be used as the Puppet resource name.

As the name attribute is omitted, Puppet will use the name for the Puppet resource name as well as for the user account name.

Declaring the following statement in the Puppet manifest would result in the Jakob user account being created in the system, as the name attribute would take priority over the Puppet resource name Elisa:

```
user { 'Elisa':
  ensure => 'present',
  name    => 'Jakob',
}
```

This produces an output that is similar to the following, although the numeric information in the output may vary between the systems:

```
uid=501(Elisa) gid=501(Elisa) groups=501(Elisa)
```

Next, we can remove the account Elisa from the system by setting the ensure attribute value to absent.

```
puppet resource user Elisa ensure=absent
```

Assuming that the command executes successfully, you should see the following output:

This output is very similar to how we created the user account Elisa except that line 1 confirms that the user account Elisa was removed and line 3 has the ensure attribute value set to absent, which results in the account being removed when declaring a resource in the Puppet manifest file.

To confirm whether Puppet really removed the account, you can run the command id Elisa again, which will confirm that the account no longer exists in the system.

The command `id Elisa` should produce the following output:

```
id: Elisa: No such user
```

Congratulations! You just did two system configuration changes using Puppet. It wasn't hard, right?

Puppet dry run

Sometimes, you want to simulate configuration changes without applying the changes to the system. This can be done by adding the `--noop` parameter after the resource keyword in the Puppet command.

To simulate account creation without creating the account, we can extend the previous user account creation command with the `--noop` option:

```
puppet resource user Elisa ensure=present --noop
```

Line1 in the output tells us that the user account does not exist in the system, and if you run the following command without the `--noop` option, Puppet would create an account:

```
Notice: /User[Elisa]/ensure: current_value absent, should be present
(noop)
user { 'Elisa':
  ensure => 'absent',
}
```

The `--noop` option comes in handy when testing Puppet commands for a syntax. To demonstrate this, we declare an invalid value `removed` for the attribute `ensure`:

```
puppet resource user Elisa ensure=removed --noop
```

Puppet will return an error that tells you that we have used an invalid value for the `ensure` attribute:

Use Puppet to examine the current state of resources

Puppet can also be used to query resources from the system. Information produced by the query can be helpful when we are uncertain about what syntax we should be using to create a resource.

Earlier, we created a user account called `Elisa`. This account was created without a password, which means that the account cannot be used for interactive logins. Let's recreate the user account and use the `password` attribute to set a password for the account.

As passwords on Linux are encrypted, we must provide them to the `password` attribute in the encrypted format.

We know that the user account root on the Learning VM uses the password `puppet`, but we yet don't know how the password would look like in the encrypted format.

No problem, as we can query the password with the command and then use the encrypted password when recreating the user account `Elisa`.

The following command shows all the attributes for the `root` user account:

```
Puppet resource user root
```

The preceding command produces the following output:

```
learn_puppet_centos-6.5 (very-latest) [Running] - Oracle VM VirtualBox
[root@learning ~]# puppet resource user root
user { 'root':
  ensure           => 'present',
  comment          => 'root',
  gid              => '0',
  home             => '/root',
  password         => '$1$jrm5tnjw$h8JJ9mCZLmJvIxvDLjw1M/',
  password_max_age => '99999',
  password_min_age => '0',
  shell            => '/bin/bash',
  uid              => '0',
}
[root@learning ~]#
```

Now we can create the user account `Elisa` with the `password` attribute, which is the same as the value of the `password` attribute for the user `root`.

The following command will create the user account `Elisa` that uses the password `puppet`:

```
puppet resource user Elisa ensure=present \
managehome=true \
password='$1$jrm5tnjw$h8JJ9mCZLmJvIxvDLjw1M/'
```

I've split the command into three lines with the backslash character at the end of the first two lines.

> The `$1$jrm5tnjw$h8JJ9mCZLmJvIxvDLjw1M/` string is a hash of the password `puppet`. Please note that we have to use single quotes around the password hash `'$1$jrm5tnjw$h8JJ9mCZLmJvIxvDLjw1M/'` because the string contains characters that the Linux command line otherwise interprets as a control character.

Now we can test whether we can log on to the system as the user `Elisa`.

Log out from the system using the `logout` command. Then, log in with the username `Elisa` and password `puppet`. You will see the following welcome screen, which confirms that the login of `Elisa` was successful:

Puppet is run as a user root

The root account in Linux is equivalent to an administrator account in the Windows operating system. This is the user account that is commonly used for system configuration changes.

The user account `Elisa` that we created does not have the same amount of privileges as the root account.

To change the system configuration in the protected areas of the operating system, we must run Puppet as a root user.

If you are still logged onto the system as user `Elisa`, you can try creating a user account and see what happens.

As the user `Elisa` is not configured to run Puppet, we will do our test using the Linux `adduser` command.

Let's see what response we get if we try to create a user called Jakob using the user Elisa:

```
useradd Jakob
```

The output of the preceding command shows you that the user Elisa did not have sufficient permissions to add a new user to the system:

```
/usr/sbin/useradd: Permission denied
```

To avoid possible permission issues on Puppet managed systems, Puppet runs as a user root that provides Puppet full control of the system to add and remove users, install and uninstall software packages, as well as manage system services.

In the end, Puppet is your new system administrator, which manages the system according to the instructions you have provided from the command line or in the form of the Puppet manifest.

Puppet DSL and manifests

I've mentioned Puppet manifests earlier, but I haven't yet explained what manifests are. Puppet manifests are text files that declare one or more Puppet resources. Instead of running Puppet resource commands on the command line, you can declare resources in the manifest file and apply the manifest to the system.

Puppet manifests uses the Puppet **Domain Specific Language** (DSL) and resource statements in the manifest file, which are described in a syntax that looks very similar to a Hash data type in the Ruby language.

We can use our user account Elisa as a simple example of the Puppet manifest syntax.

First, log out from the user account Elisa by running the logout command. Then, log on to the system as a root user and remove the user Elisa from the system with the following command:

```
puppet resource user Elisa ensure=absent
```

Then, inspect the state of the user account `Elisa` with the following commands:

```
puppet resource user Elisa
user { 'Elisa':
  ensure => 'absent',
}
```

In the Ruby language, if we try to declare a hash called `User` that contains a key `Elisa` with the value of the `ensure` attribute as `absent`, we will declare it using the following syntax:

```
User = { 'Elisa' =>
  { 'ensure' => 'absent' }
}
```

If you compare the preceding two code blocks, you can see that the Puppet DSL syntax looks similar to the Ruby language syntax, but it is slightly simpler and easier to read than the Ruby equivalent.

The output of the preceding Puppet resource command is spread across three lines only in order to make it easier for us to read. The Puppet parser that reads the manifest file doesn't care about the line feed characters.

The preceding user resource can be declared on a single line as follows:

```
user { 'Elisa': ensure => 'absent', }
```

We now have the Puppet DSL representation of the user resource `Elisa`.

Managing resources with the puppet apply command

We can apply this resource to the `--execute` (or `-e`) puppet apply command, which will remove the user `Elisa` from the system.

As `Elisa` no longer exists in the system, let's change the `ensure` attribute value to `'present'` so that Puppet can create the user `Elisa`:

```
puppet apply --execute "user { 'Elisa':  ensure => 'present', }"
```

Puppet will display the following output on the screen:

As you might have noticed, the output of the puppet apply command looks different from the puppet resource command that we used earlier to create user Elisa. Let's examine the output line by line:

- **Line 1:** Notice: Compiled catalog for learning.puppetlabs.vm in environment production in 0.12 seconds

  The Puppet report shows that the manifest was compiled successfully in 0.12 seconds. The manifest was compiled for the learning.puppetlabs.vm Puppet host. The learning.puppetlabs.vm Puppet host is a member of the Puppet environment called production.

- **Line 2:** Notice: /Stage[main]/Main/User[Elisa]/ensure: created

  The Puppet report shows that the user Elisa was created successfully on the system.

- **Line 3:** Notice: Finished catalog run in 0.22 seconds

  The Puppet report shows that the Puppet run was completed successfully in 0.22 seconds.

The preceding three lines relate to the following different stages of the Puppet run:

1. Before Puppet can apply the manifest or a set of manifests, it performs an operation where it compiles a catalogue. A catalogue is a collection of Puppet manifests. During the compilation stage, Puppet looks for possible errors in the manifest files and ensures that the manifests were correctly formatted.

2. Once the catalogue is compiled, Puppet moves on to the second stage where it applies the catalogue to the system.

3. The last step of the process is to produce a report of the results of the Puppet run.

Creating Puppet manifests

We covered the Puppet DSL syntax that is used in the Puppet manifests. Let's try to create a manifest and learn how to apply it to the system.

> The simplest way to create a manifest is to use the `puppet resource` command to create the resource definition and redirect the output of the command to the manifest file.

The following are the steps to create a manifest:

1. Use the `puppet resource` command to declare a user resource and redirect the command output to a file using a single greater than character `>` followed by the filename:

    ```
    puppet resource user Jakob > user.pp
    ```

    This command won't return any message to the screen as you have redirected the command output to a file called `user.pp`.

2. Before we inspect the contents of the `user.pp` file, let's add another user definition to `user.pp` with the following commands. This time, the output redirection is done using the double greater than characters `>>`. The difference between the single and the double greater than characters is how the output file is managed. The `>` character overwrites the file contents if the file already exists, while the `>>` characters append to the file:

    ```
    puppet resource user Markus >> user.pp
    ```

3. Let's take a look at the content of the `user.pp` file. To view the content, we can open the file in the text editor. Linux systems usually come with multiple text editors, such as Vi, but we'll use another editor called Nano, which is easier to use than Vi.

4. You can open the `user.pp` file in the Nano text editor by typing the following command:

    ```
    nano user.pp
    ```

5. You will see that the `user.pp` file contains two user definitions: the first definition is for the user `Jakob` and the second definition is for the user `Markus`. Currently, both the resources have the `ensure` attribute value as `absent`, which corresponds to the current state of the user accounts on the system.

Here is the content of the file in the Nano text editor:

```
user { 'Jakob':
  ensure => 'absent',
}
user { 'Markus':
  ensure => 'absent',
}
```

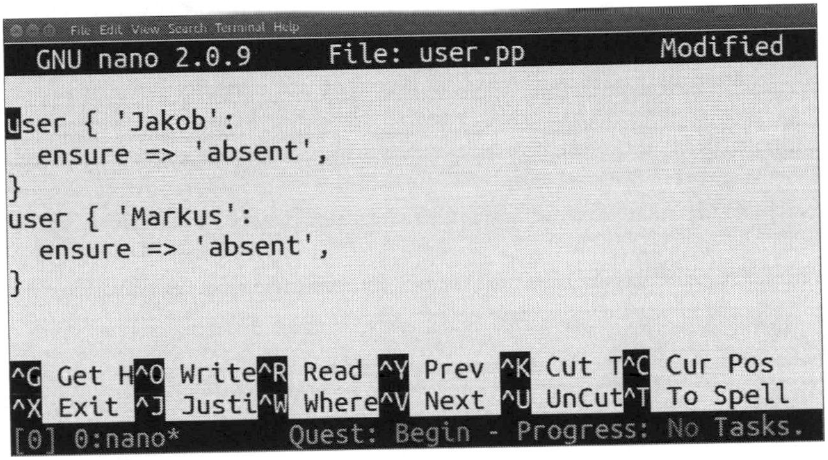
File Edit View Search Terminal Help
GNU nano 2.0.9 File: user.pp Modified
user { 'Jakob':
ensure => 'absent',
}
user { 'Markus':
ensure => 'absent',
}
^G Get H^O Write^R Read ^Y Prev ^K Cut T^C Cur Pos
^X Exit ^J Justi^W Where^V Next ^U UnCut^T To Spell
[0] 0:nano* Quest: Begin - Progress: No Tasks.

6. Using the arrow keys on the keyboard, you can move the cursor around the text file. Change both the `ensure` attribute values to `present`.
7. Once the `ensure` attribute values for both the user resources have been changed, the content of the file should be as follows:

```
user { 'Jakob':
  ensure => 'present',
}
user { 'Markus':
  ensure => 'present',
}
```

8. Now press *Ctrl* + *X* on the keyboard and save the changes by pressing *Y* and then *Enter*.

   Well done! You have just created your first manifest file that manages two resources. Now it's time to apply the manifest with the following command:

```
puppet apply user.pp
```

The following is the output generated by the preceding command:

```
learn_puppet_centos-6.5 (very-latest) [Running] - Oracle VM VirtualBox
[root@learning ~]# puppet apply user.pp
Notice: Compiled catalog for learning.puppetlabs.vm in environment production i
0.13 seconds
Notice: /Stage[main]/Main/User[Jakob]/ensure: created
Notice: /Stage[main]/Main/User[Markus]/ensure: created
Notice: Finished catalog run in 0.29 seconds
[root@learning ~]#
```

You must have probably noticed that this time we ran the puppet apply command without the --execute option. The --execute option is only used to provide the manifest content from the command line. Now that we have created the manifest file, and if we want to apply it, the --execute option can be omitted. Typically, the --execute option is used to pass parameters to the Puppet class that is declared in the manifest. We will discuss the Puppet classes more in detail later on in this book.

Idempotency

Let's run the command again, and you will notice the difference in the command output compared to the previous Puppet run:

```
puppet apply user.pp
```

This time, the output is shorter. The lines that notify us that the users Jakob and Markus were created are missing in this Puppet run:

```
Notice: Compiled catalog for learning.puppetlabs.vm in environment
production in 0.14 seconds
Notice: Finished catalog run in 0.27 seconds
```

This is due to the idempotent nature of Puppet. As the users Jakob and Markus already exist in the system, Puppet doesn't attempt to recreate these accounts. Idempotency in Puppet means that you can apply the same manifest as many times as you like, and only when the state of the resource in the system is different from the state of the resource declared in the manifest, will Puppet ensure that the required configuration changes are performed according to the manifest.

To demonstrate how Puppet handles idempotency, we will remove the user Markus with the following command, which we are familiar with:

```
puppet resource user Markus ensure=absent
```

Then, apply the manifest again with the `puppet apply user.pp` command, and you can see that the user `Jakob`, which we did not remove earlier, does not appear in the output but the user `Markus` is recreated.

Here is the command again:

```
puppet apply user.pp
```

The output of the command is as follows:

```
Notice: Compiled catalog for learning.puppetlabs.vm in environment
production in 0.15 seconds
Notice: /Stage[main]/Main/User[Markus]/ensure: created
Notice: Finished catalog run in 0.35 seconds
```

Puppet command line versus Puppet manifests

So far, we have practiced how to manage system resources from the command line with puppet resource command, and also learned how to manage resources with the Puppet manifest and puppet apply command. When we start expanding our environment with new hosts and increase the number of resources that Puppet manages on these hosts, you will notice that the Puppet command line doesn't scale very well. The Puppet command line typically manages a single resource, such as user `Elisa` or user `Jakob`. Each of these resources was created with its own command. If I have 100 user accounts to be managed, then that would result in the same amount of commands to be run, which would be a very tiring job for anyone to do.

Puppet is a configuration management and automation tool that helps you eliminate repetitive tasks, such as creating 100 user accounts. Instead of running the puppet resource command 100 times, it is better if we add all our users once to a single manifest file, call the file with a puppet apply command, and let the Puppet do the hard work for us. Puppet manifests are types of recipes for your system configuration. Once you have described your system configuration in the form of a manifest, you can easily transfer the recipe onto another host and apply the configuration with a single command.

Managing files and directories with a file resource

The phrase "everything is a file" that is often associated with the Linux operating system makes it an ideal environment for Puppet to manage. Puppet is very good at managing files. Puppet's file resource can create files from static source files. You can define the file content with the `content` attribute, or you can create files with a dynamic content using templates. A file resource can also be used to manage directories and links.

The syntax of a file resource is very similar to the user resource syntax, only the set of available attributes is different. Here is a simple example of how to create an empty directory called `/root/Documents`:

```
file {  '/root/Documents':
  ensure => directory;
}
```

The first line defines the type of resource we want Puppet to manage, followed by the name of the directory that Puppet creates.

The `ensure` attribute on line two says that the file resource must be a directory. If we omit the `ensure` attribute, Puppet will create a file instead of a directory.

The closing curly brace } on the third and the last line ends the file resource statement.

Let's do a practical experiment with the file resource and write a manifest file that sets a log in greeting message when the user `Jakob` logs in. In order to do this, our manifest must fulfill the following two criteria:

- The user `Jakob` must have a home directory to store the login greeting message
- The user `Jakob` must have a custom `.bash_profile` file present under the home directory

To start with, let's remove the user `Jakob` from the system so that we can easily recreate the account with a password, and tell Puppet to create a home directory for the user:

```
puppet resource user Jakob ensure=absent
```

Now when the user Jakob has been removed, let's generate a user resource for Jakob and redirect the output to the file called jakobs-login.pp. Again, we use the single > character to create a new file:

```
puppet resource user Jakob > jakobs-login.pp
```

Then, using the >> notation to redirect the output to the jakobs-login.pp file, we can generate the file resource snippet for the .bash_profile file that will be placed under the home directory of Jakob with the following command:

```
puppet resource file /home/Jakob/.bash_profile >> jakobs-login.pp
```

Now that we have the manifest body ready for editing, we can open the jakobs-login.pp file in the Nano editor:

```
nano jakobs-login.pp
```

On opening the file, you should see the following file content:

```
user { 'Jakob':
  ensure => 'absent',
}
file { '/home/Jakob/.bash_profile':
  ensure => 'absent',
}
```

Let's begin by changing the ensure attribute value from absent to present for the user resource Jakob.

Then, to tell Puppet to create the home directory for the user, we need to use the managehome attribute and set its value to true. The managehome attribute is specific to a user resource, and we can use it to tell Puppet to create a home directory for the user under the /home directory. The home directory is needed to store the .bash_profile file, which we will take a look at shortly.

Finally, to enable Jakob to log in using the password puppet, we should set the encrypted password attribute value to 1jrm5tnjw$h8JJ9mCZLmJvIxvDLjw1M/.

This is how the user resource for Jakob should look like after the changes:

```
user { 'Jakob':
  ensure => 'present',
  managehome => true,
  password => '$1$jrm5tnjw$h8JJ9mCZLmJvIxvDLjw1M/',
}
```

Before we move on to the file resource, let's save the changes with *Ctrl + X* and hit *Enter*. Then, apply the manifest to the `puppet apply` command:

```
puppet apply jakobs-login.pp
```

If the Puppet run was successful, you should see the following output:

```
Notice: Compiled catalog for learning.puppetlabs.vm in environment
production in 0.63 seconds
Notice: /Stage[main]/Main/User[Jakob]/ensure: created
Notice: /Stage[main]/Main/File[/home/Jakob/.bash_profile]/ensure:
removed
Notice: Finished catalog run in 0.35 seconds
```

If we take a look at the third line of the output, we can see that Puppet removed the /home/Jakob/.bash_profile file although we had not yet created it. This is because of the `managehome` attribute that we declared for the user `Jakob`, which results in the Linux environment to create the file when the user is created. Because we haven't yet modified the file resource for /home/Jakob/.bash_profile in the manifest, the `ensure` attribute value is `absent`. This results in Puppet removing the file.

Don't worry, as we will now tell Puppet to recreate the file with the content that we specify:

1. Open the `jakobs-login.pp` manifest file using the Nano editor using the following command:

    ```
    nano jakobs-login.pp
    ```

2. Using the arrow keys, move to the file resource that currently has the following content:

    ```
    file { '/home/Jakob/.bash_profile':
      ensure => 'absent',
    }
    ```

3. Instead of updating the `ensure` attribute value from `absent` to `present`, we can remove the attribute altogether and replace it with the `content` attribute. To greet the user `Jakob` with his name when he logs in, we can specify the `content` attribute in the following way:

    ```
    file { '/home/Jakob/.bash_profile':
      content => 'echo Hello $(logname)',
    }
    ```

4. When you are done with the changes, you can save the file using *Ctrl + X* and press *Enter*.

5. Now let's apply the most recent changes from the manifest;

```
puppet apply jakobs-login.pp
```

The output is as follows:

```
Notice: Compiled catalog for learning.puppetlabs.vm in
environment production in 0.22 seconds
Notice:/Stage[main]/Main/File[/home/Jakob/.hash_profile]/ensur
e: defined content as '{md5}7af0d63debeedf19adbd8bb239f5ab36'
Notice: Finished catalog run in 0.53 seconds
```

6. Now, it is the big moment to test whether our configuration changes work as expected. Log out with the `exit` command and then log in as user `Jakob` using the password `puppet`.

   If the configuration changes were successful, you should see the bottom of the login banner, showing the message `Hello Jakob`.

Puppet configuration

So far, we have discussed how to configure a system using Puppet. But what about Puppet's own configuration? Can the Puppet configuration be managed by Puppet itself?

The answer is yes, but if you decide to do so, do it with caution. Test your Puppet configuration changes thoroughly in isolation, and test it multiple times before pushing it into a live environment. It only requires a minor error in your configuration, and your Puppet agents become non-functional.

There are two ways to manage the Puppet configuration. The Puppet configuration can be managed from the command line by running the puppet `config` commands. Or the configuration can be changed by editing the file in `/etc/puppetlabs/puppet/puppet.conf`, if you are using the Puppet Enterprise edition as we are doing. In the open source Puppet, the configuration file path is `/etc/puppet/puppet.conf`.

Let's view the contents of the file with the utility called `less` , which enables us to browse the file with the arrow keys:

```
less /etc/puppetlabs/puppet/puppet.conf
```

The content of the `puppet.conf` file is similar to the `ini` configuration files, which are commonly used with Windows applications. The data structure basically is a key value pair separated by the = equivalence sign.

There are also sections in the configuration file that are marked with the section name wrapped inside the block brackets. The sections are as follows:

- The `[main]` section
- The `[master]` section
- The `[agent]` section

The `[main]` section contains the configuration that is shared by the `[master]` and `[agent]` sections.

The `[master]` section contains the configuration for the Puppet master, which we will discuss in detail later in this book.

The `[agent]` section contains the configuration for the Puppet agent, which we have already been using when managing resources on the command line.

When you take a look at the second line in the `/etc/puppetlabs/puppet/puppet.conf` file, you can see a configuration key called `certname` with the `learning.puppetlabs.vm` value. Using the arrow keys, when scrolling down to the `[agent]` section, we find a key called environment with the value `production`.

Do you recall seeing these values before? You probably do from the output of the `puppet apply` command that we ran earlier. Here is the output that I'm referring to:

```
Notice: Compiled catalog for learning.puppetlabs.vm  in environment
production in 0.15 seconds
```

The `Compiled catalog for learning.puppetlabs.vm` string and the environment production are defined in the Puppet configuration file. When running Puppet in the standalone mode, as we are at this point, the configuration is not that relevant; but later on in this book, when we link the Puppet Agents with the Puppet Master, we will benefit from knowing how to change the Puppet configuration.

To change the Puppet Agent configuration, we can use the Nano text editor and edit the file manually, but as an alternative, we can use the Puppet command-line utility to change the configuration.

As an exercise, we can change the Puppet Agent's identity with the following command:

```
puppet config set certname brandnew
```

While we are at it, let's change the environment as well. As we are developing Puppet, a suitable environment name for it is development, which we can set with the following command:

```
puppet config set environment development
```

Puppet expects to find an environment-specific directory in the filesystem, so let's create one with the following command:

```
mkdir /etc/puppetlabs/puppet/environments/development
```

Now run the puppet apply user.pp command, and you can see that the configuration changes have become effective:

```
Notice: Compiled catalog for brandnew in environment development in
0.13 seconds
Notice: Finished catalog run in 0.27 seconds
```

Now we can try changing the configuration manually in the Nano editor. Open the configuration file:

```
nano /etc/puppetlabs/puppet/puppet.conf
```

Press *Ctrl + W* to search for a certname key and replace the brandnew value with the learning.puppetlabs.vm string.

Then, search for an environment key name, and Nano will take you a couple of lines down to the end of the [main] configuration section. This line got added when we changed the configuration with the puppet config set command. Now repeat the search with *Alt + W*, and you will find another key called environment in the [agent] configuration block with the original value production. Why duplicate keys? Well, by default, the puppet config set command manages the configuration under the [main] block of the configuration file. The keys specified in this section will take priority over the configuration in the [master] and [agent] sections.

. So, to revert to the environment value production, we can just remove the environment development from the [main] configuration block.

Once the line has been removed, save the puppet.conf file by pressing *Ctrl + X*, confirm the save operation by pressing *Y* for Yes, and then press *Enter*.

To confirm that the configuration changes were successfully applied, we can query specific keys in the configuration file with the puppet config print command:

```
puppet config print certname environment
```

The output of the command should show that the configuration was successfully changed. Here is a screenshot of the `puppet config print certname environment` command before and after the change.

Summary

In this chapter, we thoroughly covered the basics of Puppet, such as how to run Puppet on the command line, and how to use, generate, and edit manifests. We also learned how to get the development environment up and running quickly with a little installation effort using VirtualBox.

In the next chapter, we will be adding a little bit more functionality to VirtualBox, and then start experimenting with the new type of Puppet resources; mainly, let's take a look at how to remove resources with Puppet. This will contribute toward the goal, which is to build a Puppet-managed environment that consists of multiple virtual machines.

Managing Packages in Puppet

This chapter is not just about learning how to manage packages in Puppet, although the package management is one of the key deliverables of this chapter. Before we dive into this, we have to revert our machine image to the snapshot revision that we created in *Chapter 1, Puppet Development in Isolation*, so that all of the changes we made in the virtual machine earlier are wiped out.

Once we have reverted to the snapshot, we will take a look at how to configure shared folders and host-only networking that will be used later in this book.

Moving on, we'll do more "snapshotting", and learn how to create a virtual machine clone from the snapshot, which will be used for our web server node that we are going to build in *Chapter 3, My First Puppet Module*.

Once the virtual machine clone is run, we will purge software packages from the system to create the slimmed down version of the Puppet Learning VM that has a smaller memory footprint than the original Puppet Learning VM.

In this chapter, we will be doing a fair amount of VirtualBox-related tasks, but once the chapter is completed, you will have the development environment fully configured, and we can focus 100 percent on Puppet. We will cover the following topics in this chapter:

- Introducing the VirtualBox Guest Additions
- Configuring shared folders
- Configuring the host-only-network interface
- Creating the Puppet-agent node
- Configuring Puppet environment and the certname
- Purging package resources

Restoring a snapshot

In *Chapter 1, Puppet Development in Isolation,* we learned how to snapshot the virtual machine before we started to work on it. To go back to the original state of the virtual machine, we need to restore the snapshot. In order to restore a snapshot, you should shut down the virtual machine if it is currently running. This can be done from the command line on the virtual machine with the `poweroff` command. Alternatively, we can shut down the virtual machine using the VirtualBox Manager by navigating to **Machine | Close | Power Off**:

Once the virtual machine has shut down, we can restore the snapshot that we created in *Chapter 1, Puppet Development in Isolation*:

1. Click on the **Snapshots** button in the top right-hand corner.
2. Select the snapshot to restore. In *Chapter 1, Puppet Development in Isolation*, I called it **Base image**.

3. Click on the Restore Snapshot button.

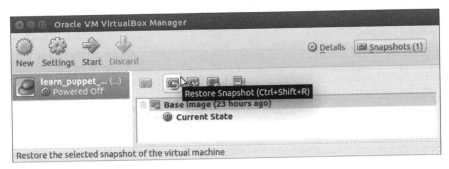

Introducing VirtualBox Guest Additions

The VirtualBox Guest Additions is a package that unlocks a couple of handy features in the virtual machine that makes our development environment more usable. The features enabled by Guest Additions are the shared folders, mouse pointer integration, paravirtualized videocard, timesync, and shared clipboard. At the moment, we can only access the virtual machine through the console window that is provided by the VirtualBox Manager. Writing Puppet manifests using the text editor running inside the virtual machine is a bit clunky. Also, manifests that we create will get deleted when we restore the snapshot.

Shared folders

The VirtualBox Guest Additions provides a service called shared folders that enables us to share folders from the machine that VirtualBox is running on and access them directly from the virtual machine. This means that we are no longer bound to use the text editor inside the virtual machine, as we can use better text editors, such as Notepad++ on Windows or Gedit on Linux. As the files stored in the shared folders are stored outside the virtual machine on the host computer's hard drive, and not in the virtual disk file used by the VM, we are guaranteed that the files are preserved when we revert to the previous snapshot or delete the virtual machine.

Another advantage of shared folders is that folders can be attached to multiple virtual machines simultaneously. This makes the manifest distribution easy as we can write the manifest once, and we can then apply the manifest across all the virtual machines by running the `puppet apply` command on each VM, pointing each to the manifest file stored in the `Shared Folders` directory.

Host-only networking

In addition to shared folders, VirtualBox provides the so-called host-only networking feature that enables us to attach virtual network interfaces to the virtual machine. This feature is handy as we can create a private network inside the VirtualBox environment, where virtual machines can communicate with each other directly. Virtual machines that have the so-called host-only network adapter attached to them can operate in isolation, and they are able to connect to each other using private IP addresses that are allocated by the DHCP server built into the VirtualBox. When addresses are allocated by the VirtualBox, there is no dependency to external routers. The host-only networking feature enables us to spin up the development environment when we are working offline, without any connectivity to Wi-Fi or the Internet.

Configuring shared folders

The shared folders service enables us to access files that are stored on the host computer from the virtual machine. To configure shared folders, you need to decide which directory you want to share and what mount point to use inside the virtual machine to access the directory. In the following example, I'll share the /home/jussi/learning directory on the host computer and use the /learning mount point on the virtual machine.

Select the Puppet Learning VM from the list of virtual machines:

1. Click on the **Machine** menu and select **Settings**.

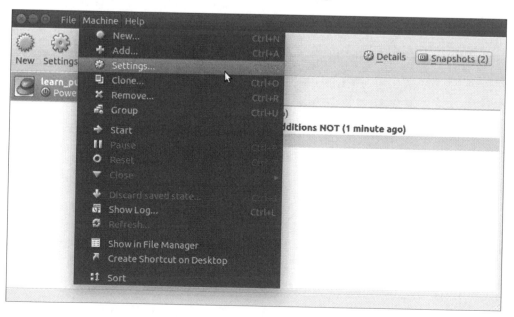

2. Select the **Shared Folders** setting from the left-hand side pane.

3. In the **Folders List** view, click on the blue icon that has a green plus sign on it.

4. In the **Add Share** view, we have to configure the following four properties:

   - **Folder Path**: This specifies the folder to be shared on the host computer, for example, `/home/jussi/learning`. You can click on the arrow sign at the end of the text field to go to the folder you wish to share.

   - **Folder Name**: VirtualBox should automatically populate this field with the name of the folder.

   - The **Read-only** checkbox should be left unchecked.

   - The **Auto-mount** checkbox should be checked.

5. Click on **OK** to save the settings.

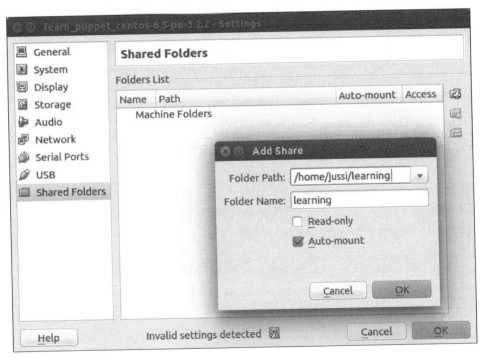

Configuring the host-only network interface

The host-only network interface enables a virtual machine to communicate with other virtual machines that are connected to the same virtual network. We will make use of this later in the book when we run multiple virtual machines in parallel and configure them to communicate with each other.

First, we should confirm that VirtualBox has the host-only network interface that we can assign to the virtual machine:

1. Open the **File** menu and go to **Preferences**.
2. In **Preferences**, click on the **Network** option.
3. Go to the **Host-only Networks** tab.
4. If the host-only networks list is empty, we need to add a network. If that list is not empty, we need not add a network and can skip through the following steps.
5. Create a host-only network by clicking on the icon that has a green plus sign on it.
6. Once a host-only network appears on the list, we should enable the DHCP server.
7. Go to the **Host-only Network** setting by double-clicking on it.
8. The IPv4 address value on the **Adapter** tab should be set to 192.168.56.1.
9. On the **DHCP Server** tab, click on the **Enable Server** checkbox, then fill out the following details:

   - **Server Address**: 192.168.56.1
   - **Server Mask**: 255.255.255.0
   - **Lower Address Bound**: 192.168.56.10
   - **Upper Address Bound**: 192.168.56.20

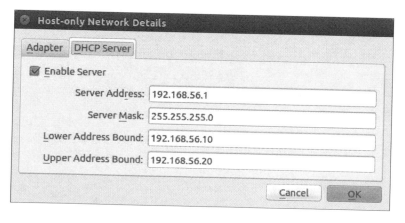

10. Click on **OK** to close the host-only network configuration, and close the settings view by clicking on **OK**.

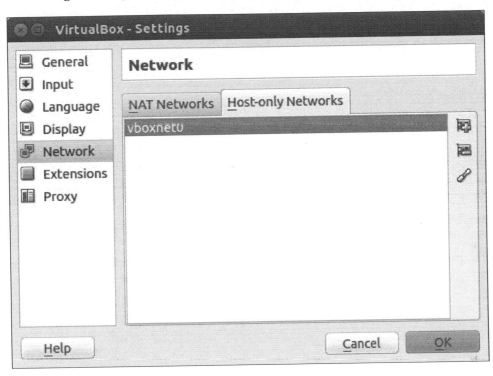

11. Restart the VirtualBox Manager (exit and start the VirtualBox Manager) to ensure that the DHCP Server is activated.

Next, we should attach the host-only network interface with the virtual machine:

1. In the virtual machine settings, select the **Network** settings from **Machine | Settings**.

2. Select the **Adapter 2** tab, and check the **Enable Network Adapter** checkbox.

3. In the **Attached to:** field, select **Host-only Adapter** from the drop-down menu.

4. Ensure that the **Name** field has the value **vboxnet0** (Linux) or **VirtualBox Host-Only Ethernet Adapter** (Windows).

5. Click on **OK** to save the **Network** settings.

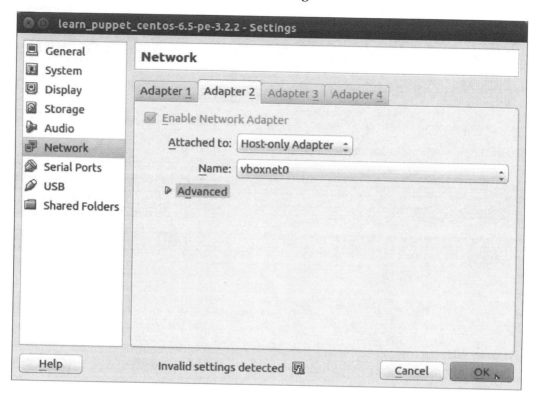

Testing shared folders

Let's take a look at whether the shared folders are available on the Puppet Learning VM. Start the virtual machine and log on with the username `root` and the password `puppet`.

We can check whether the shared folder configuration was successful by running the following command:

```
df
```

If the shared folders are working, you should see a `/media/sf_learning` mount point appearing at the bottom of the view, as shown in the following screenshot:

```
learn_puppet_centos-6.5 (Base image) [Running] - Oracle VM VirtualBox
[root@learning ~]# df
Filesystem                  1K-blocks      Used  Available Use% Mounted on
/dev/mapper/vg00-rootvol      9037088   8041080    1296296  87% /
tmpfs                          969436         0     969436   0% /dev/shm
/dev/sda1                       99150     28465      65565  31% /boot
learning
                            232459240 149207260   83251980  65% /media/sf_learning
[root@learning ~]#
```

Using the file resource to configure network interface on the virtual machine

Before the virtual machine can start using the host-only network interface that we added, we have to create a file that tells the operating system how the new network interface should be configured.

We will configure the host-only network interface as a device name `eth1` on the virtual machine, set it to use the DHCP network address, and enable it when the system boots up.

Such a configuration can be done by creating a `/etc/sysconfig/network-scripts/ifcfg-eth1` file with the following content:

```
DEVICE="eth1"
BOOTPROTO="dhcp"
ONBOOT="yes"
```

 Red Hat-based Linux distributions store the network configuration files under `/etc/sysconfig/network-scripts`.

Instead of creating the file manually, we can use Puppet's file resource to create the file. Here's a file resource that does the configuration for us:

```
file {
  '/etc/sysconfig/network-scripts/ifcfg-eth1':
    content => 'DEVICE="eth1"
BOOTPROTO="dhcp"
ONBOOT="yes"',
  }
```

The preceding file resource may initially look a bit messy, but let's take a look at it in detail and try to make some sense out of it:

- Line 1 begins with the file resource.
- Line 2 defines the file path of the filename that will be created on the target machine.
- Line 3 begins with the `content` attribute. As you may guess, the `content` attribute defines the content of the file. Unlike the earlier Puppet resource examples, line 3 does *not* end with a quote and a colon because the `content` attribute value is spread over lines 4 and 5.
- Line 4 is part of the `content` attribute value and it declares the second line of the file.
- Line 5 defines the third line of the file and terminates the `content` attribute with a quote and a comma.
- Line 6 closes the file resource statement.

Now add the preceding file resource statement to the `network.pp` manifest file and apply the manifest:

1. Open a new file in the Nano editor with the `nano network.pp` command.
2. Add the file resource that we created into the file.
3. Save the file by pressing *Ctrl + X*, then press *Y* and *Enter* to exit the Nano editor.
4. Apply the manifest with the `puppet apply network.pp` command.

If no errors occurred while the manifest was applied, Puppet reports the following lines:

```
Notice: Compiled catalog for learning.puppetlabs.vm  in environment
production in 0.12 seconds
Notice: /Stage[main]/Main/File[/etc/sysconfig/network-scripts/ifcfg-
eth1]/ensure: defined content as '{md5}f98d0b3852ba630aeb2b7d37f8c74b26'
Notice: Finished catalog run in 0.27 seconds
```

Restart networking

To tell the operating system to refresh the network configuration, we can use the following command:

```
service network restart
```

If the network was restarted successfully, you should see the following information printed on the virtual machine console:

```
[root@learning ~]# service network restart
Shutting down interface eth0:                              [  OK  ]
Shutting down interface eth1:                              [  OK  ]
Shutting down loopback interface:                         [  OK  ]
Bringing up loopback interface:                            [  OK  ]
Bringing up interface eth0:
Determining IP information for eth0... done.
                                                           [  OK  ]

Bringing up interface eth1:
Determining IP information for eth1... done.
                                                           [  OK  ]

[root@learning ~]#
```

Creating the puppet-agent node

We have now arrived at the point where we are going to "branch" the Puppet Learning VM to create a slimmed down version of the Puppet Learning VM, which I'll be referring to as the puppet-agent node. The slimmed down version of the Learning VM is based on the current state of the Puppet Learning VM, but it will have a smaller memory footprint than the original Puppet Learning VM, as we will remove some of the packages that are preinstalled on the Puppet Learning VM. The Puppet Learning VM in its current state will be used as the puppetmaster node that manages the puppet-agent nodes. In *Chapter 6*, *Scaling Up the Puppet Environment*, we will learn how to connect the puppet-agent nodes with the puppetmaster node, but for now, we'll focus on how to branch the virtual machine and remove packages from it using Puppet.

Take a snapshot of the virtual machine

To avoid having to repeat the fairly challenging task of configuring the host-only network interface, I'd recommend that you create a new snapshot of it now.

Let's run through the steps one more time, and see how to create a snapshot of the virtual machine:

1. Shut down the virtual machine from command line with the `poweroff` command, or alternatively, select the **ACPI Shutdown** option under the **Machine** menu at the top of the virtual machine window.

2. Once the virtual machine is powered off, click on the **Snapshot** button in the top right-hand corner of the **VirtualBox Manager** window.

3. Click on the Take Snapshot button and provide a name for the snapshot. The name I will use this time for the snapshot is `host-only-networking`.

Branch the virtual machine by creating a clone from the snapshot

In order to create a clone of the virtual machine, it must be powered off. Once the virtual machine is powered off, you can create a clone by performing these steps:

1. Go to the **Snapshots** view of the virtual machine.

2. Select the snapshot that has the shared folders and host-only networking configured on it. On my machine, I will select the snapshot called **host-only-networking**.

3. Then, click on the Clone button (*Ctrl + Shift + C*) to open the **Clone Virtual Machine** dialog box.

4. Provide a name for the clone. For example, you can call it puppet-agent.

5. Below the name field, you can see a checkbox for **Reinitialize the MAC address of all network cards**. It is important to remember to check this box to avoid an IP address conflict when running multiple virtual machine clones in parallel.

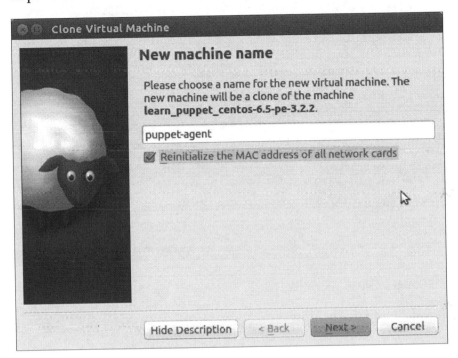

6. Click on the **Next** button to move on to the **Clone type** view. Here, you can see two options for the type of the clone: the **Full clone** (default) and the **Linked clone**. We will go with the default **Full clone**.

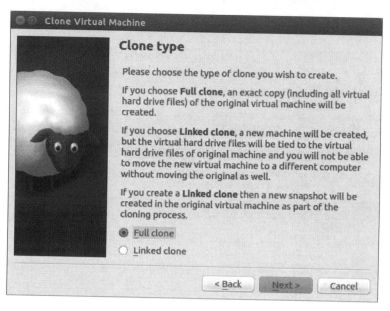

7. Click on **Next** to go to the next view, where you are given options to clone the **Current machine state** or **Everything**. We should choose the default **Current machine state** option, and then click on the **Clone** button.

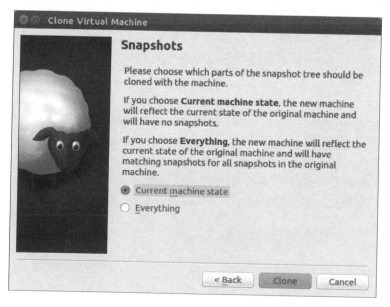

8. Cloning shouldn't take more than a minute or two, and once cloning is complete, you should see a new virtual machine appearing in the **VirtualBox Manager** view.

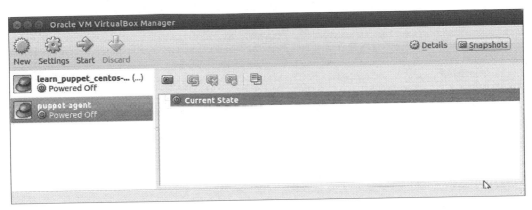

Purging package resources

You should power on the new virtual machine so that we can take a look at what packages can be removed to reduce the memory usage on the virtual machine.

Select the **puppet-agent** virtual machine from the list, and click on the **Start** button. Once the machine has booted up, log in using the user name `root` and the password `puppet`.

Once you have logged in, you can check the current memory consumption by running the `free -m` command.

```
puppet-agent [Running] - Oracle VM VirtualBox
[root@learning ~]# free -m
             total       used       free     shared    buffers     cached
Mem:          1893       1844         49          0         10        262
-/+ buffers/cache:       1570        322
Swap:         4095          0       4095
[root@learning ~]#
```

The command output shows the current memory usage of 1570 MB, and the virtual machine has only 322 MB of free memory space. We should be able to halve the memory consumption by removing packages that are not needed by the puppet-agent node.

We want to remove all the packages that are used by the puppetmaster and only retain the `puppet` and `mcollective` client packages that are needed to run the puppet-agent node.

Here is the complete list of packages that we can safely remove from the system:

- `pe-puppet-dashboard`
- `pe-puppetserver`
- `pe-puppet-license-cli`
- `pe-puppetdb`
- `pe-puppetdb-terminus`
- `pe-memcached`
- `pe-postgresql`
- `pe-activemq`
- `pe-console-services`

Earlier, when we removed a file, we did it with an attribute called `ensure`. To remove packages, we will also use the `ensure` attribute but with a value `purge`. As all the package resources share the same attribute value, we should consolidate the removal of all the packages into one package resource using an array of package names as the Puppet resource name.

In the following example, I've split the package name array on multiple lines to make it easier to read:

```
package {
  ['pe-puppet-dashboard',
   'pe-puppetserver',
   'pe-puppet-license-cli',
   'pe-puppetdb',
   'pe-puppetdb-terminus',
   'pe-memcached',
   'pe-postgresql',
   'pe-activemq',
   'pe-console-services']:
     ensure => 'purged';
}
```

The preceding package resource contains the following elements:

- Line 1 begins with the package resources.
- Lines 2-10 declare the array of packages that we want Puppet to manage. You will notice that the shutdown is much faster now due to the removal of the packages.

We have already practiced quite a few times how to take a snapshot of the virtual machine, so I will just provide you with a quick overview of the steps without screenshots:

1. Ensure that the virtual machine is powered off.
2. Click on the **Snapshots** button in the top right-hand corner of the **VirtualBox Manager** window.
3. Click on the Take Snapshot button.
4. Provide a meaningful name for the snapshot. I call my snapshot `puppet-agent-web`.
5. Then, click on **OK** to create the snapshot.

Summary

I want to congratulate you for completing the development environment setup. I hope that this chapter provided you with some new skills in the areas of VirtualBox, Linux command line, and most importantly, how to manage packages using Puppet. From now on, we will shift our focus away from VirtualBox, and start building our development environment using Puppet.

Now, it is a good time to have a cup of tea and do a recap before diving into *Chapter 3*, *My First Puppet Module*. I'll see you there!

3
My First Puppet Module

So far, we have learned how to manage Puppet resources with Puppet manifests. In *Chapter 1*, *Puppet Development in Isolation*, we created a manifest called user.pp that manages the user accounts for us. In *Chapter 2*, *Managing Packages in Puppet*, we wrote more manifests, such as network.pp, to configure host-only network interface and uninstall.pp to purge packages that are not needed on puppet-agent node.

Together with all the manifest files that we created so far, there are several of them already, and we haven't yet started to develop Puppet manifests. As the number of manifests expand, one may start wondering how files can be distributed and applied efficiently across multiple systems.

This chapter will introduce you to Puppet modules and show you how to prepare a simple web server environment with Puppet.

In this chapter, we will focus on the following key areas:

- Introduction to puppet modules
- Making use of Puppet modules that are available in the public Puppet Forge repository
- Creating your own module (wrapper)
- Deploying a web server with a single Puppet command
- Introduction to facts and Puppet templates

Introducing the Puppet module

The Puppet module is a collection of code and data that usually solves a particular problem, such as the installation and configuration of a web server. A module is packaged and distributed in the **TAR (tape archive)** format. When a module is installed, Puppet extracts the archive file on the disk, and the output of the installation process is a module directory that contains Puppet manifests (code), static files (data), and template files (code and data).

Static files are typically some kind of configuration files that we want to distribute across all the nodes in the cluster. For example, if we want to ensure that all the nodes in the cluster are using the same DNS server configuration, we can include the /etc/resolv.conf file in the module and tell Puppet to apply it across all the nodes. This is just an example of how static files are used in Puppet and not a recommendation for how to configure DNS servers.

Like static files, template files can also be used to provide configuration. The difference between a static and template file is that a static file will always have the same static content when applied across multiple nodes, whereas the template file can be customized based on the unique characteristics of a node. A good example of a unique characteristic is an IP address. Each node (or a host) in the network must have a unique IP address. Using the template file, we can easily customize the configuration on every node, wherever the template is applied.

It's a good practice to keep the manifest files short and clean to make them easy to read and quick to debug. When I write manifests, I aim to keep the length of the manifest file in less than a hundred lines. If the manifest length exceeds 100 lines, then this means that I may have over-engineered the process a little bit. If I can't simplify the manifest to reduce the number of lines, then I have to split the manifest into multiple smaller manifest files and store these files within a Puppet module.

The Puppet module structure

The easiest way to get familiar with a module structure is to create an empty module with the puppet module generate command. As we are in the process of building a web server that runs a web application, we should give our module a meaningful name, such as learning-webapp.

The Puppet module name format

Before we create our first module, let's take a quick look at the Puppet module naming convention. The Puppet module name is typically in the format of `<author>-<modulename>`. A module name must contain one hyphen character (no more, no less) that separates the `<author>` and the `<modulename>` names. In the case of our `learning-webapp` module that we will soon create, the author is called `learning` and the module name is `webapp`, thus the module name `learning-webapp`.

As we create more modules during the course of this book, we will always use the same author name so that each module that we create gets tagged as being written by the same author.

Generating a Puppet module

Let's take a look at the following steps to create the `learning-webapp` Puppet module:

1. Start the puppet-agent virtual machine.

2. Using the `cd` command, navigate to the directory that is shared via the shared folder.

3. On my virtual machine, my shared folder appears as `/media/sf_learning`, and I can move to the directory by running the following command:

    ```
    # cd /media/sf_learning
    ```

4. Then, I'll create an empty puppet module with the command `puppet module generate learning-webapp --skip-interview` and the command returns a list of files and directories that the module contains:

    ```
    # puppet module generate learning-webapp --skip-interview
    Notice: Generating module at /media/sf_learning/learning-webapp
    Notice: Populating templates...
    Finished; module generated in learning-webapp.
    learning-webapp/metadata.json
    learning-webapp/Rakefile
    learning-webapp/manifests
    learning-webapp/manifests/init.pp
    learning-webapp/spec
    ```

```
learning-webapp/spec/spec_helper.rb
learning-webapp/spec/classes
learning-webapp/spec/classes/init_spec.rb
learning-webapp/Gemfile
learning-webapp/tests
learning-webapp/tests/init.pp
learning-webapp/README.md
```

5. To get a better view of how the files in the directories are organized in the `learning-webapp` module, you can run the `tree learning-webapp` command, and this command will produce the following tree structure of the files:

```
puppet-agent (agent-deployed) [Running] - Oracle VM VirtualBox
root@learning /media/sf_learning]# tree learning-webapp/
learning-webapp/
├── Gemfile
├── manifests
│   └── init.pp
├── metadata.json
├── Rakefile
├── README.md
├── spec
│   ├── classes
│   │   └── init_spec.rb
│   └── spec_helper.rb
├── tests
    └── init.pp

4 directories, 8 files
root@learning /media/sf_learning]#
```

Here, we have a very simple Puppet module structure. Let's take a look at the files and directories inside the module in more detail:

- `Gemfile`: A file used for describing the Ruby package dependencies that are used for unit testing. This book does not cover unit testing.

  For more information on `Gemfile`, visit `http://bundler.io/v1.3/man/gemfile.5.html`.

- `manifests`: A directory for all the Puppet `manifest` files in the module.

- `manifests/init.pp`: A default `manifest` file that declares the main Puppet class called `webapp`.

- `metadata.json`: A file that contains the module metadata, such as the name, version, and module dependencies.
- `README.md`: A file that contains information about the usage of the module.
- `Spec`: An optional directory for automated tests.
- `Tests`: A directory that contains examples that show how to call classes that are stored in the manifests directory.
- `tests/init.pp`: A file containing an example how to call the main class `webapp` in file `manifests/init.pp`.

A Puppet class

A Puppet class is a container for Puppet resources. A class typically includes references to multiple different types of resources and can also reference other Puppet classes.

The syntax for declaring a Puppet class is not that different from declaring Puppet resources. A class definition begins with the keyword `class`, followed by the name of the class (unquoted) and an opening curly brace ({). A class definition ends with a closing curly brace (}).

Here is a generic syntax of the Puppet class:

```
class classname {
}
```

Let's take a look at the `manifests/init.pp` file that you just created with the `puppet module generate` command. Inside the file, you will find an empty Puppet class called `webapp`. You can view the contents of the `manifests/init.pp` file using the following command:

```
# cat /media/sf_learning/learning-webapp/manifests/init.pp
```

The `init.pp` file mostly contains the comment lines, which are prefixed with the # sign, and these lines can be ignored. At the end of the file, you can find the following declaration for the `webapp` class:

```
class webapp {
}
```

The `webapp` class is a Puppet class that does nothing as it has no resources declared inside it.

Resources inside the Puppet class

Let's add a `notify` resource to the `webapp` class in the `manifests/init.pp` file before we go ahead and apply the class. The `notify` resource does not manage any operating system resources, such as files or users, but instead, it allows Puppet to report a message when a resource is processed.

As the `webapp` module was created inside shared folders, you no longer have to use the Nano editor inside the virtual machine to edit manifests. Instead, you can use a graphical text editor, such as a Notepad on Windows or Gedit on the Linux host. This should make the process of editing manifests a bit easier and more user friendly.

The directory that I shared on the host computer is `/home/jussi/learning`. When I take a look inside this directory, I can find a subdirectory called `learning-webapp`, which is the Puppet module directory that we created a moment ago. Inside this, there is a directory called `manifests`, which contains the `init.pp` file.

Open the `init.pp` file in the text editor on the host computer and scroll down the file until you find the `webapp` class code block that looks like the following:

```
class webapp {
}
```

 If you prefer to carry on using the Nano editor to edit manifest files (I salute you!), you can open the `init.pp` file inside the virtual machine with the `nano /media/sf_learning/learning-webapp/manifests/init.pp` command.

The `notify` resource that we are adding must be added inside the curly braces that begins and ends the class statement; otherwise, the resource will not be processed when we apply the class.

Now we can add a simple `notify` resource that makes the `webapp` class look like the following when completed:

```
class webapp {
  notify {  'Applying class webapp':
  }
}
```

Let's take a look at the preceding lines one by one:

- Line 1 begins with the webapp class, followed by the opening curly brace.
- Line 2 declares a notify resource and a new opening curly brace, followed by the resource name. The name of the notify resource will become the message that Puppet prints on the screen when the resource from a class is processed.
- Line 3 closes the notify resource statement.
- Line 4 indicates that the webapp class finishes here.

Once you have added the notify resource to the webapp class, save the init.pp file.

Rename the module directory

Before we can apply our webapp class, we must rename our module directory. It is unclear to me as to why the puppet module generate command creates a directory name that contains a hyphen character (as in learning-webapp). The hyphen character is not allowed to be present in the Puppet module directory name. For this reason, we must rename the learning-webapp directory before we can apply the webapp class inside it.

As the learning-webapp module directory lives in the shared folders, you can either use your preferred file manager program to rename the directory, or you can run the following two commands inside the Puppet Learning VM to change the directory name from learning-webapp to webapp:

```
# cd /media/sf_learning
# mv learning-webapp webapp
```

Your module directory name should now be webapp, and we can move on to apply the webapp class inside the module and see what happens.

Applying a Puppet class

You can try running the puppet apply webapp/manifests/init.pp command but don't be disappointed when nothing happens. Why is that?

The reason is because there is nothing inside the init.pp file that references the webapp class. If you are familiar with object-oriented programming, you may know that a class must be instantiated in order to get services from it. In this case, Puppet behaves in a similar way to object-oriented programming languages, as you must make a reference to the class in order to tell Puppet to process the class.

Puppet has an `include` keyword that is used to reference a class. The `include` keyword in Puppet is only available for class resources, and it cannot be used in conjunction with any other type of Puppet resources.

To apply the `webapp` class, we can make use of the `init.pp` file under the tests directory that was created when the module was generated. If you take a look inside the `tests/init.pp` file, you will find a line `include webapp`. The `tests/init.pp` file is the one that we should use to apply the `webapp` class.

Here are the steps on how to apply the `webapp` class inside the Puppet Learning VM:

1. Go to the parent directory of the `webapp` module:

   ```
   # cd /media/sf_learning
   ```

2. Apply the `webapp` class that is included in the `tests/init.pp` file:

   ```
   # puppet apply --modulepath=./ webapp/tests/init.pp
   ```

3. When the class is applied successfully, you should see the `notify` resource that was added to the `webapp` class that appears on lines 2 and 3 in the following Puppet report:

   ```
   Notice: Compiled catalog for web.development.vm in environment
   production in 0.05 seconds

   Notice: Applying class webapp

   Notice: /Stage[main]/Webapp/Notify[Applying class webapp]/message:
   defined 'message' as 'Applying class webapp'

   Notice: Finished catalog run in 0.81 seconds
   ```

Let's take a step back and look again at the command that we used to apply to the `webapp` class:

```
# puppet apply --modulepath=./ webapp/tests/init.pp
```

The command can be broken down into three elements:

- `puppet apply`: The `puppet apply` command is used when applying a manifest from the command line.
- `modulepath=./`: This option is used to tell Puppet what filesystem path to use to look for the `webapp` module. The `./` (dot forward slash) notation means that we want our current `/media/sf_learning` working directory to be used as the `modulepath` value.
- `webapp/tests/init.pp`: This is the file that the `puppet apply` command should read.

Installing a module from Puppet Forge

Puppet Forge is a public Puppet module repository (`https://forge.puppetlabs.com`) for modules that are created by the community around Puppet. Making use of the modules in Puppet Forge is a great way to build a software stack quickly, without having to write all the manifests yourself from scratch.

One of the key deliverables of this chapter is to build a fully functioning web server, and we can do this very easily by building the web server from modules that are available in Puppet Forge.

The web server that we are going to install is a highly popular Apache HTTP Server (`http://httpd.apache.org/`), and there is a module in Puppet Forge called `puppetlabs-apache` that we can install. The `Puppetlabs-apache` module provides all the necessary Puppet resources for the Apache HTTP Server installation.

Note that the puppet module installation requires an Internet connection. To test whether the Puppet Learning VM can connect to the Internet, run the following command on the command line:

```
# host www.google.com
```

On successful completion, the command will return the following output:

```
www.google.com has address 216.58.211.164
www.google.com has IPv6 address 2a00:1450:400b:801::2004
```

> Note that the reported IP address may vary. As long as the host command returns `www.google.com has address ...`, the Internet connection works.

Now that the Internet connection has been tested, you can now proceed with the module installation.

Before we install the `puppetlabs-apache` module, let's do a quick search to confirm that the module is available in Puppet Forge. The following command will search for the `puppetlabs-apache` module:

```
# puppet module search puppetlabs-apache
```

When the search is successful, it returns the following results:

Then, we can install the module. Follow these steps to install the
puppetlabs-apache module:

1. In the Puppet Learning VM, go to the shared folders /media/sf_learning
    directory by running the cd /media/sf_learning command.

2. Then, run the following command:

    ```
    # puppet module install --modulepath=./ puppetlabs-apache
    ```

    The --modulepath=./ option specifies that the module should be installed in
    the current /media/sf_learning working directory

3. The installation will take a couple of minutes to complete, and once it is
    complete, you will see the following lines appear on the screen:

    ```
    Notice: Preparing to install into /media/sf_learning ...
    Notice: Downloading from https://forgeapi.puppetlabs.com ...
    Notice: Installing -- do not interrupt ...
    /media/sf_learning
    └─┬ puppetlabs-apache (v1.2.0)
      ├── puppetlabs-concat (v1.1.2)
      └── puppetlabs-stdlib (v4.8.0)
    ```

Let's take a look at the output line by line to fully understand what happened during
the installation process:

*   Line 1 tells us that the module is going to be installed in the
    /media/sf_learning directory, which is our current working directory.
    This directory was specified with the --modulepath=./ option in the puppet
    module install command.

- Line 2 says that the module is going to be installed from `https://forgeapi.puppetlabs.com/`, which is the address for Puppet Forge.

- Line 3 is fairly self-explanatory and indicates that the installation process is running.

- Lines 4 and 5 tell us that the `puppetlabs-apache` module was installed in the current `/media/sf_learning` working directory.

- Line 6 indicates that as part of the `puppetlabs-apache` module installation, a `puppetlabs-concat` dependency module was also installed.

- Line 7 lists another dependency module called `puppetlabs-stdlib` that got installed in the process.

Now you can run the `tree -L 1` command to see what new directories got created in `/media/sf_learning` as a result of the `puppet module install` command:

```
# tree -L 1
├── apache
├── concat
├── stdlib
└── webapp

4 directories, 0 files
```

 The argument `-L 1` in the `tree` command specifies that it should only traverse one level of directory hierarchy.

Installing Apache HTTP Server

Now that the `puppetlabs-apache` module is installed in the filesystem, we can proceed with the Apache HTTP Server installation.

Earlier, we talked about how a Puppet class can be referenced with the `include` keyword. Let's see how this works in practice by adding the `include apache` statement to our `webapp` class, and then applying the `webapp` class from the command line.

Open the `webapp/manifests/init.pp` file in your preferred text editor, and add the `include apache` statement inside the `webapp` class.

I like to place the include statements at the beginning of the class before any resource statement. In my text editor, the webapp class looks like the following after the include statement has been added to it:

Once you have saved the webapp/manifests/init.pp file, you can apply the webapp class with the following command:

```
# puppet apply --modulepath=./ webapp/tests/init.pp
```

This time, the command output is much longer compared to what it was when we applied the webapp class for the first time. In fact, the output is too long to be included in full, so I'm only going to show you the last two lines of the Puppet report, which shows you the step where the state of the Service[httpd] resource has changed from stopped to running:

```
Notice: /Stage[main]/Apache::Service/Service[httpd]/ensure: ensure changed 'stopped' to 'running'
Notice: Finished catalog run in 65.20 seconds
```

Testing the Apache HTTP Server

Assuming that the installation was successful, you can now test whether the HTTP interface on the Puppet Learning VM is accessible in a web browser on the host computer.

You must start by discovering what IP address the Puppet Learning VM uses for the host-only network interface called eth1. The discovery is the easiest to do with the facter utility that is installed as part of Puppet. We will take a look at the facts in detail shortly, but for now, we can just query a key called ipaddress_eth1, and this will return the IP address of the network interface, eth1.

Here is the command and output when I run it on my Puppet Learning VM:

```
# facter ipaddress_eth1
192.168.56.10
```

Facter shows that the host-only networking interface `eth1` uses an IP address `192.168.56.10`. Based on this information, I can type in the URL `http://192.168.56.10` in the web browser on the host computer, and the following web page will load up:

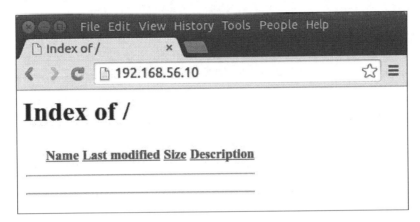

Customizing a web server with facts and templates

Installing the Apache HTTP Server was as simple as adding a line `include apache` to the `webapp` class. The `apache` class provided by the `puppetlabs-apache` module did the basic server installation for us and that's it.

To make the web server look like a real web application, we should add more functionalities to it. We will start by adding a simple landing page, which will replace the default index page, that the web server is provided with when we accessed the address `http://192.168.56.10/`.

The source code of the landing page will live inside a Puppet template, and the template will be defined as a file resource inside the `webapp` class.

Puppet templates

Puppet templates (`https://docs.puppetlabs.com/guides/templating.html`) are files that produce dynamic content for files on the target machine. Templates are written in the ERB Templating Language, which is a mixture of static text, variable references, and functions. The ERB language syntax can get complex especially when using functions, but I like simple things, so we will begin by writing a template that only contains static text, and learn how to create a file resource that populates the template. Later, we will modify the template and learn how to use variables to make the file content dynamic.

Puppet templates live inside the `templates` directory within the Puppet module. Unfortunately, the Puppet module `generate` command does not create the templates directory, so we have to create this directory by hand.

Here are the steps on how to create the templates directory inside the `webapp` module from the command line:

1. Go to root of the `webapp` module:

   ```
   # cd /media/sf_learning/webapp
   ```

2. Create the templates directory using the `mkdir` command:

   ```
   # mkdir templates
   ```

    As an alternative to the command line, you can create the `templates` directory using the file manager program on the host computer.

After the `templates` directory has been created, you will see the following directory structure inside the `webapp` module:

```
# tree -L 1
├── Gemfile
├── manifests
├── metadata.json
├── Rakefile
├── README.md
├── spec
├── templates
└── tests

4 directories, 4 files
```

Creating a template file

You can create the template file in the text editor on the host computer, or alternatively, use the Nano editor on the Puppet Learning VM to create the file. The template file that I'm creating will initially have static content, and I'll save it as `index.html.erb` under the directory `templates`.

Here is a simple HTML document that makes the content for the `index.html.erb` file:

```
<html>
  <body>
    <h1>Welcome to Puppet Learning VM</h1>
    <p>The contents of this file was generated by Puppet</p>
  </body>
</html>
```

Once you have added the content to the file, save it in the `templates` directory with the name, `index.html.erb`. Using the `.erb` file extension is not required, but it is a good way to differentiate the template files from the static files.

Creating a file resource for the template file

The template file has been created, and we have to now instruct Puppet where to find the template and where to populate the file on the target machine.

Open the `manifests/init.pp` file in the text editor on the host computer, and add the following `file` resource statement to the `webapp` class:

```
file { '/var/www/html/index.html':
  content => template('webapp/index.html.erb'),
  owner   => 'apache',
  require => User['apache'];
}
```

As we have introduced a couple of new attributes for the `file` resource, I think it is worth taking a look at the preceding resource declaration in detail:

- Line 1 begins with a new `file` resource. The name of the resource defines the path and the name of the file that Puppet will create from the template.
- Line 2 defines a `content` attribute, and the attribute value begins with a function called `template`. The function takes an argument that defines the location of the template file in the `webapp` module.

The syntax of the template file location may look a bit strange, as it doesn't specify the directory called `template`, where the template file lives. The syntax that Puppet uses for referencing templates is in the format of `<modulename>/<template>`.

- Line 3 defines an `owner` attribute that is used to specify a user account that Puppet should make as the owner of the file on the target machine. The `apache` attribute value results in the file owner to become an apache user, which is the user account that runs the Apache HTTP Server process.

- Line 4 introduces a `require` attribute, which is used to set the order for Puppet to process resources. The `User['apache']` value means that Puppet must process the `apache` user resource (declared in the `puppetlabs-apache` module) prior to processing the file resource.

  This attribute ensures that the `apache` user is created prior to setting the file owner as the `apache` user.

- Line 5 closes the file resource statement.

The `webapp` class should have the following content once a new `file` resource has been added to it:

```
*init.pp (~/learning/webapp-org/manifests) - gedit

Open    Save    Undo

*init.pp ×

1 class webapp {
2   include apache
3   file { '/var/www/html/index.html':
4       content => template('webapp/index.html.erb'),
5       owner   => 'apache',
6       require => User['apache'];
7   }
8   notify {
9     'Applying class webapp':
10  }
11 }

Puppet ▾   Tab Width: 2 ▾      Ln 11, Col 2      INS
```

Apply the Puppet class and visit the new landing page.

When the file resource is added to the `webapp` class, you can reapply the class with the following two commands:

```
# cd /media/sf_learning
# puppet apply --modulepath=./ webapp/tests/init.pp
```

After a successful Puppet run, you will see the following lines on the screen:

```
# puppet apply --modulepath./ webapp/tests/init.pp
Notice: Compiled catalog for web.development.vm in environment
production in 5.97 seconds
Warning: The package type's allow_virtual parameter will be changing its
default value from false to true in a future release. If you do not want
to allow virtual packages, please explicitly set allow_virtual to false.
(at /opt/puppet/lib/ruby/site_ruby/1.9.1/puppet/type/package.rb:430:in
'block (3 levels) in <module:Puppet>')
Notice: Applying class webapp
Notice: /Stage[main]/Webapp/Notify[Applying class webapp]/message:
defined 'message' as 'Applying class webapp'
Notice: /Stage[main]/Webapp/File[/var/www/html/index.html]/ensure:
defined content as '{md5}751763924b26dc9a7f3e4c81bc4bf158'
Notice: Finished catalog run in 9.53 seconds
```

The warning message in the Puppet report output can be safely ignored.

If you open the web browser and type `http://192.168.56.10/` in the address bar, you should see your newly-designed landing page loading up in the browser:

Facts by the facter

Facter is an inventory application that comes bundled with Puppet, and it provides an interface with a range of data about your system. Earlier in the chapter, we used the `facter` command to query the IP address of an `eth1` network interface. This is just one of the many available system properties that are available via Facter.

In addition to built-in facter queries, you can also create your own facts and bundle them with the module or make Facter read values from particular files in the filesystem. We will take a look at the custom facts later in this book, but for now, we'll focus on how to make use of the built-in facts.

Facter integrates nicely with Puppet and Puppet templates. Next, we will practice how to make use of the facter to turn the currently static landing page content into a more dynamic web page and expose some of the system information on the landing page.

Facter on the command line

Let's take a look at what system information is available out of the box with Facter by running the following command:

```
# facter
```

This command will show you all the available built-in facts. If the list of facts do not fit into the window, you may view the facts page by page by extending the `facter` command in the following way, and then use the arrow keys to scroll the command output up and and down:

```
# facter | less
```

To query a specific fact, such as the name of the operating system, you simply need to provide the name of the fact as an argument for the `facter` command:

```
# facter operatingsystem
```

On the Puppet Learning VM, the preceding command will produce the following output:

```
CentOS
```

Accessing facts from the Puppet template

Accessing facts from the Puppet template is done by a reference to the variable name that matches the name of the fact. For example, to reference the fact operating system, we can do it with the following statement in the Puppet template:

```
<%= @operatingsystem %>
```

Since Puppet Version 3.x, local variable references must be prefixed with the @ sign. Although facts are not technically local variables, we can reference them as local variables with the @ prefix. An alternative and recommended way to reference nonlocal variables in Puppet 3.x is to use the `<%= scope['::operatingsystem'] %>` template syntax. I personally prefer the @ notation as it is shorter and it works just fine.

The name of the fact that we want to reference must be wrapped inside an expression that begins with the opening marker `<%=` and ends with the closing marker `%>`. When the ERB template parser reads the template and detects a character sequence `<%`, followed by `%>`, it treats its contents as a block of executable Ruby code. Any characters outside the `<%` and `%>` tags are treated as plain text.

A tag with the equals sign such as `<%=` means that the ERB template parser must substitute the expression with the result of the command output.

For example, in order to allow the Puppet template to produce a string `My operating system is CentOS`, we can use the following ERB syntax in the template file:

```
My operating system is <%= @operatingsystem %>
```

Let's add the preceding statement to the existing template, and see what happens when Puppet applies the template.

Open the `index.html.erb` file under `webapp/templates/` in the text editor, and add the statement to it. In the following example, I've wrapped the statement inside the HTML `<p>` and `</p>` tags to allow the browser to display the text with a font that is consistent with the rest of the page:

```html
<html>
  <body>
    <h1>Welcome to Puppet Learning VM</h1>
    <p>The contents of this file was generated by Puppet</p>
    <p>My operating system is <%= @operatingsystem %></p>
  </body>
</html>
```

Once you have saved the file, you can apply the changes with the following commands:

```
cd /media/sf_learning/
puppet apply --modulepath=./ webapp/tests/init.pp
```

Once Puppet has applied the new version of the template, you should refresh the browser window at http://192.168.56.10/ by pressing *F5* on the keyboard. If the changes were applied successfully, you should now have the page with the following content in front of you:

Accessing facts from Puppet manifests

Facts are accessible in the Puppet manifest file through a reference to the fact name prefixed with the `$::` (dollar and double colon) character sequence. For example, a reference to the fact `operatingsystem` can be done with the `$::operatingsystem` notation.

Let's create a local Puppet variable and store some facter values in it. We can then reference the local variable in the Puppet template, and use a simple for loop inside the template to populate the Facter values on the landing page.

We can choose any name for the variable, and as we are going to store the facter values in the variable, I'll call it `$fact_list`. A local variable in Puppet is declared by adding a dollar character as a prefix for the variable name, for example, `$fact_list`. In order to iterate through values in the variable, the variable type has to be an array, which is created with the following syntax:

```
$fact_list = []
```

The preceding example creates an empty array. Let's add some content to the array with double-quoted strings separated by comma characters:

```
$fact_list = ["IP address $::ipaddress_eth1", "Uptime
$::uptime"]
```

The `$fact_list` array now contains two elements. The first element in the array begins with a string IP address, followed by a reference to the fact called `ipaddress_eth1`. The second array element contains an `Uptime` string and a reference to the fact `uptime`.

Before we move on to editing the template file, you should add the `$fact_list` array to the `webapp` class in the `manifests/init.pp` file. Once the array is added to the `webapp` class, it should have the following content:

```
1 class webapp {
2     $fact_list = ["IP address $::ipaddress_eth1", "Uptime $::uptime"]
3     include apache
4     file { '/var/www/html/index.html':
5         content => template('webapp/index.html.erb'),
6         owner   => 'apache',
7         require => User['apache'];
8     }
9     notify {
10        'Applying class webapp':
11    }
12 }
```

A simple for loop in the Puppet template

We now have a `$fact_list` array with two elements but nothing yet references the variable. Next, we are going to modify the `templates/index.html.erb` file, and learn how to reference the local variable from the template and iterate through elements that are stored in the array.

A local variable reference in a template is done in exactly the same manner as referencing facts, by adding the @ prefix to the variable name. The iteration over the array can be done with the method `each`, which is a method provided by an array data type in the Ruby programming language.

The referencing and iteration can be done with the following code block:

```
<% @fact_list.each do | fact | %>
<p> <%= fact %> </p>
<% end %>
```

I'll explain what the preceding three lines do:

- Line 1 contains a reference to the variable facts, which we defined in the init.pp manifest file. Variable facts call the Ruby array method each that results in iteration over the array. Each element in the array is referenced with the local variable called fact for which you can find a reference on line 2.

- Line 2 begins with an HTML <p> tag, followed by a reference to the fact local variable that was instantiated on line 1. The line ends with closing the HTML </p> tag.

- Line 3 has the end statement that terminates the iteration created by the each method.

Now it's time to try this out in action. Once you have added the preceding code block to the templates/index.html.erb directory, the file should have the following content, where the latest code addition is highlighted in red:

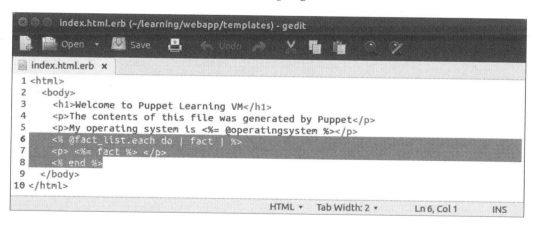

After you have saved the template file, apply the template with the following commands:

```
# cd /media/sf_learning/
# puppet apply --modulepath=./ webapp/tests/init.pp
```

Once Puppet has applied the new template, you will see the IP address and the `Uptime` information displayed on the landing page when you reload the page.

Here's a screenshot showing you the landing page content after the changes were applied successfully:

If you wait for a minute and try rerunning the `puppet apply` command and reload the landing page, you should see that the `Uptime` value gets updated at every Puppet run.

Testing repeatable deployment

One great thing about Puppet is that it makes the deployment process repeatable across multiple machines. Once you have described the deployment process in the form of Puppet manifests, you can quickly deploy a cluster of machines that share the common configuration. For example, we can easily build a cluster of web servers that are deployed by the `webapp` module. Let's try this in action and create two web servers that incorporate the `webapp` module.

The high-level plan is as follows:

1. Shut down the currently running puppet-agent virtual machine.
2. Revert the machine state to the previous snapshot.
3. Reduce the virtual machine memory allocation.
4. Create a linked virtual machine clone from the snapshot.
5. Power on both the virtual machines.
6. Apply the `webapp` class to the virtual machines.

Shut down the virtual machine

We have already shut down the virtual machine a few times, but as a reminder, you can power off the machine from the command line by running the following command:

```
# poweroff
```

Alternatively, you can shut down the virtual machine by choosing the **ACPI Shutdown** option under the **Machine** menu from the virtual machine console.

Revert the machine state to the previous snapshot

Restoring a snapshot only reverts the data that is stored on the virtual disk of the virtual machine. Puppet modules that are stored in the shared folders will remain available after the snapshot has been restored.

You can restore the snapshot by performing these steps:

1. In the VirtualBox Manager window, select the **puppet-agent** virtual machine.
2. Click on the **Snapshots** button in the top right-hand corner of the window.
3. Select the snapshot called **puppet-agent-web** that was created earlier.
4. Click on the **Restore snapshot** button.
5. Uncheck the **Create a snapshot of the current machine state** option.
6. Click on the **Restore** button.

Reduce memory allocation for the virtual machine

Reducing the memory allocation for the virtual machine is optional. If the host computer has more than 4 GB of free memory, you may skip this step, but I'd recommend that you reduce the allocation because the virtual machine runs just as well with less memory; hence, we removed Puppet Enterprise packages in *Chapter 2, Managing Packages in Puppet*.

The memory allocation can be changed in the following way:

1. Select the **puppet-agent** virtual machine from the list in the VirtualBox Manager view.
2. Click on **Settings**.
3. Select the **System** option from the left-hand side pane.

4. Reduce the **Base Memory** down to **512 MB**, and then click on **OK**:

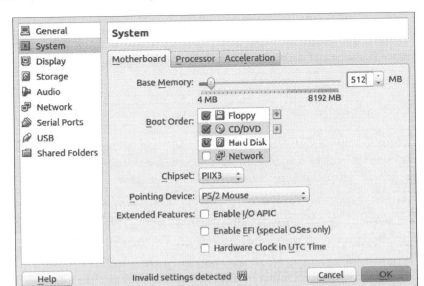

Create a linked virtual machine clone from the snapshot

There are two types of virtual machine clones that can be created in VirtualBox. Earlier, we created the so-called Full clone, but now we will try the other method called a Linked clone, which is a faster way to clone virtual machines.

Here are the steps on how to create a Linked clone virtual machine:

1. In the VirtualBox Manager window, select the **puppet-agent** virtual machine.
2. Click on the **Snapshots** button in the top right-hand corner of the window.
3. Select the snapshot called **puppet-agent-web**.
4. Click on the **Clone** button above the snapshot list view.
5. Provide a name for the new virtual machine. I'll call it `puppet-agent-web-clone`.
6. It is important to remember to check the **Reinitialize the MAC address of all network cards** option.
7. Click on **Next** and choose the **Linked clone** option in the **Clone type** view.
8. Click on the **Clone** button to complete the cloning process.

You may notice that the creation of a Linked clone happens much quicker than creating the Full clone.

Power on both the virtual machines and apply the webapp class

You should now see three virtual machines in the list of VMs in the VirtualBox Manager view. These machines are called:

- learn_puppet_centos-6.5
- puppet-agent
- puppet-agent-web-clone

Power on the **puppet-agent** and the **puppet-agent-web-clone** virtual machines by selecting the machine and then clicking on the **Start** button.

Once both the machines have booted up, you should find the IP address information for each host displayed on the log on the screen under the section called **My IP information**. Make a note of the IP address from the IP address range 192.168.56.x for both the hosts. You will need this information in a little while after you have applied the webapp class to both the hosts.

The following screenshot shows that the virtual machines that I powered on use IP addresses 192.168.56.11 and 192.168.56.12:

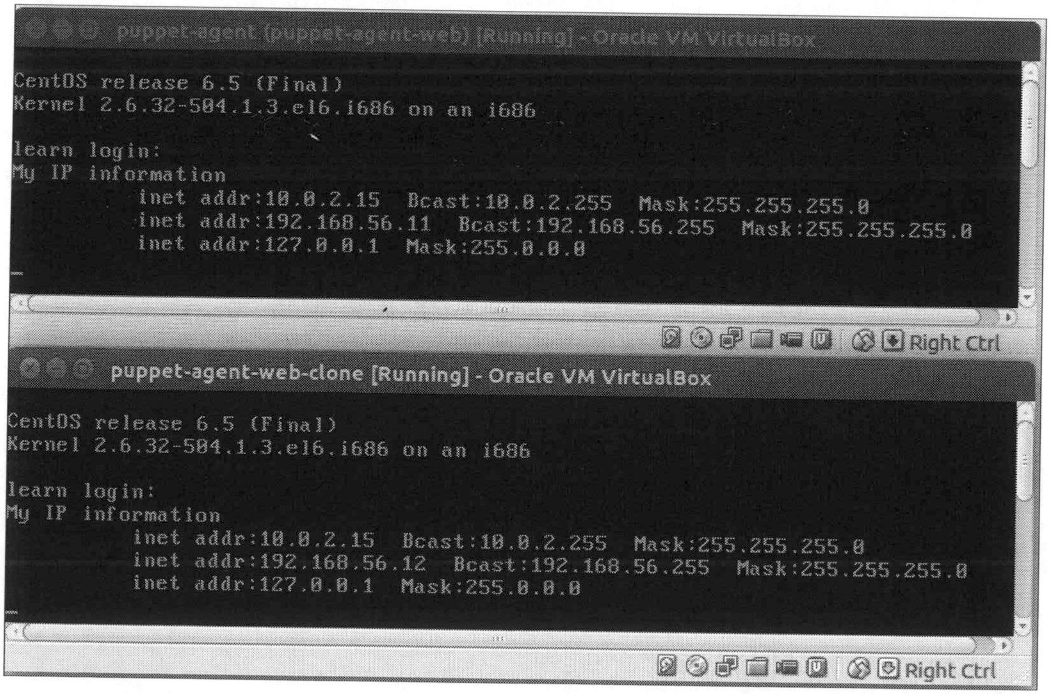

Now log on to both the virtual machines using these login details:

- Username: root
- Password: puppet

Then, apply the webapp class by running the following two commands on both the machines:

```
# cd /media/sf_learning
# puppet apply --modulepath=./ webapp/tests/init.pp
```

Once the webapp class has been applied to both hosts, you can check whether the landing page is available on both machines by opening the web browser on the host computer and accessing http://<ipaddress>, where the <ipaddress> should correspond to the IP address of your virtual machines.

The following screenshot shows the landing page from both the web servers, following the successful deployment:

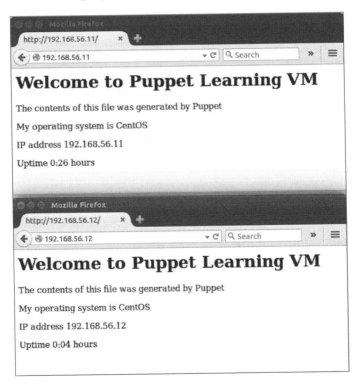

Summary

So we have now come to the end of this chapter. I hope you found the content useful and not too challenging. One of the key deliverables of this chapter was to experiment with Puppet modules and learn how to create your own module as well as make use of modules that other people have written. We also took a look at Puppet templates and facts, which are fundamental building blocks of Puppet modules. There are surely areas that you may feel I didn't cover in enough detail, but try not to worry about it at this stage, as we will be revisiting modules, templates, and facts throughout the course of this book.

Monitoring Your Web Server

For applications to be considered production-ready, they should include monitoring that actively collects performance metrics and raises alerts when things go wrong.

Not so long ago, applications were deployed on a shared, beefy hardware that was capable of running multiple applications and workloads in parallel. Software deployments were done manually by the operations guy according to instructions written by the developer. If the instructions were properly written, they also included a step to set up monitoring for the application. The entire process was carried out manually, which was fine when deployments only happened on a weekly, monthly, or quarterly basis.

But deployments started to be more frequent when virtualization technologies gained popularity, and it became easier to deploy each application on its own virtual machine to make it more resilient against issues that were common with applications deployed on the shared hardware.

The self-service infrastructure model introduced by cloud providers such as Amazon changed the game even more. Nowadays, it isn't just the operations people who carry out deployments, developers also deploy software in the cloud themselves. The availability of pay-as-you-go charging options, as well as the easy to use self-service infrastructure models, encourages us to launch instances of virtual machines on demand and tear them down when instances are no longer needed.

Instead of deploying software on a weekly or monthly basis like we used to, today, deployments are done on daily basis, or even more often. As deployments are becoming more frequent, it is not viable to do things manually any more, and that's why we use modern tools such as Puppet to automate deployments. The *goal should be to automate everything, including the monitoring*.

In this chapter, we'll look at how Puppet can help you to make monitoring part of the deployment process.

The chapter will cover the following topics:

- Monitoring the architecture
- Creating a Nagios module that provides client and server classes
- Deploying a Nagios server on the monitoring server host
- Deploying a Nagios client on the web server host
- Managing Nagios resources with Puppet's built-in types
- Creating checks for the the web server host
- Creating a custom type to easily create Nagios checks

Monitoring the architecture

The monitoring aspect will be built on an open source project called Nagios, which is a very popular monitoring tool and fits well in Puppet managed environments, as Puppet has built-in resource types for Nagios resources that make configuration easy.

Nagios uses a client-server architecture where the server issues monitoring check commands to the client that runs on the monitored host and the client returns check results back to the server. Nagios Server runs a database where it stores information about Nagios resources, such as clients, what checks to be run on each client, and the status of checks. Nagios Server also provides a web interface for administrators to view the current status of checks and look at the metrics of checks in the form of simple charts. One of the key features of the server is to trigger monitoring alerts when status of checks changes. Alerts can be configured to be delivered by e-mail, SMS, or by making a request to the API.

Nagios Client in comparison to the server is much simpler. Clients receive check commands from the server, perform the check, and return results back to the server for processing. Nagios Client daemon, the process that listens to incoming requests from the Nagios Server, is called **Nagios Remote Plugin Executor**, which is commonly referred to as **NRPE**. The NRPE daemon listens on TCP port 5666.

The Nagios client-server architecture that we will create in this chapter can be illustrated with the following diagram:

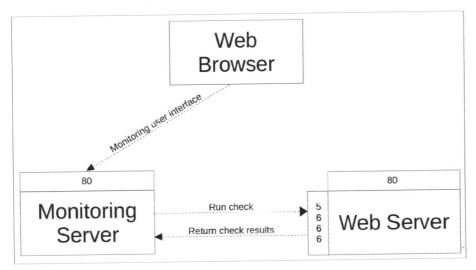

Creating a Nagios module for the client and server

In *Chapter 3, My First Puppet Module*, we practiced creating our first Puppet module for the web server that was deployed by the class called webapp. Now, we'll create another module for Nagios that incorporates a parent class called nagios and two subclasses, one for the Nagios Server called nagios::server and another for the Nagios Client called the nagios::client.

Puppet dictates the class names that we can use within the module. Let's take an example of the class nagios::server that we will create. The double colon (::) notation in the class name acts as a separator between the *parent class* and the *subclass*. In this case, server is a subclass of the parent class called nagios. This nagios parent class must reside in the Puppet module called nagios, or else Puppet won't be able to find the class. If you would declare the class nagios inside the webapp class that was created in *Chapter 3, My First Puppet Module*, and apply it, then Puppet would report the **Error: Could not find class nagios** error.

To avoid any problems with Puppet finding the nagios::server and nagios::client classes, the module name must be nagios. Before we go ahead with module creation, let's create a new clean virtual machine that can be used for Nagios module development.

A recap on the state of virtual machines and snapshots

Let's do a quick recap on the current state of virtual machines and snapshots before we create a new clone. In the **VirtualBox Manager** view, I can see the following three virtual machines:

- **learn_puppet_centos-6.5-pe**: This is the original Puppet Learning VM image that we downloaded in *Chapter 1, Puppet Development in Isolation*. This virtual machine has two snapshots:
  - The base image, which was taken at a very early stage in *Chapter 1, Puppet Development in Isolation*, before we started to work on the virtual machine
  - Host-only-networking, which was created after host-only networking was configured

- **puppet-agent**: This virtual machine was created as a clone from the host-only-networking snapshot of the original Puppet Learning VM. This virtual machine has two snapshots:
  - The base image, which contains the state of the virtual machine before any web server-specific changes
  - **puppet-agent-web**, which is the light version of the Puppet Learning VM that only contains the minimal set of packages needed to run Puppet manifests

- **puppet-agent-web-clone**: This virtual machine was created as a linked clone from the snapshot **puppet-agent-web** that belongs to the **puppet-agent** virtual machine

I'll include a screenshot of the VirtualBox Manager view on my machine, so you can compare it with the view on yours:

In the the preceding screenshot, you can see that I've highlighted the snapshot **puppet-agent-web** of the virtual machine **puppet-agent**. This is the snapshot we should use as the base to create a new clone for the Nagios module development.

Cloning the virtual machine for Nagios module development

You may already be familiar with how to clone the virtual machine from the snapshot, but just in case you need a reminder, here are the steps to carry out the task:

1. In the **VirtualBox Manager** window, select the **puppet-agent** virtual machine.

2. Click the **Snapshots** button in the right-hand top corner of the window.

3. Select the snapshot called **puppet-agent-web**.

4. Click on the **Clone** button above the snapshot list view.

5. Provide a name for the new virtual machine. I'll call it `puppet-agent-nagios`.

6. It is important to remember to tick the option **Reinitialize the MAC address of all network cards**.

7. Click on **Next** and choose the **Linked clone** option in the **Clone type** view.

8. Click on the **Clone** button to complete the cloning process.

Once the clone is created, you should see a fourth virtual machine appearing on the list called **puppet-agent-nagios**. Before you launch the new virtual machine, create a new snapshot called `Base image` that can be used to roll back the machine state in the case of an emergency. I trust the you are familiar with the snapshot creation by now so I won't instruct it again, but if you feel unsure, you may revisit the *Snapshot of the virtual machine* section in *Chapter 1*, *Puppet Development in Isolation*, that instructs the process.

I'd also advise to lower the system memory allocation for the puppet-agent-nagios virtual machine. This can be done in the virtual machine settings (shortcut keys *Ctrl + S*) by selecting the **System** category and reducing the **Base Memory** to 512 MB.

Now, let's launch the virtual machine and start writing our new Nagios module.

Generating the Nagios module

Once the puppet-agent-nagios virtual machine is running, you can log in with the username root and password puppet. Next, you need to change the directory to /media/sf_learning and generate the Nagios module template files. This can be done with the following command sequence:

```
# cd /media/sf_learning
# puppet module generate learning-nagios --skip-interview
```

The puppet module generate command will produce the following output:

```
Notice: Generating module at /media/sf_learning/learning-nagios
Notice: Populating templates...
Finished; module generated in learning-nagios.
learning-nagios/metadata.json
learning-nagios/Rakefile
learning-nagios/manifests
learning-nagios/manifests/init.pp
learning-nagios/spec
learning-nagios/spec/spec_helper.rb
learning-nagios/spec/classes
learning-nagios/spec/classes/init_spec.rb
learning-nagios/Gemfile
learning-nagios/tests
learning-nagios/tests/init.pp
learning-nagios/README.md
```

As in *Chapter 3*, *My First Puppet Module*, we renamed the webapp module so that Puppet is able to find the module from the module path. We must also rename the Nagios module directory so that the part learning- is not present. Use the following command to rename the module directory learning-nagios to nagios:

```
# mv learning-nagios nagios
```

Using the command, ls, you can list files and directories in the current working directory. After renaming the learning-nagios module directory, we'll have the following list of modules:

```
# ls
apache  concat  nagios  stdlib  webapp
```

Puppetize the Nagios Server installation

Nagios Server installation is very easy with Puppet as it only requires a couple of resources to be declared in the manifest. To install Nagios Server, we need a manifest file that installs the Nagios Server package and the Apache HTTP Server provided by the Apache module that we used in *Chapter 3, My First Puppet Module*. The manifest file also must declare a configuration file for the Nagios administration web interface.

We will wrap these resources into the Puppet class called nagios::server and place the class into the file nagios/manifests/server.pp.

Here is the definition for the class nagios::server, which I'll explain more in detail after the snippet:

```
class nagios::server {
  include apachc
  include apache::mod::php
package { ['nagios','nagios-plugins-nrpe']:
    require => Package['httpd'],
    ensure  => installed;
  }
  file fil { '/etc/httpd/conf.d/nagios.conf':
      require => Package['nagios'],
      notify  => Service['httpd'],
      source => "puppet:///modules/nagios/nagios.conf";
  }
  cxcc { 'set-default-username':
    require => Package['nagios'],
    command => '/bin/echo default_user_name=nagiosadmin >> /etc/
nagios/cgi.cfg',
    unless  => '/bin/grep default_user_name=nagiosadmin /etc/nagios/
cgi.cfg',
    notify  => Service['nagios'];
  }
  service { 'nagios':
    require => Package['nagios'],
    ensure  -> running;
  }
}
```

To make it easier to explain the preceding code block, I've prefixed lines with line numbers, which you should omit when writing the file `server.pp`:

- Line 1 begins the `nagios::server` class definition.

- Line 2 references the Apache module that we already used once when building the web server in *Chapter 3, My First Puppet Module*. The Nagios Server web interface also runs on the Apache HTTP server, so we install it on the Nagios Server as well.

- Line 3 references a class `apache::mod::php` that is provided by the Apache module. The Nagios Server web interface is written in the PHP programming language, and in order to make web interface functional, we must enable PHP module on the web server.

- Line 4 declares two package resources. The first package called `nagios` installs the Nagios Server. The `nagios-plugins-nrpe` package installs NRPE plug-in on the server that enables it to communicate with NRPE clients.

- Line 5 sets order in which resources must be processed. The `require` attribute specifies that the web server installation package called `httpd` must be processed prior to processing package `nagios`.

- Line 6 uses `ensure` attribute to indicate that package `nagios` must be installed.

- Line 7 closes the `package` resource statement.

- Line 8 begins with a file resource statement for the file `/etc/httpd/conf.d/nagios.conf` on the target machine. This file will contain the Nagios web interface configuration information for Apache HTTP Server.

- Line 9 defines that the package `httpd`, which creates the directory `/etc/httpd/conf.d`, must be processed before Puppet populates the file `nagios.conf`.

  If this line was omitted, it could potentially cause an ordering issue where Puppet tries to populate the file `nagios.conf` before the target directory is created by the `httpd` package.

- Line 10 uses the `notify` attribute to set the resource processing order in a similar manner as the `require` attribute. The `notify` attribute is slightly more advanced in the sense that it can be used to send a signal to the named resource when originating resource state changes.

  In this case, the file resource notifies the service httpd when the file content changes and the notify signal results in the process httpd to be restarted.

- Line 11 declares a `source` attribute, which defines the source file to be used to populate target file `/etc/httpd/conf.d/nagios.conf`.

- Line 12 closes the file statement.

- Line 13 begins an `exec` resource that sets the default username for the Nagios Server web user interface in the file `/etc/nagios/cgi.cfg`.

  By default, the Nagios installer configures a default username `guest`, that provides limited access to the web interface.

- Line 14 sets the resource processing order so that Nagios package that provides the file `/etc/nagios/cgi.cfg` is installed before the `exec` resource attempts to edit it.

- Line 15 specifies the command that Puppet should execute on the command line. This command uses the `/bin/echo` utility to print the string `default_user_name=nagiosadmin` and the command output is redirected into the file `/etc/nagios/cgi.cfg`.

- Line 16 makes the `exec` resource idempotent using the `unless` attribute. The command specified as the attribute value tells Puppet to only execute the command on line 15 *unless* the result of the command specified as the attribute value is `true`.

  This command uses the `/bin/grep` utility to check whether the string `default_user_name=nagiosadmin` is already present in the file `/etc/nagios/cgi.cfg`.

  - If the string is found, the command returns the value `true` and the command on line 15 is not executed.

  - If the string is not found, the command returns the value `false` and the command on the line 15 is executed.

- Line 17 uses the `notify` resource to signal the Nagios Server process to restart in case the Exec resource modified the configuration.

- Line 18 closes the `exec` resource block.

- Line 19 defines a `service` resource for the Nagios Server process called `nagios`. This resource must be declared so that the `exec` resource `set-default-username` can notify the the Nagios service.

- Line 20 sets the ordering so that the package `nagios` is installed before the `service` resource is processed.

- Line 21 specifies that the Nagios Server process should be in the `running` state.

- Line 22 closes the `service` resource declaration.

- Line 23 marks the end of the class `nagios::server`.

You hopefully now have a better understanding of what the `nagios::server` class does. Now, it's your turn to create the file `server.pp`. You can create the file inside the puppet-agent-nagios virtual machine using the Nano editor, or you can create it on the host computer using the graphical text editor.

Here is the screen capture from text editor on my computer after I've added the content to `server.pp`:

```puppet
class nagios::server {
  include apache
  include apache::mod::php
  package { ['nagios','nagios-plugins-nrpe']:
    require => Package['httpd'],
    ensure  => installed;
  }
  file { '/etc/httpd/conf.d/nagios.conf':
    require => Package['nagios'],
    notify  => Service['httpd'],
    source  => "puppet:///modules/nagios/nagios.conf";
  }
  exec { 'set-default-username':
    require => Package['nagios'],
    command => '/bin/echo default_user_name=nagiosadmin >> /etc/nagios/cgi.cfg',
    unless  => '/bin/grep default_user_name=nagiosadmin /etc/nagios/cgi.cfg',
    notify  => Service['nagios'];
  }
  service { 'nagios':
    require => Package['nagios'],
    ensure  => running;
  }
}
```

Before we can test the `nagios::server` class, we need to create the configuration source file for `nagios.conf` and place it inside the `files` directory within the Nagios module. Because the `puppet module generate` command doesn't create the `files` directory automatically, we must create it by hand. You can create the directory in the file manager program on your machine, or alternatively, create the directory on the command line inside the puppet-agent-nagios virtual machine. Here are the commands for creating the `files` directory on the command line:

```
# cd /media/sf_learning
# mkdir nagios/files
```

Configuring the Nagios Server web interface

The module should now have the `files` directory in place where we can store the `nagios.conf` configuration file that the `nagios::server` class references. The following example enables Nagios web interface on Apache HTTP Server.

For clarity, I've prefixed each line with a line number, which you should omit when creating the file `nagios/files/nagios.conf`:

```
ScriptAlias /nagios/cgi-bin/ /usr/lib/nagios/cgi-bin/
<Directory /usr/lib/nagios/cgi-bin/>
    Options ExecCGI
    Allow from all
</Directory>
Alias /nagios /usr/share/nagios/html
<Directory /usr/share/nagios/html>
    Allow from all
</Directory>
```

Although the preceding configuration has very little to do with Puppet, I'd still like to take a moment to explain what these configuration statements do:

- Line 1 creates an alias for script execution on the web server.
- Line 2 begins a directive for directory `/usr/lib/nagios/cgi-bin` that holds scripts used by Nagios Server web interface.
- Line 3 enables scripts in directory `/usr/lib/nagios/cgi-bin` to be executable by the web server.
- Line 4 makes the directory unrestricted and accessible from any host.
- Line 5 closes the `Directory` directive.
- Line 6 creates a web server resource alias `/nagios`. In practice, this means that when you access the URL `http://192.168.56.10/nagios`, the web server will provide web documents from directory `/usr/share/nagios/html`.
- Line 7 begins a configuration block for `Directory /usr/share/nagios/html`.
- Line 8 configures the directory to be accessible for everyone.
- Line 9 closes the `Directory` directive.

Now, go ahead and create the file `nagios.conf` with the preceding content. Once you have added all lines into the file, the contents should look very similar to the following screenshot:

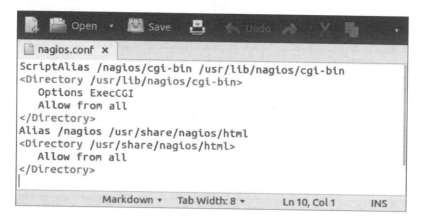

Applying the nagios::server class

 A virtual machine must have a working Internet connection to successfully apply the class.

Now we are ready to try out the new `nagios::server` module. As you may recall from *Chapter 3, My First Puppet Module*, we used the file `tests/init.pp` to apply the class. Similarly, here we will use the `tests/init.pp` file to apply the `nagios::server` class. The only problem is that file `tests/init.pp` doesn't yet have a statement in it that references class `nagios::server`. That's not really a problem as we can easily change the file content.

When you open the `tests/init.pp` file, you will find the following statement inside it that references class `nagios`, which is an empty class in file `manifests/init.pp`.

```
include nagios
```

Change the include statement to reference the class `nagios::server` instead with the following statement:

```
include nagios::server
```

Now we can apply the file `tests/init.pp` and Puppet should be able to locate the `nagios::server` class. Run the following two commands inside the puppet-agent-nagios virtual machine to apply the class:

```
# cd /media/sf_learning
# puppet apply --modulepath=./ nagios/tests/init.pp
```

At the first run, you will get a fairly long report from Puppet due to amount of packages, files, and other type of resources that Puppet has to process. Applying `init.pp` the second time will produce a lot shorter report that looks like the following:

```
# puppet apply --modulepath=./ nagios/tests/init.pp
Notice: Compiled catalog for web.development.vm in environment production in 7.23 seconds
Notice: Finished catalog run in 11.39 seconds
```

Verifying Nagios Server installation

If Puppet didn't report any errors (errors are highlighted in red) during the Puppet run, you should now have Nagios Server web interface accessible from your web browser.

So that we can work out the address for the web interface, we should check what IP address Nagios Server is using. You can use the `ifconfig` command to display the IP address information on the host. Running the command without arguments would print out IP address information from all network interfaces, but to query information from particular interface, such as the host-only network interface that uses device ID eth1, we can use the following command:

```
# ifconfig eth1
```

The IP address that we are interested in is displayed on line 2 with name `inet addr:` in the following output:

```
eth1      Link encap:Ethernet  HWaddr 08:00:27:7A:63:99
          inet addr:192.168.56.10  Bcast:192.168.56.255
Mask:255.255.255.0
```

Based on the IP information that I just extracted, I can construct an URL `http://192.168.56.10/nagios`. When I put this address into the web browser's address bar and hit *Enter*, the following page will load up:

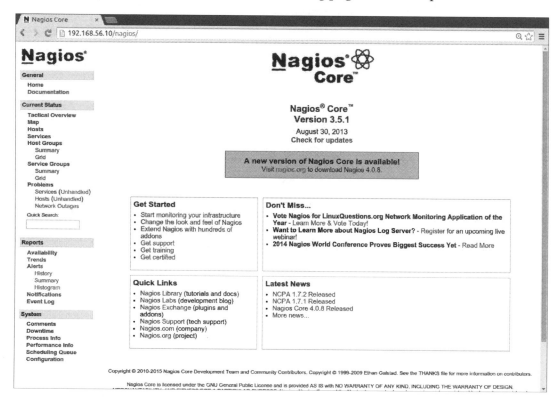

Creating nagios::client class

I hope you managed to get the Nagios Server installed and the web interface running on your machine. Now you can spend some time exploring the Nagios user interface using the links on the left hand side of the view. There is not much to see at this point as we yet haven't configured any resources on the server. There are some resources created by default that you can have a look right away.

If you click the `Services` link that can be found in the navigation pane on your left you will find a list of checks that are run on the host called `localhost`. The `localhost` is the Nagios Server and it has some checks on it that all flag up as CRITICAL.

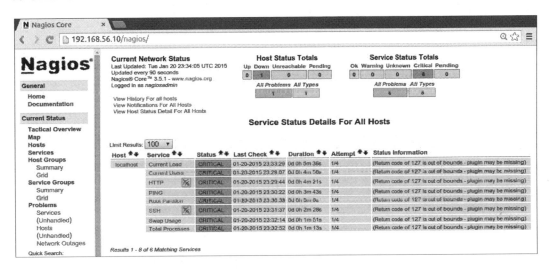

There is a reason why all checks are in CRITICAL status, and that is because there is no Nagios Client installed on the monitoring server and that's why the Nagios Server is unable to check the state of it.

Next, we'll have a look at how to hook a Nagios Client with the server. Earlier in the chapter, I mentioned the acronym NRPE, which is the name of the package that makes a host a Nagios Client. Our mission now is to install the NRPE package, configure it, and tell Puppet to start the process.

To begin the process, you should create a new file called `client.pp` and save it into the directory called `manifests` inside the Nagios module. In the `client.pp` file, create a class called `nagios::client` that does the installation, configuration, and service management for us.

Here is how the content of the file should look like:

```
class nagios::client {
  package { 'nrpe'']:
      ensure => installed;
  }
    package { [
      'nagios-plugins-http',
      'nagios-plugins-ping',
      'nagios-plugins-ssh',
      'nagios-plugins-disk',
      'nagios-plugins-users',
      'nagios-plugins-swap',
      'nagios-plugins-procs',
      'nagios-plugins-load',
      ]:
        ensure  => installed,
        require => Package['nrpe'];
    }
  exec { 'allowed-hosts'
    command => '/bin/sed -i 's/^allowed_hosts=127.0.0.1//g''/etc/
nagios/nrpe.cfg",
    onlyif  => '/bin/grep ^allowed_hosts=127.0.0.1 /etc/nagios/nrpe.
cfg',
    require => Package['nrpe'],
    notify  => Service['nrpe'];
  }
  service { 'nrpe':
    ensure => running,
    enable => true;
  }
}
```

Lines 1 to 20 look fairly straight forward but the exec resource on lines 21 to 27 may look a bit messy. Not to worry though, as I'll do my best to explain what each line inside the class is for.

- Line 1 begins the new class nagios::client that we can associate with every host we want to monitor.

- Line 2 specifies the package nrpe that provides the NRPE daemon installation files.

- Line 3 defines that packages must be installed on the system.

- Line 4 closes the package resource statements.

- Lines 5 to 14 define another package resource. Package resource name is an array of Nagios plug-ins that we want to install.

- Line 15 contains an attribute `ensure => installed` to indicate that we want all packages to be installed.

- Line 16 dictates the order which is to install `package ['nrpe']` before attempting to install plug-ins.

- Line 17 closes the `package` resource.

- line 18 begins an `exec` resource called `allowed-hosts`.

- Line 19 specifies the `command` to be run on the command line by Puppet.

  This command uses utility called `sed`. **Sed** stands for **stream editor** and it is powerful tool used for editing files from the command line.

  The argument `-i` that follows the `/bin/sed` command specifies that the file `/etc/nagios/nrpe.cfg`, which is named as the final argument of the command, should be edited "in place". Running the command without the `-i` argument would only print out the edited content of the file without actually editing the file.

  The argument `'s/^allowed_hosts=127.0.0.1//g'` specifies the text `^allowed_hosts=127.0.0.1` that we want to find and replace with empty string that uses the notation `//`. For example, if we would like to find the text `find_me` and replace it with the text `replace_with`, we would use the expression `'s/find_me/replace_with/g'`.

- Line 20 introduces a new attribute called `onlyif` which sets a condition for the `exec` resource in similar manner as the `unless` attribute that we used in `exec` resource inside the class `nagios::server`.

  The difference between `onlyif` and `unless` attributes is that the command specified by the `command` attribute is executed only if the command specified as the value of `onlyif` attribute returns `true`. In the case of `unless` attribute, the command specified by the `command` attribute is executed, unless the command in `unless` attribute returns `true`.

- Line 21 uses `require` attribute to define that the package `nrpe` must be installed before `exec` resource is processed.

- Line 22 specifies a `notify` attribute that results in the service `nrpe` to be restarted in case `exec` resource command is executed.

- Line 23 closes the `exec` resource statements.

- Line 24 creates a service resource that manages the nrpe service.
- Line 25 sets the state of the service to be running which means that Puppet will start the service unless it has been already started.
- Line 26 defined an attribute enable => true which means that service must be started automatically when system boots up.
- Line 27 closes the service resource statement.
- Line 28 closes the class nagios::client.

Now it's time to start typing and to create the client.pp under the manifests directory. Here is a screenshot that shows the content of the file client.pp:

```puppet
class nagios::client {
  package { 'nrpe':
    ensure => installed;
  }
  package { [
    'nagios-plugins-http',
    'nagios-plugins-ping',
    'nagios-plugins-ssh',
    'nagios-plugins-disk',
    'nagios-plugins-users',
    'nagios-plugins-swap',
    'nagios-plugins-procs',
    'nagios-plugins-load',
    ]:
    ensure  => installed,
    require => Package['nrpe'];
  }
  service { 'nrpe':
    ensure => running;
  }
  exec { 'allowed-hosts':
    require => Package['nrpe'],
    command => "/bin/sed -i 's/^allowed_hosts=127.0.0.1//g' /etc/nagios/nrpe.cfg",
    onlyif  => "/bin/grep ^allowed_hosts=127.0.0.1 /etc/nagios/nrpe.cfg",
    notify  => Service['nrpe'];
  }
}
```

Puppet ▾   Tab Width: 2 ▾   Ln 27, Col 4   INS

Testing the nagios::client class

 You will need an Internet connection to test the nagios::client class.

The nagios::client is now ready to be applied. Let's test it first on the puppet-agent-nagios virtual machine before we try to apply it on the web server host.

The easiest way to apply the class is to add an include nagios::client statement into the file tests/init.pp, that currently only includes the nagios::server class, and then apply the file with puppet apply command.

Open the nagios/tests/init.pp in text editor and add include nagios::client statement into the file. Once it's been added, the nagios/tests/init.pp should have the following content:

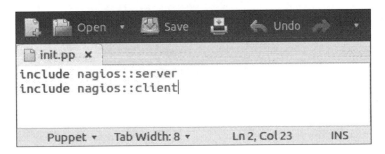

Once the nagios/tests/init.pp file has been saved, you can apply it with the following commands:

```
# cd /media/sf_learning
# puppet apply --modulepath=./ nagios/tests/init.pp
```

If the nagios::client class is applied successfully, Puppet will produce the following report:

```
Notice: Compiled catalog for web.development.vm in environment production
in 6.22 seconds
Notice: /Stage[main]/Nagios::Client/Package[nrpe]/ensure: created
Notice: /Stage[main]/Nagios::Client/Exec[allowed-hosts]/returns: executed
successfully
Notice: /Stage[main]/Nagios::Client/Package[nagios-plugins-all]/ensure:
created
Notice: /Stage[main]/Nagios::Client/Service[nrpe]/ensure: ensure changed
'stopped' to 'running'
Notice: Finished catalog run in 53.20 seconds
```

If you now go back to Nagios Server web interface and click the service link again, you should see that the checks on the host `localhost` are slowly starting to change from state **CRITICAL** to state **OK**, as seen in the following screen capture:

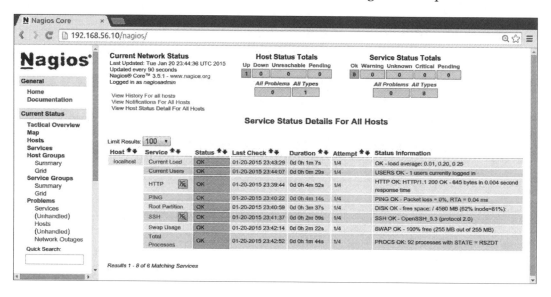

Enable monitoring on the web server

So, the monitoring server is now fully up and running, and so far it monitors one host — the monitoring server itself. What we are most interested in is monitoring the web server that we built in *Chapter 3, My First Puppet Module*. On a high level, the process is the following.

- Configure web server host and checks on the Nagios Server
- Apply nagios::client class on the web server

Let's tackle the first bullet point first and add the web server host and the checks for it on the Nagios Server.

Configuring the web server host and checks on the Nagios Server

Nagios resources such as hosts and checks have built-in resource types in Puppet. Nagios hosts are configured with the resource type called `nagios_host` and checks are configured with the resource type `nagios_service`.

Monitoring checks in Nagios terminology are called services.

Creating a Nagios host

Every host that we want to monitor must be configured on the Nagios Server. Nagios host resource requires two pieces of information:

- Name of the host
- IP address of the host

The name can be whatever you like, and it does not have to match the host name of the host. I like descriptive names, so I'll choose the name web-server for the web server host.

The IP address is slightly trickier as we don't know for sure what IP address the web server will get from the DHCP server when it boots up. For now, let's assume that the web server gets the next available IP address from the DHCP server, which is 192.168.56.11. The IP address ending with .10 is allocated to the Nagios Server at the moment. Later in the book we will have a look at how hosts can export resources that enable Puppet to dynamically adjust the IP address when it changes.

So, we have chosen the name web-server and the IP address 192.168.56.11, and we can now create the host with the following resource definition:

```
nagios_host { 'web-server':
  host_name    => 'web-server',
  address      => '192.168.56.11',
  use          => 'linux-server',
  target       -> '/etc/nagios/conf.d/hosts.cfg',
  notify       => File['/etc/nagios/conf.d'],
  require      => Package['nagios'],
}
```

Let's walk through the nagios_host resource definition so that we know what each attribute does:

- Line 1 declares a nagios_host resource called the web-server.
- Line 2 defines the host_name attribute which sets the name for the Nagios host that will appear in the Nagios Server web interface.
- Line 3 defines the IP address that Nagios Server should use when contacting the agent.
- Line 4 specifies a use attribute that acts as a reference to Nagios host template that provides default values for a variety of attributes associated with the host.

- Line 5 defines the target filename where Nagios host resource should be stored in.

  Target is used to override the default location of the Nagios configuration files that Puppet uses. By default Puppet uses directory `/etc/nagios` to store configuration files in to. The problem is that Nagios Server is not configured to read configurations from this directory. Nagios Server, however, is configured to look for configuration files that use the `.cfg` file extension within the directory `/etc/nagios/conf.d`, and that's why we specify the target file `/etc/nagios/conf.d/resources.cfg` as part of the host resource definition.

- Line 6 creates a `notify` relationship with a file resource for directory `/etc/nagios/conf.d` which we will create in a moment.

- Line 7 requires the package `nagios` that creates the directory `/etc/nagios/conf.d`, to be installed prior to processing this resource. Puppet cannot create the target file `/etc/nagios/conf.d/hosts.cfg` if the directory does not exist.

- Line 8 closes the `nagios_host` resource definition.

Before we add the above `nagios_host` definition into the manifest file, we should have a look at the `nagios_service` definition that will go into the same manifest file and create a check for the web server:

```
nagios_service { 'HTTP':
  host_name           => 'web-server',
  service_description => 'HTTP',
  check_command       => 'check_http',
  use                 => 'local-service',
  target              => '/etc/nagios/conf.d/services.cfg',
  notify              => File['/etc/nagios/conf.d'],
  require             => Package['nagios'],
}
```

- Line 1 declares a `nagios_service` resource called HTTP.

- Line 2 defines a `host_name` attribute that associates the check with the `web-server` host

- Line 3 defines the service name for the check that is displayed in the Nagios Server web interfaces.

- Line 4 specifies the NRPE plug-in name to be used to perform the check. Plug-in `check_http` is used for checking the availability of web server interfaces.

- Line 5 references the Nagios service template called `local-service`.
- Line 6 defines the target file where the Nagios service resource is going to be stored in.
- Line 7 creates a `notify` relationship to file resource `/etc/nagios/conf.d` which is the directory where this `nagios_service` resource is stored in.
- Line 8 requires the package `nagios`, that creates the directory `/etc/nagios/conf.d`, to be installed prior to processing this resource. Puppet cannot create the target file `/etc/nagios/conf.d/hosts.cfg` if the directory does not exist.
- Line 9 closes the `nagios_service` resource definition.

There is one more resource that must accompany the `nagios_host` and `nagios_service` resources, and that is the file resource `/etc/nagios/conf.d`, which was referenced with the `notify` attribute from both Nagios resources. This resource resets the file ownership information so that the Nagios process is able to read the files stored in the directory `/etc/nagios/conf.d`. Here is how to define the file resource:

```
file { '/etc/nagios/conf.d':
  recurse   => true,
  owner     => 'nagios',
  require   => Package['nagios'],
  notify    => Service['nagios'];
}
```

- Line 1 begins the file resource statement for directory `/etc/nagios/conf.d`.
- Line 2 uses `recurse` attribute which is specific to directories that we want to manage recursively.
- Line 3 sets the directory owner as user nagios which is the user account that runs the Nagios Server process.
- Line 4 requires the package `nagios` to be installed prior to processing the `file` resource. Directory `/etc/nagios/conf.d` is created by the nagios installer, and that's why the installation must happen before Puppet tries to change the ownership of the directory.
- Line 5 notifies the `nagios` process to restart in case of any of the files inside the directory had their owner information changed.
- Line 6 closes the `file` resource definition.

Now, create a file `nagios/manifests/resources.pp` and add the preceding three resources into the file wrapped inside the class `nagios::resources`.

The content of file `nagios/manifests/resources.pp` should look like the following after all resources have been added into it:

```
1 class nagios::resources {
2   nagios_host { 'web-server':
3     host_name       => 'web-server',
4     address         => '192.168.56.11',
5     use             => 'linux-server',
6     target          => '/etc/nagios/conf.d/hosts.cfg',
7     notify          => File['/etc/nagios/conf.d'],
8     require         => Package['nagios'],
9   }
10  nagios_service { 'HTTP':
11    host_name           => 'web-server',
12    service_description => 'HTTP',
13    check_command       => 'check_http',
14    use                 => 'local-service',
15    target              => '/etc/nagios/conf.d/services.cfg',
16    notify              => File['/etc/nagios/conf.d'],
17    require             => Package['nagios'],
18  }
19  file { '/etc/nagios/conf.d':
20    recurse   => true,
21    owner     => 'nagios',
22    require   => Package['nagios'],
23    notify    => Service['nagios'];
24  }
25 }
```

Once the file has been created, you should add the `include nagios::resources` statement into the file `nagios/tests/init.pp` before you apply the file. Here's how the content of the `nagios/tests/init.pp` file should look like after modification:

```
include nagios::server
include nagios::client
include nagios::resources
```

Next, we can apply the class on the Nagios Server with the following two commands:

```
# cd /media/sf_learning
```

```
# puppet apply --modulepath=./ nagios/tests/init.pp
```

We are almost done with setting up the monitoring for the web server. Nagios Server has been configured to monitor the HTTP interface on the web server but the web server is not running at this point and there is no NRPE agent installed on it.

However, this issue can be easily rectified by including the class `nagios::client` in the class `webapp` which is found in the file `webapp/manifests/init.pp`.

This is how the beginning of the class `webapp` looks like once I've added the statement `include nagios::client` into it:

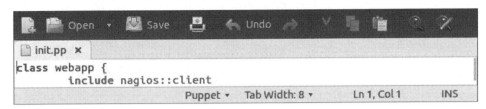

Once the file `webapp/manifests/init.pp` has been saved, power on the virtual machine puppet-agent in its current state, not from the snapshot, and once virtual machine is powered on, log on to the machine as a user `root` using the password `puppet`. Then, apply the `webapp/tests/init.pp` file with the following commands:

```
# cd /media/sf_learning
# puppet apply --modulepath=./ webapp/tests/init.pp
```

Once the `webapp` class has been applied on the web server node, you can go back to Nagios Server web interface at `http://192.168.56.10/nagios`. After refreshing the browser window by clicking the services link, a new host called web-server should appear on the list.

Here's a screenshot from the Nagios Server web interface that shows the HTTP check on the host `web-server` in OK state:

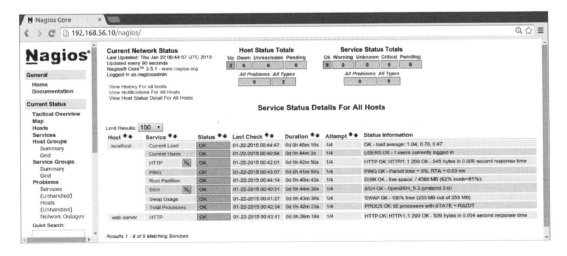

Summary

In this chapter, we learned how to create a Nagios module that includes subclasses. Subclasses provide two streams of deployment logic. We used `nagios::server` class to deploy the Nagios Server, and we installed Nagios Client on the web server by including class `nagios::client` in the `webapp` module. We also had a look at how to configure Nagios hosts and services with Puppet's built-in resource types, `nagios_host` and `nagios_service`.

In the next chapter, we will continue to expand the cluster by adding a load balancer node in front of the web and monitoring servers. The load balancer will provide a single point of access to web interfaces of both servers.

5
Load Balancing the Cluster

Modern clusters running on cloud infrastructure are easy to scale up and down on demand using tools such as Puppet. When new hosts are added in and older hosts are removed from the cluster, it becomes increasingly difficult and impractical to access the cluster services directly on the hosts. A common way to deal with this issue is to add a load balancer or a proxy host in front of services that provides a single point of entry for the user to access the variety of services behind it.

In this chapter you will learn how to make the cluster more resilient and easier to use by adding a load balancer in front of the cluster. The load balancer is going to be built on the Apache web server module that we have already used on the web server and the monitoring server. We will create a new Puppet module for load balancer that interacts with the Apache module by passing class parameters which is a common way to change the behavior of a Puppet class.

This chapter will cover the following topics:

- Parameterized classes
- Defined types
- Load balancing architecture
- Installing proxy server and load balancer
- Creating parameterized class

Let's begin with an introduction to parameterized classes and defined types as we will be using both of these in this chapter. Parameterized classes and defined types are similar in the sense that both are used as a wrapper for Puppet resources.

In *Chapter 4, Monitoring Your Web Server*, we created the `nagios::server` class and added multiple Puppet resources into it, such as the package and the service called `nagios`. If we wanted, we could have created a defined type called `nagios::server`, which first installs the Nagios package, and then starts the `nagios` service; this would have worked as well as the class `nagios::server`. However, since we only need a single instance of a `nagios::server` class, it makes more sense to do this as a class.

If we needed multiple instances of `nagios::server` running on the same host, we would have used defined type instead of the class because defined type can be called multiple times, whereas the class can only be instantiated once per Puppet run.

The parameterized class

The `class` parameter is a mechanism to alter the default behavior of a Puppet class. Typically, parameters are some kind of configuration information that is provided to the class when it is instantiated. For example, installing a database server with a parameterized Puppet class could provide you a parameter that defines how much memory to allocate to the database server process. Or, if a database server process should run as a certain user, you could provide a user parameter to the class, which will then create the user account and start the process as the user.

Calling a class with parameters

When calling a class without parameters, we will use the `include` keyword followed by the class name, for example, `include apache`.

When calling a class with parameters, the `include` key word is replaced with the key word `class` and the syntax used with `class` key word becomes analogous to any other type of Puppet resource. For example, by calling a class `bicycle` with the parameter `wheels` and the parameter `value` 2, we would use the following syntax:

```
class { 'bicycle':
    wheels => '2',
}
```

Perhaps you find traditional bicycles a bit dull and unexciting and decide to go for a unicycle; in which case, you call the class with parameter `wheels => '1'`. Or if you are a family person like I am, and you need more space for kids and groceries, you may prefer a tricycle which you can get with parameter `wheels => '3'`.

This is just an example of how `class` parameters can help to have a single implementation of a class that caters for multiple needs.

Creating a parameterized class

Now, we know how to call class with parameters, but before we can do this, the class must be written in way that it understands the parameters that we are passing in.

Let's implement the `bicycle` class and add a simple `exec` resource into it, which executes a fictional command that orders a bicycle from a nonfictional shop called `The School Run Centre` (my local bike retailer based in Cambridge, UK):

```
class bicycle {
  exec { 'bicycle-order':
  command => "/usr/bin/the-school-run-centre order wheels=2"
}
```

The class `bicycle` in its current form doesn't yet understand parameters passed into it, and if you're calling the class without parameters, using the `include` key word, it will always place an order for a traditional two-wheel bike.

To make the `bicycle` class accept the parameter `wheels` and to make use of the parameter value in `exec` resource, we must do the following alterations to the class:

```
class bicycle ($wheels='2') {
  exec { 'bicycle-order':
    command => "/usr/bin/the-school-run-centre order wheels=$wheels"
  }
}
```

Let's have a look at the preceding class definition more in detail:

1. Line 1 declares a class `bicycle` and class accepts a parameter called `wheels`. The parameter `wheels` has a default value 2, which means that if parameter is not provided, its value will be 2.

   To make the parameter obligatory, you should omit the default value and specify the parameter as `$wheels`. Only in this case will Puppet report an error if the user doesn't supply the parameter when calling the class.

2. Line 2 begins the `exec` resource statement `bicycle-order`.

3. Line 3 specifies the command that Puppet executes when the class is called. The command ends with a reference to input parameter `$wheels`.

4. Line 4 closes the `exec` resource block.

5. Line 5 ends the `bicycle` class definition.

The defined type

The defined type is a user-defined Puppet resource type that works in a very similar manner as the parameterized class with exception that it can be called multiple times. Continuing with our bicycle example, if we would create a defined type called `bicycle`, we could use it to order more than one type of bicycle at the time. In other words, you can order a unicycle and a tricycle in one go. But if you're using a class `bicycle`, I can only order a unicycle for you or tricycle for me.

Calling the defined type

The defined type is referenced with the exactly the same syntax as when referencing Puppet built-in resource types such as the `exec`, `file`, or the user resource.

To reference the defined type called `bicycle`, we'd do it in the following way:

```
bicycle { 'unicycle':
    wheels => '1';
}
```

As you can see, the syntax is almost identical to the `bicycle` class reference. The only difference is that here we don't begin the definition with a class key word because we are not referencing the `class` resource type. Instead, our resource type is called `bicycle`, and the name of the resource, here I used unicycle, can be whatever you like as long as the resource name is unique.

The preceding snippet would order a unicycle for you. But what if I also wanted a bicycle, one that has 3 wheels? Well, this could be done with another bicycle resource definition that looks like the following:

```
bicycle { 'tricycle':
    wheels => '3';
}
```

Now we have references to two different types of bicycles: one has 1 wheel and another has 3 wheels. That's fine as long as the bicycle resource names are unique. And this criteria is fulfilled as the first `bicycle` is called unicycle and the other one is called tricycle.

Now, we know how to reference a defined type, but how does it look from the other end of the tunnel? Let's have a look at how the type bicycle can be implemented.

Creating the defined type

Creating the defined type is quite similar to creating a class. There is one tricky bit to remember though when creating your own types and I've highlighted that part of the code in the following declaration that creates the type bicycle:

```
define bicycle ($wheels='2') {

  exec { "bicycle-order-${name}":

    command => "/usr/bin/the-school-run-centre order wheels=$wheels"

  }

}
```

The tricky bit that I mentioned is found at the end of the line 2, but I'll run you through the preceding type definition line by line and compare it to the class definition:

1. Line 1 begins with the keyword define, which is used when we want to define a new type in Puppet. For the bicycle class, we used the key word class. For defined types, we must use the key word define.

2. Line 2 begins an exec resource definition that executes a command on the command line every time the type is called. When comparing this definition to the exec resource definition inside the class bicycle, we find that there are two important changes.

3. The name of the exec resource is wrapped inside double quotes (") to enable variable interpolation. In the bicycle class, we used single quotes ('), which Puppet interprets as string literal. Because the resource name in the bicycle type references the $name variable, we must use double quotes.

4. Reference to the $name variable helps to make the exec resource name unique and avoid resource name clashes when the type is called multiple times. The variable $name used in the defined type is a reference to the name that the user defines when the type is called.

5. When the type bicycle is referenced with the name unicycle, the $name variable value in the exec resource name becomes unicycle; thus, the exec resource name is interpolated as bicycle-order-unicycle.

6. When the type `bicycle` is referenced the second time with the name `tricycle`, the `exec` resource name is interpolated as `bicycle-order-tricycle`.

7. Line 3 is identical to the line 3 found in the class `bicycle`. This specifies the command that Puppet executes when the type is called.

8. Line 4 closes the `exec` resource.

9. Line 5 ends the type definition of `bicycle`.

I believe that's all we need to know about parameterized classes and defined types before we move on and use them in real-life scenario.

The load balancing architecture

Before we dive into the Puppet module world again, let's have a quick look at the system architecture and how the load balancer fits into it. The load balancer will be installed on a dedicated virtual machine, which sits in front of the web and the monitoring servers.

First, we will configure the load balancer in the so-called proxy mode, which means that the load balancer is acting like a router for HTTP requests that it forwards to the appropriate backend server based on the URL that the user is accessing.

For example, when a user requests resource `http://loadbalancer_ipaddress/nagios`, the load balancer forwards the request to the monitoring server, and when the requested resource is `http://loadbalancer_ipaddress/webapp`, the request is routed to the web server.

Later, we will configure the load balancer, do some real load balancing between two web server nodes and experience how load balancer makes services more resilient against outages when one of the web servers suddenly drops offline.

The following diagram illustrates the layout of the cluster that we will build now:

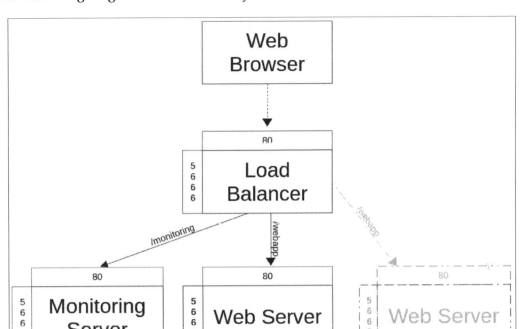

The top element in the preceding diagram is the web browser that runs on the user's computer. The web browser connects to TCP port 80 on the load balancer machine. The load balancer forwards the request either to the monitoring server or the web server node based on the address that the user typed into the web browser.

If a user requests a web page, `http://loadbalancer-ipaddress/monitoring`, the load balancer forwards the request to the monitoring server. If the requested web page is `http://loadbalancer-ipaddress/webapp`, the load balancer routes the request to the web server 1 node.

The 5th element in the diagram that is greyed out is the second web server node that we will boot up later in the chapter when testing the load balancing functionality. Once load balancing is enabled, the load balancer will forward and request for `http://loadbalancer-ipaddress/webapp` to either one of the web server nodes.

Building the load balancer node

Now we know how the cluster will look once the load balancer node has been added to the cluster. To create the load balancer node, we will first create a new virtual machine clone that will be used as the development environment for the load balancer Puppet module development. Let's get on with it then.

Cloning a new virtual machine for the load balancer

If you have any virtual machines running at the moment, I'd recommend to shut them down now to reduce the memory usage on the host computer. We will begin by creating a new clean virtual machine for the load balancer module development using the following steps:

1. Select the virtual machine puppet-agent.
2. Click the **Snapshots** button.
3. Choose the `puppet-agent-web` snapshot.
4. Click the **Clone** button.
5. Provide a name for the new virtual machine, for example, `puppet-agent-loadbalancer` and tick the box **Reinitialize the MAC address of all network cards**.
6. Click on **Next**.
7. In the **Clone type** view, select **Linked clone**.
8. Click on **Clone**.
9. You should now see a new virtual machine called `nagios-agent-loadbalancer` appearing on the virtual machine list.

Reducing the virtual machine memory allocation

Reduce the memory size of the machine by opening virtual machine settings (*Ctrl + S*). Navigate to the **System** view and reduce the **Base memory allocation** to 512 MB.

Creating a snapshot and starting the virtual machine

Once the memory allocation has been reduced, I'd recommend that you create a snapshot of the new virtual machine so that we can quickly restore the virtual machine into its original state if we happen to break it during the development process.

By now, you probably know well how to create virtual machine snapshot in VirtualBox, but as a reminder here are the steps on how to create a snapshot:

1. Select the new virtual machine from the list.
2. Click on the **Snapshots** button.
3. Click on the **Take Snapshot** button.
4. Provide a name of the snapshot, for example, Base Image.

Now we are ready to start the virtual machine. When the virtual machine comes up, you can log in using the username root and password puppet.

Creating a load balancer module

After starting the virtual machine, now we'll create a new Puppet module for load balancer that will use the apache module from Puppetlabs to do the base install of the Apache HTTP Server and enable load balancing on it. In addition to the base installation, we will add our own custom configuration that specifies which backend services and nodes the load balancer should link to.

Once you have logged on to the virtual machine, you can create the load balancer module with the following commands:

```
cd /media/sf_learning
puppet module generate learning-loadbalancer --skip-interview
```

The command `puppet module generate` will create a new module directory called `learning-loadbalancer` that we must rename as `loadbalancer` so that Puppet is able to locate the module. Assuming your current working directory is `/media/sf_learning`, you can rename the directory `learning-loadbalancer` by issuing an `mv` command in the following way:

```
mv learning-loadbalancer loadbalancer
```

 As an alternative to the command line, you can rename the `learning-loadbalancer` directory in the file manager program on the host computer. On my machine, the folder is located in the following path: `/home/jussi/learning/learning-loadbalancer`

Once the module directory has been renamed, you should have six modules in the directory `/media/sf_learning`. You can list the directory content with the `ls` command and the command should produce the following list of Puppet modules:

```
[root@learn /media/sf_learning]# ls
apache concat loadbalancer nagios stdlib webapp
```

Installing the load balancer using class parameters

Now that the `loadbalancer` module has been created, we can start adding deployment logic into the class `loadbalancer`, which you can find inside the file `loadbalancer/manifests/init.pp`:

 To make it easier to keep track of the lines in the file `init.pp`, I've removed all comment lines (lines beginning with #) and enabled line numbers in Gedit text editor.

Open the file `init.pp` in text editor and add the following content to it:

```
 1 class loadbalancer {
 2   include apache
 3   apache::vhost { 'loadbalancer':
 4     ip          => $::ipaddress_eth1,
 5     docroot     => '/var/www/html',
 6     proxy_pass  => [
 7                   { 'path' => '/nagios', 'url' => 'http://192.168.56.11/nagios' },
 8                   { 'path' => '/webapp', 'url' => 'http://192.168.56.12/' },
 9                 ]
10   }
11 }
```

It only takes as little as 11 lines of Puppet configuration to turn the load balancer node into a proxy server.

Let's look at the preceding `loadbalancer` class more in detail:

1. Line 1 begins the `loadbalancer` class definition.

2. Line 2 calls the `apache` class without passing any parameters to it. With this statement, we express that we want Puppet to do the basic installation of Apache HTTP Server.

3. Line 3 makes a reference to defined type called `vhost` that is provided by the class `apache`. To make a reference to a type `vhost` that is declared inside a class `apache`, Puppet uses notation `apache::vhost` followed by the name of the type, in this case named as `loadbalancer`.

4. Line 4 sets a parameter `ip` that we pass into the type `vhost`. The value of the parameter defines the address that the load balancer node is listening on for incoming HTTP requests. For this, we use fact called `ipaddress_eth1`, which is a reference to the IP address of the `Host-Only Network` interface on the load balancer virtual machine. In my environment load balancer, the node uses IP address `192.168.56.10` for the `Host-Only Network` interface.

5. Line 5 defines parameter `docroot` which is one of the required parameters by the `apache::vhost`. The value of the parameter is not important for the functionality of the load balancer, we just must provide the parameter with some value when calling the type `apache::vhost`.

6. Line 6 defines a parameter `proxy_pass`, which is used to create a route via load balancer to the web server and the monitoring server. The value of the parameter begins with `[` sign, which in the Puppet language means that the parameter value is a list of items. Lines 7 and 8 specifies the items on the list.

7. Line 7 defines the first item on the list, which is a dictionary type of data where the data is presented in the format of key—value pairs. With this configuration, we tell the load balancer to forward all requests for the resource `/nagios` on the load balancer to the monitoring server URL `http://192.168.56.11/`.

   The first key is called `path` and the value is `/nagios`.

   The second key is called `url` and the value of the url is `http://192.168.56.11/nagios`.

8. Line 8 specifies another set of key—value pairs for the Web Server interface at http://192.168.56.12/.

   The dictionary entry path has a value /webapp.

   The second dictionary entry url has the value http://192.168.56.12.

9. Line 9 ends the list with a closing block bracket].

10. Line 10 closes the block apache::vhost.

11. Line 11 ends the loadbalancer class definition.

So, now you should have rough idea of what is involved in the initial deployment of the load balancer node. Next, we can try this in action.

Deploying the load balancer

Load balancer deployment requires Internet connectivity, so make sure that you are connected to the Internet before you carry on.

We will begin by deploying the load balancer node before we boot up the Web and the monitoring server nodes. As we are have used hardcoded IP addresses in the loadbalancer class, we have to be careful with the order in which we boot up the virtual machines in our cluster so that the nodes get allocated the correct IP addresses from the DHCP server on VirtualBox.

Virtual machines should be started in the following order:

1. The load balancer node being the first node in the cluster should get IP address 192.168.56.10.

2. The monitoring server started as the second in order should get IP address 192.168.56.11.

3. The web server is started as the third node and it should get IP address 192.168.56.12.

 The load balancer node should be already up and running. If not, then start it up now, but before you do this, make sure that you haven't got other virtual machines running on VirtualBox.

Now that we have only the load balancer node running, we can apply the class loadbalancer with the following commands:

```
cd /media/sf_learning
puppet apply --modulepath=./  loadbalancer/tests/init.pp
```

The deployment should last a maximum of couple of minutes and it will produce quite verbose Puppet report, which I'll not disclose here in full as it would take up too much space in this chapter. Instead, I'll include the last two lines of the Puppet report that are printed when the deployment is completed successfully:

```
Notice: /Stage[main]/Apache::Service/Service[httpd]/ensure: ensure
changed 'stopped' to 'running'
Notice: Finished catalog run in 17.36 seconds
```

The first line reports the final step of the deployment where Puppet changes the state of the Apache HTTP Server process from `stopped` to `running`. The last line shows that the load balancer deployment on my machine took `17.36 seconds`.

Verifying the load balancer deployment

Analyzing the Puppet report is one way to know whether the deployment was successful, but what is more important is to know whether the service works in real life. To verify the load balancer functionality, we will spin up the web and monitoring servers and see whether we can access both web interfaces via load balancer node's IP address.

But before we do this, let's do a quick test that shows whether the load balancer node is trying to route request to the backend services:

Open the web browser on the host computer. Type in the URL `http://192.168.56.10/webapp` and hit *Enter*.

If you get immediate response of `404 Not Found` displayed at the top of the browser window, then that's a sign that deployment was not successful. If this is the case, I'd advise you to review the content of the class `loadbalancer` and check the syntax of each line in the class.

However, if the request takes a few seconds to process and you then receive message 503 **Service Temporarily Unavailable**, this means that the load balancer attempted to route the request to the web server interface but as the node is not yet running, the request timed out. The following screenshot shows example 503 response:

Testing end-to-end functionality

Next, we will verify the functionality end-to-end and launch.

Depending on how much free memory you have on the host computer, you may have to reduce the memory allocation in the virtual machine settings, which you can access by pressing *Ctrl + S* and adjusting the Base Memory value under the **System** category. You can reduce the amount of memory down to 256 MB and virtual machines should still boot up fine.

Once the monitoring server comes up, you should see the IP address information displayed on the log in prompt. The IP information shows that the monitoring server has got IP address 192.168.56.11 from the DHCP server as shown in the following screenshot:

Similarly, in the login prompt on the web server, the IP address information shows that the web server is using the IP address 192.168.56.12:

If for any reason web and monitoring server nodes came up with different IP addresses, you should reconfigure the load balancer node by adjusting the lines 7 and 8 in the file loadbalancer/manifests/init.pp, and point the /nagios and /webapp resources to appropriate IP addresses. In case you made changes to the loadbalancer class, you should apply your changes with the command puppet apply --modulepath=./ loadbalancer/tests/init.pp on the load balancer node.

Before we do our end-to-end tests, let's do a Puppet run on the other two nodes to make sure that all services are started properly.

Log on to the web server node using the username `root` and password `puppet`. Then, run the following two commands:

```
cd /media/sf_learning
puppet apply --modulepath=./ webapp/tests/init.pp
```

Then, log on to the monitoring server node using the same login details and apply the `nagios::server` class with the following set of commands:

```
cd /media/sf_learning
puppet apply --modulepath=./ nagios/tests/init.pp
```

Now that all three virtual machines have been updated by Puppet, it is time to check whether we can access monitoring and web server interfaces via the load balancer node. In the class `loadbalancer`, we configured resource `/nagios` for the monitoring server and the resource `/webapp` for the web server.

Open the web browser on the host computer type in the URL `http://192.168.56.10/nagios`. This should give you the nagios server front-page:

Then, try the URL http://192.168.56.10/webapp and see whether the web server landing page loads up. The following screenshot demonstrates the proxy functionality quite nicely. If you look at the page content, it shows the web server's IP address 192.168.56.12, but the IP address in the address field on the web browser points to the IP address 192.168.56.10:

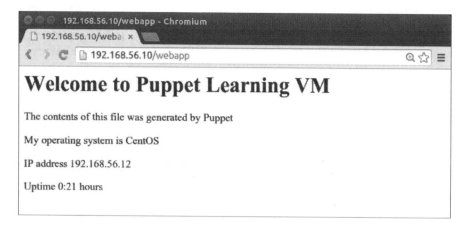

That's it. I hope your end-to-end tests were as successful as mine. Next, we will focus on how to make the loadbalancer class more configurable by turning it into the parameterized class.

Adding parameters to the loadbalancer class

The load balancer node is now working, but the configuration is quite static in the sense that the HTTP end points /nagios and /webapp are bound to back-end services defined in the class loadbalancer. What if the web server's IP address changes or we wanted to change the name of the end points? We could adjust the loadbalancer class, but the better option is to make the loadbalancer class to accept parameters that enables us to specify the end points and backend service URLs when we call the class.

We currently use the following "hardcoded" URL mappings in the class loadbalancer:

```
{ 'path' => '/nagios', 'url' => 'http://192.168.56.11/nagios' }
```

This links the resource /nagios with URL http://192.168.56.11/nagios:

```
{ 'path' => '/webapp', 'url' => 'http://192.168.56.12/' }
```

This links the resource /webapp with URL http://192.168.56.12/.

To make the path and the url parameters configurable when calling the class, we will add four input parameters to the class loadbalancer, which you can find on lines 1 to 4 in the following screenshot:

```
init.pp  ×

 1 class loadbalancer ($nagios_path = '/nagios',
 2                     $nagios_url  = 'http://192.168.56.11/nagios',
 3                     $webapp_path = '/webapp',
 4                     $webapp_url  = 'http://192.168.56.12/') {
 5   include apache
 6   apache::vhost { 'loadbalancer':
 7     ip         => $::ipaddress_eth1,
 8     docroot    => '/var/www/html',
 9     proxy_pass => [
10                    { 'path' => $nagios_path, 'url' => $nagios_url },
11                    { 'path' => $webapp_path, 'url' => $balancer_url },
12                   ]
13   }
14 }
```

Puppet ▾   Tab Width: 2 ▾   Ln 14, Col 2   INS

Let's focus on the lines that were added or changed in the class loadbalancer:

1. Line 1 begins the class loadbalancer and defines the first input parameter $nagios_path that we reference on line 10. The parameter $nagios_path has a default value nagios, which we can override with our own value when calling the class. If we don't provide the parameter $nagios_path, then the default value will be used.

2. Line 2 defines the second input parameter $nagios_url and sets a default value http://192.168.56.11/nagios. The parameter is referenced on line 10.

3. Line 3 defines the third input parameter $webapp_path and gives it a default value /webapp. The parameter is referenced on line 11.

4. Line 4 defines the fourth and the last input parameter $webapp_url with the default value http://192.168.56.12/ and the reference to the parameter can be found on line 11.

5. Line 10 contains references to input parameters `$nagios_path` (line 1) and `$nagios_url` (line 2).

6. Line 11 references input parameters `$webapp_path` (line 3) and `$balancer_url` (line 4).

That's all the changes required in the class `loadbalancer` to make it parameterized. As all input parameters have default values, it is fully backwards compatible, and we are not forced to provide parameters when calling the class.

But we of course want to try how parameters add functionality to the class, and this we can do on the command line by applying the `loadbalancer` class with extra options. In the following example, the path to the web server is changed from `/webapp` to `/web` on the load balancer node.

On the load balancer node, move to the directory `/media/sf_learning` with the following command:

```
cd /media/sf_learning
```

Then, apply the `loadbalancer` class with class parameters using the `-e` option:

```
puppet apply --modulepath=./ -e "class { 'loadbalancer': webapp_path
=> '/web' }"
```

When Puppet run is completed successfully, the default path value `/webapp` will stop working and you should be able to access the web server interface using the URL `http://192.168.56.10/web`.

To pass two or more parameters to the class, you can provide a comma separated list of parameters in following way:

```
puppet apply --modulepath=./ -e "class { 'loadbalancer': nagios_path
=> '/', nagios_url => 'http://192.168.56.11/nagios/' }"
```

This command configures the root resource (/) to point to nagios server interface

After the command has been applied, you should now be able to access the `nagios` web interface in the URL `http://192.168.56.10`:

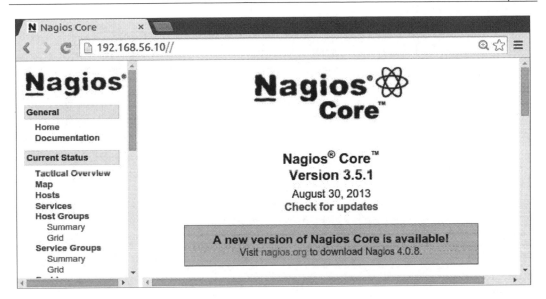

If you want to revert the configuration to the default, just use the same command syntax without passing any parameters to the class. Here's the example command:

```
puppet apply --modulepath=./ -e "class { 'loadbalancer': }".
```

The same command in simpler format using the `include` keyword looks like this:

```
puppet apply --modulepath=./ -e "include loadbalancer"
```

That's how parameterized classes are created and instantiated. The class parameters adds flexibility to how Puppet classes can be used and configuration changes becomes quicker and easier to apply when we can change the configuration with parameters instead of having to change the content of the class itself.

The load balancer node is now working as a proxy server for the web server and monitoring server nodes. Next, we will have a look how we can turn the load balancer node into a proper load balancer that spreads the requests across multiple web server nodes.

Load balancing web server nodes

Load balancing is used to make services more resilient and scalable. In a typical scenario, we have a cluster of nodes such as web servers. All of the servers provides the same service, which means that incoming requests received from clients can be processed on any of the servers in the cluster. So that the user doesn't have to decide which server to send the request to, we add a load balancer in front of the cluster which makes the decision and routes the requests to one of the cluster nodes. When nodes in the cluster start to struggle with the number of incoming requests, and we need to scale up the service, it is easy to add a new node in to the cluster. Then, we can tell the load balancer that a new member node has joined the cluster and the load balancer start routing requests to new node. At some point, when the number of incoming requests goes down again, and the cluster can manage with fewer member nodes, we just remove nodes from the cluster and the load balancer automatically stops forwarding requests to decommissioned nodes. This is called horizontal scaling of the service.

The following diagram illustrates how requests **Req.1**, **Req.2**, and **Req.3** are load balanced across three web servers in cluster:

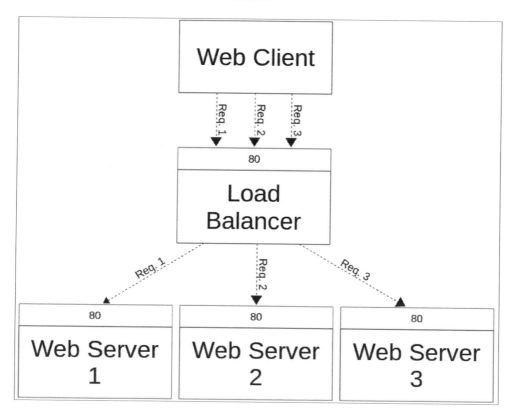

Next, we can try out this load balancing scenario in our virtual machine environment and set up a cluster of two web servers and configure the load balancer node to route requests to them. To achieve this, we must first make a couple of modifications in the loadbalancer class and then create a new class called loadbalancer::create that constructs the load balancer object and adds member nodes to it.

Enabling load balancing on the loadbalancer class

To enable load balancing in the class loadbalancer, we will add couple of new variables in to the class that we can reference from the class loadbalancer::create that we will soon create.

Here's how the latest version of the class loadbalancer in file loadbalancer/manifests/init.pp looks after variables and variable references have been put in place:

```puppet
1 class loadbalancer ($nagios_path = '/nagios',
2                     $nagios_url  = 'http://192.168.56.11/nagios',
3                     $webapp_path = '/webapp',
4                     $webapp_url  = 'http://192.168.56.12/') {
5   include apache
6   $balancer_name = 'webapp'
7   $balancer_url  = "balancer://${balancer_name}"
8   include loadbalancer::create
9   apache::vhost { 'loadbalancer':
10    ip         => $::ipaddress_eth1,
11    docroot    => '/var/www/html',
12    proxy_pass => [
13                  { 'path' => $nagios_path, 'url' => $nagios_url },
14                  { 'path' => $webapp_path, 'url' => $balancer_url },
15                  ]
16  }
17 }
```

Let's walk through the lines that were added or changed since the previous version of the class:

1. Line 6 defines a string variable called $balancer_name that is referenced on the line 7. The same variable will be also referenced from the class loadbalancer::create later in the chapter.

2. Line 7 declares another string variable `$balancer_url` that references the variable `${balancer_name}` defined on line 6. The variable `$balancer_url` is referenced on line 14 by the `url` attribute value.

   Please note that variables in Puppet can be referenced with syntax `$variable` or as `${variable}`. Both work the same way, but the added curly braces in variable reference makes. The later variant `${variable}` is recommended by Puppet Language Style Guide (`https://docs.puppetlabs.com/guides/style_guide.html`).

3. Line 8 references the class `loadbalancer::create` that we will create in a moment.

4. Line 14 that previously referred to the web server URL is now referencing the variable `${balancer_url}`, which translates to string `balancer://webapp`.

Let's not try to apply the `loadbalancer` class yet as it would produce an error during Puppet run due to missing the class `loadbalancer::create` that we need to create now.

In the text editor, create a new file `loadbalancer/manifests/create.pp`. The file defines the class `loadbalancer::create` that creates the `load balancer` object and adds two member nodes into it.

Here's the content for the file `loadbalancer/manifests/create.pp` and I'll explain its functionality more in detail after the screenshot:

```puppet
1 class loadbalancer::create {
2   apache::balancer { $::loadbalancer::balancer_name:
3     collect_exported => false;
4   }
5   apache::balancermember { "web1":
6       balancer_cluster => $::loadbalancer::balancer_name,
7       url              => 'http://192.168.56.12/',
8   }
9   apache::balancermember { "web2":
10      balancer_cluster => $::loadbalancer::balancer_name,
11      url              => 'http://192.168.56.13/',
12  }
13 }
```

Here's the break down of the file `loadbalancer/manifests/create.pp`:

1. Line 1 begins the class `loadbalancer::create`. This class doesn't accept any parameters.

2. Line 2 references defined type `apache::balancer` that is provided by the Apache module. The name of the type in this case becomes `webapp` that we defined at the time when we added the variable `$balancer_name` into the class `loadbalancer` in previous paragraph.

3. Puppet variables have "a scope" and we can reference variables from other classes with syntax `${::classname::variablename}`. We will talk about variable scope more in detail in the next chapter.

4. Line 3 sets a Boolean value `false` for input parameter `collect_exported`. With this parameter, we tell the defined type `apache::balancer` not to collect exported resources.

5. Exported resources are not yet available in our Puppet environment, but we will enable them and learn how to use them in *Chapter 7, Making the Configuration Dynamic*.

6. Line 4 closes the defined type `apache::balancer` definition.

7. Line 5 begins the first of the two `apache::balancermember` definitions. Type `apache::balancermember` is used to describe the URL where the load balancer should forward requests to. For the first balancer member, we give a name `web1`.

8. Line 6 defines the name of the cluster that this balancer member belongs to. With the attribute `balancer_cluster`, we assign this balancer member to the cluster that we created in the preceding `apache::balancer` block.

9. Line 7 sets the URL where requests are routed to.

10. Line 8 closes the first `apache::balancermember` block.

11. Line 9 begins the second balancer member definition for which I've given a name `web2`.

12. Line 10 assigns the balancer member `web2` to the the same cluster as the balancer member `web1`.

13. Line 11 sets the URL to forward requests to on the node `web2`.

14. You may need to adjust this IP address if the node comes up with a different address when it started up.

15. Line 12 closes the second balancer member definition.

16. Line 13 ends the class `loadbalancer::create`.

We now have all the assets ready for load balancer deployment. Make sure that the class `loadbalancer::create` is saved as `create.pp` in the directory `loadbalancer/manifests` so that Puppet is able to locate the class. Next, we will apply the class `loadbalancer` and see how load balancing works in practice.

Applying and testing the load balancer

Let's apply the class `loadbalancer` first to see that we got the syntax right before we join the second web server node in the cluster.

On the load balancer node, run the following two commands:

```
cd /media/sf_learning/
puppet apply --modulepath=./ loadbalancer/tests/init.pp
```

This time the `puppet apply` command will produce couple of warning messages, which you can safely ignore.

The first message `Warning: You cannot collect exported resources without storeconfigs` being set is related to exported resource collection, which we haven't yet enabled in our environment.

The second message `Critical: Scope(Concat::Fragment[01-webapp-proxyset]): No content, source or symlink specified` is produced by the type `concat::fragment`What. This message doesn't have functional impact on the deployment so you can safely ignore this.

What you should ensure is that Puppet bounces the service HTTPD at the end of the Puppet run, which is an indication that deployment was successful. On successful run, the Puppet report will include the following two lines at the end:

```
Notice: /Stage[main]/Apache::Service/Service[httpd]: Triggered
'refresh' from 1 events
Notice: Finished catalog run in 13.42 seconds
```

Before we launch the second web server node, let's do a quick test to ensure that the first web server is accessible via load balancer in the URL `http://192.168.56.10/webapp`.

I've checked it and it works for me. Does it also work in your environment?

Launching the second web server node

In *Chapter 3, My First Puppet Module*, we created the virtual machine called `puppet-agent-web-clone`, which we can use as our secondary web server node. If you have deleted it, you can easily recreate by following the process described in *Chapter 3, My First Puppet Module*.

Launch the virtual machine puppet-agent-web-clone and once it's up and running, perform the following three things on the virtual machine:

1. Check that second web server node got an IP address `192.168.56.13` from the DHCP Server. The IP information is displayed in the login prompt. If it reports a different IP address than `192.168.56.13`, then you need to adjust the line 11 in `loadbalancer/manifests/create.pp` and set the `url` attribute value accordingly.

2. Run Puppet on the virtual machine to bring the configuration up to date with the following commands:

    ```
    cd /media/sf_learning/
    puppet apply --modulepath=./ webapp/tests/init.pp
    ```

3. Then open the web browser and go to the address `http://192.168.56.10/webapp`. If you keep refreshing the browser window (press *F5*), you should notice from the IP address field that each odd request is routed to web server 1 at `192.168.56.12` and that even requests are routed to web server 2 at `192.168.56.13`.

    The following screenshot shows how two requests are forwarded to different back end servers:

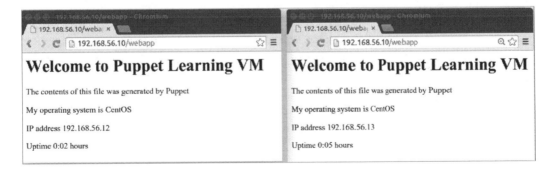

Summary

In this chapter, we discussed the use of parameters with Puppet classes and defined types that makes Puppet modules more configurable and able to cater for multiple use cases. We also had a look how to make an application cluster more scalable by enabling load balancing on it.

In the next chapter, we will introduce Puppet environments that help us to manage larger Puppet environments more efficiently and to make the configuration of hosts more dynamic through exported resources.

6
Scaling Up the Puppet Environment

Comparing our progress with football, we have reached the half way line in the field, and we have scored quite a few goals in the game already. I hope you have had your half time team talk, refueled yourself with cold drinks, and have stretched your muscles for the second half action that is about to begin.

Until now, we have learned how to set up the development environment where we can build new Puppet modules easily and test them in the cluster that consists of multiple nodes. The environment was fully configured with Puppet, and in the process, we got to experiment with various building blocks such as built-in resource types, facts, variables, parameterized classes, and defined types.

But I believe that not all of this has been easy or problem free, not for me at least. For example, when the cluster members (hosts) sometimes get new IP address from the DHCP server and we then have to adjust the IP configuration in the manifest files to enable nodes to communicate with each other. This is because the Puppet configuration at the moment is standalone. There is no mechanism in place yet that enables nodes to discover other members in the cluster and the services each member provides.

This chapter introduces the concept of Puppet environments on the Puppet Master that enables nodes to discover and share resources with each other. We will cover the following key areas:

- Puppet Master and its components
- Setting the Puppet resource processing order with arrow notation
- Out-of-scope variables

- Conditional statements
- Puppet environments and node classification
- Bootstrapping Puppet Agent and Puppet Master
- Linking Puppet Agent with the Master
- Puppet certificate management

Puppet Master

Like the famous song *Master of Puppets* in the late 90s by the heavy metal band Metallica that goes on saying "Master of Puppets I'm pulling your strings", Puppet Master in Puppet world *pulls the strings* on the Puppet Agent nodes. In other words, Puppet Master coordinates with what manifests and classes will be applied to any given Puppet Agent node.

The concept is quite simple. Instead of deploying Puppet modules locally on Puppet Agent nodes, like we have done so far through Shared Folders, we will deploy modules on the Puppet Master node. When Puppet Agent connects to Puppet Master, the agent identifies itself using so-called Puppet certificates. Once Puppet Master knows the identity of the agent, it compiles manifests into a catalogue and hands over the catalog to the agent node for processing. One of the benefits of using Puppet Master is that it makes resource distribution easy. We have to install the Puppet module only once on the Puppet Master and it distributes the logic contained in manifests and other types of Puppet resources across multiple Puppet Agents automatically.

In addition to distributing resources to agents, Puppet Master provides services such as authentication and authorization, deployment orchestration, reporting, and perhaps most importantly, the ability to export and import resources between Puppet Agent nodes. The mechanism to export and import resources is called `exported resources`, which we will discuss more in detail in the next chapter.

Puppet Master can be started from the same `puppet` binary that we used before to apply Puppet manifests. All you need to do is issue the command `puppet master --verbose –no-daemonize`. This command starts Puppet in the `master` mode that uses a web server that is built-in to the `puppet` binary. Starting Puppet Master from `puppet` binary is sufficient for testing purposes when you have only a handful of Puppet Agents to manage, but it doesn't scale up well when the number of agents increases. This is due to limitation in the built-in web server library called `WEBrick`, that is, `single-threaded`, and it therefore cannot handle concurrent connections.

To overcome the issue with concurrency, it is recommended that you run Puppet Master as a web application on a high-performance web server such as Apache HTTP Server. The Puppet Learning VM that this book is based on comes bundled with Puppet Master and Apache HTTP Server, so we don't have to worry about the installation and configuration. If you are interested in the installation process, there is good documentation available online that you can find by doing a search with the key words `puppetmaster` and `rack`.

The Puppet Master components

The Puppet binary running inside the Apache HTTP Server is responsible for distribution of Puppet resources to the clients. But what about the other services that I briefly mentioned in the previous paragraph? Well, there is a separate component for each of the services, which we should discuss now in few words.

Certificate Authority for authorization

Certificate Authority (CA) manages SSL certificates that are used to authenticate nodes and encrypt HTTP connections between Puppet Agent and Puppet Master. Before Agent can connect to Puppet Master, it must have a valid SSL certificate that is signed by the CA, which is installed on the Puppet Master.

If Agent hasn't got a valid certificate, Puppet Master will reject the connection from the Agent. The certificate signing process can be fully automated so that Puppet Master automatically processes certificate signing requests that it receives from the Agents. But for added security and control over which Agents are allowed to connect to the Puppet Master, you can choose to manually sign the certificates on the command line on the Puppet Master or in Puppet Enterprise Console.

Mcollective for orchestration

Orchestration is needed when we want to have a better control over the deployment process in the environment that consists of multiple Puppet Agent nodes. As an example, our cluster that consists of Load Balancer, Web Server, and Monitoring Server nodes we could use orchestration to sequence the deployment in the following three steps:

1. First, run Puppet on the Web Server node to deploy the web app.
2. Then, run Puppet on the Load Balancer node.
3. Finally, run Puppet on the Monitoring Server node to add Web Server and the Load Balancer node into monitoring after the Web Server and Load Balancer nodes are up and running to avoid unnecessary alerts to be raised by the Monitoring Server.

The orchestration component in Puppet is called Mcollective, which is a message queue application built atop of an open source software called ActiveMQ. Message queue is running on the Puppet Master node, and Puppet Agents that run Mcollective clients registers with the message queue and consumes messages that are sent to the queue by Puppet Master.

PuppetDB for exported resources, PuppetDB queries, and reporting

Functionality-wise, I'd rate PuppetDB as the most interesting and exciting component of all. Like the name implies, PuppetDB is a database application that stores various information about Puppet Agents, such as the services they provide, facts, and in what state the Puppet Agents are in.

PuppetDB helps to make cluster configuration more dynamic and automated in a way that it enables Puppet to adjust the configuration at runtime. Every time Puppet is run on the Puppet Agent node, the information in PuppetDB gets updated. For example, if the IP address of a Puppet Agent changes, say as a result of Puppet Agent node being rebooted, the new IP address gets updated into PuppetDB under *fact* called ipaddress. In addition to facts, PuppetDB also keeps record on what resources (for example, files and classes) have been applied on each node. Information about resources is useful when we want to discover what services each node is running. For example, PuppetDB can tell us that the Web Server node has the class webapp applied on it and the Load Balancer node includes the class loadbalancer.

Information stored in PuppetDB can be queried in the Puppet manifest file and we can utilize this information during the deployment. Instead of specifying static IP address for the Web Server node in the loadbalancer class, we can write a PuppetDB query that returns the IP address of the node that the class webapp has applied on it. So, when the IP address of the Web Server node changes, we don't have to tweak the configuration in the manifest and reapply it. Instead we just rerun Puppet on the Load Balancer node, which results in new query to be made and PuppetDB returns back the new IP address as a query result.

Another useful feature provided by PuppetDB is called exported resources. Exported resources enable Puppet Agent nodes to export resources to PuppetDB from where other nodes can collect or import *exported resources*. Here, the PuppetDB query is used for exchanging information between nodes, and exported resources are used for passing resources from node to another. We will look into exported resources and PuppetDB more in detail and learn how to use them in *Chapter 7, Making the Configuration Dynamic*.

Before we can use any of these features, we have to link up Puppet Agent nodes with the Puppet Master.

Connecting Puppet Agent with Puppet Master

Before Puppet Agent can connect to Puppet Master, it has to find out the host name of the Puppet Master and that host name must resolve an IP address that belongs to the Puppet Master node. Our Puppet Master is currently configured to acquire an IP address from DHCP server. This is not ideal because if the IP address changes on the Puppet Master node, we have to reconfigure Puppet Agents to make the connection to Puppet Master work again. To avoid this problem, it is good practice to configure Puppet Master with a static IP address.

We will also create a new *environment* on the Puppet Master node and configure Agent nodes to join this environment. As we have to do couple of tweaks on the Puppet Master node as well as on the Puppet Agent nodes, I feel that it's best that we consolidate all the *bootstrap* logic in a new Puppet module, which we'll call the bootstrap.

Creating the bootstrap module for Puppet Master and Puppet Agent

The module bootstrap will be created inside the shared folders, which is mounted as /media/sf_learning across all nodes. You can use any of the existing virtual machines to create the module, but I've decided that I will create a new module on the Puppet Master node, which is called learn_puppet_centos-6.5 in VirtualBox Manager.

First, launch the virtual machine, and then run the following commands to create the bootstrap module:

1. Go to the shared folder directory:

   ```
   # cd /media/sf_learning
   ```

2. Create a module learning-bootstrap:

   ```
   # puppet module generate learning-bootstrap --skip-interview
   ```

3. Rename the module directory to remove the prefix `learning-`:

   ```
   # mv learning-bootstrap bootstrap
   ```

4. Create a `templates` directory for Puppet templates:

   ```
   # mkdir bootstrap/templates
   ```

5. Using the command `tree`, we can verify that the directory was successfully created, and it displays the following content:

```
learn_puppet_centos-6.5 (host-only-networking) [Running] - Oracle VM VirtualBox
[root@learning ~]# tree /media/sf_learning/bootstrap/
/media/sf_learning/bootstrap/
├── Gemfile
├── manifests
│   └── init.pp
├── metadata.json
├── Rakefile
├── README.md
├── spec
│   ├── classes
│   │   └── init_spec.rb
│   └── spec_helper.rb
├── templates
└── tests
    └── init.pp

5 directories, 8 files
[root@learning ~]#

[0] 0:*                                        Quest: Begin - Progress: No Tasks.
                                                              Right Ctrl
```

Configuring static IP address on Puppet Master

The first task for us is to change the network configuration on Puppet Master node in a way that it uses static IP address instead of dynamic IP address. When the IP address is fixed, it is easier for us to configure Puppet Agent nodes to connect to known IP address.

Defining resource processing order with the arrow notation

Resource processing order can be defined within the resource with `require` and `notify` attributes. If you have many resources that requires strict ordering, it may be difficult to manage resources with these attributes.

Puppet provides an alternative syntax, which I call the *arrow notation*, to order resources outside the resource definition block.

Let's take a look at an example where we have two Puppet resources: `file { 'myfile':}` and `service { 'myservice': }`.

If we want the `file` resource to be processed before the `service` resource, we need to traditionally declare the `require` attribute inside the service resource in the following way:

```
file { 'myfile': }
service { 'myservice':
  require => File['myfile'];
}
```

With the *arrow notation*, we can express the same ordering by removing the `require` attribute and adding an arrow in between resources:

```
file { 'myfile': } -> service { 'myservice': }
```

Another form of the preceding arrow notation is an arrow with a tilde character `~>`. The arrow using tilde is an analog to the `notify` attribute. If we would like the `service { 'myservice': }` to be restarted only in the case that the resource `file { 'myfile': }` changes, we can express it with the `notify` attribute in the following way:

```
file { 'myfile':
  notify => Service['myservice']
}
service { 'myservice': }
```

The same results can be achieved with the tilde arrow notation like this:

```
file { 'myfile': }~> service { 'myservice': }
```

Next, we will try this in practice by ordering resources in the class `bootstrap::master` using the arrow notation.

Creating class bootstrap::master

All Puppet Master-related configuration can be contained within a subclass called `bootstrap::master`, which we will create in the file `bootstrap/manifests/master.pp`.

Now, create a new file in the text editor with the following content and save it as `master.pp` under the `manifests` directory.

```
1 class bootstrap::master {
2   # Add user pe-puppet to group vboxfs to allow process pe-puppetserver access to Shared Folders
3   user { 'pe-puppet':
4       groups => 'vboxsf';
5   }
6   # Create Puppet environment (a directory) called development
7   file { '/etc/puppetlabs/puppet/environments/development':
8     ensure => directory;
9   }
10  ->
11  # Link manifests with Shared Folders after directory development is created
12  file { '/etc/puppetlabs/puppet/environments/development/manifests':
13    ensure => link,
14    target => '/media/sf_learning/manifests/';
15  }
16  ->
17  # Link modules with Shared Folders after manifests link is created
18  file { '/etc/puppetlabs/puppet/environments/development/modules':
19    ensure => link,
20    target => '/media/sf_learning';
21  }
22  # Apply ifcfg-eth1 template and notify (with notation ~>) service network
23  file { '/etc/sysconfig/network-scripts/ifcfg-eth1':
24      content => template("${module_name}/ifcfg-eth1.erb"),
25  }
26  ~>
27  # Restart service network only if ifcfg-eth1 file changed
28  service { 'network': }
29 }
```

The preceding `master.pp` file creates a class `bootstrap::master` that contains a bunch of Puppet resources. Let's look at them more in detail:

- Line 1 declares a class `bootstrap::master`.

- Line 2 is a comment related to the `user` resource on lines 3-6. Comments in manifests must be prefixed with the # sign.

- Line 3 begins a `user` resource for user account `pe-puppet`. The `pe-puppet` user runs the process `pe-puppetserver`, which is the Puppet Master process.

- On Line 4, the `groups` attribute defines the name of the group that the user account `pe-puppet` should be member of.

- Line 5 closes the `user` resource statement.

- Line 6 is another comment line. You may leave the comment out if you like but comments can be helpful when revisiting manifest again in future.

- Line 7 declares a `file` resource `/etc/puppetlabs/puppet/environments/development`. The file resource creates a Puppet environment called `development`.

- Line 8 sets an `ensure` attribute with value `directory`, which means that the file resource type is a directory (instead of a file).

- Line 9 closes the file resources.

- Line 10 sets the resource order. With the arrow notation `->`, we tell Puppet that the `/etc/puppetlabs/puppet/environments/development` directory must be created before the link `manifests` is created inside the directory.

- Lines 12 to 15 specify another type of `file` resources, which is defined as a link using the `ensure` attribute (on line 13). The link uses the `target` attribute (on line 14) to specify a file or directory that `link` should be pointed to.

  These resources create a link `/etc/puppetlabs/puppet/environments/development/manifests` that points to the directory `/media/sf_learning/manifests` in shared folders, which we will create shortly.

- Line 16 adds another ordering constraint. Here, we tell Puppet that the link specified on lines 12 to 15 must be processed before the link defined on lines 18 to 21.

- Lines 18 to 21 create another link /etc/puppetlabs/puppet/environments/ development/modules that points to the shared folder directory /media/ sf_learning.

- Line 23 begins the statement for a file resource /etc/sysconfig/network-scripts/ifcfg-eth1, which is the file that defines the network interface configuration for host-only network interface eth1.

- Line 24 references the template function that generates the content from the template file ifcfg-eth1.erb, which we will create shortly. Here, I'm using Puppet's built-in variable ${module_name} to reference the name of the module where the template file lives in. In this instance, the value of the variable becomes bootstrap. I like to use the ${module_name} variable in the template function because I can reuse it easier in other modules.

- Line 25 closes the file resources definition.

- Line 26 creates order constraint between the file resource and the service resource using arrow notation ~>. As mentioned in the previous paragraph, the arrow notation ~> (tilde greater than) is a shorthand for the notify attribute.

- Line 28 creates a service resource called network, which we want to restart after the IP address on the host has been changed.

- As this resource has no attributes, we can define it as a one line statement to make manifest more compact.

- Line 29 ends the bootstrap::master class definition.

Once you have added all these lines into the file, save it as master.pp inside the directory bootstrap/manifests directory.

Referencing an out-of-scope variable from Puppet template

Next, we'll have to create the template file that the bootstrap::master class is referencing (on line 24 in master.pp). In this template file, we will use the so-called out-of-scope variable reference, which in Puppet terminology means a variable that is declared in an external Puppet class.

You can find the out-of-scope variable references on lines 4 and 5 in the following screenshot:

Let's have a look at the content of the template file `bootstrap/templates/ifcfg-eth1.erb`:

- **Line 1**: The DEVICE parameter specifies the name of the network interface that we want to configure. The interface eth1 is the name of the host-only network interface that we added on the host in *Chapter 2, Managing Packages in Puppet*.

- **Line 2**: BOOTPROTO specifies the protocol that network interface should be using. The previous value of the parameter was dhcp, but as we are no longer using DHCP, we set this to none.

- **Line 3**: The ONBOOT parameter value yes means that the network interface should be activated at boot time.

- **Line 4**: IPADDR specifies the IP address that the operating system should allocate for the network interface.

  As we are in the process of disabling DHCP address and replacing it with a static IP address, we must provide the value of the address somehow. Here, we use the Puppet function scope to reference the out-of-scope variable called puppetmaster_ip that is declared in the class bootstrap. This is done with syntax such as scope['::class-name::variable_name'].

- **Line 5**: The NETMASK parameter defines the subnet mask for the network for the IP address. Here, we use another out-of-scope variable reference, which at this time references the variable puppetmaster_netmask defined in the bootstrap class.

Now, go ahead and create new file in text editor with the the preceding content and save the file as ifcfg-eth1.erb under the directory bootstrap/templates/. Then, we can move on to adjust the main bootstrap class before we apply the class on the Puppet Master node.

Conditional statements

Let's have a look at how we can add more logic into Puppet manifests by introducing conditional statements. We just created the class bootstrap::master, which we will soon apply on the Puppet Master node. A little later, we'll create a class called bootstrap::agent, which will be applied on the Puppet Agent nodes. This means that we'll have two classes for different Puppet "roles" to choose from.

In *Chapter 4, Monitoring Your Web Server*, we had a similar decision to make when we applied the nagios::server class on the Nagios Server node and the nagios::client class on the Nagios Client nodes. The decision on which class to apply on each node was done by us at the time when we ran the puppet apply command.

With conditional statements, we can hand over this decision-making task to Puppet and let Puppet to evaluate which class to apply on each node.

The two most commonly used types of conditional statements are the if and case statements. Both of these statements are used to evaluate whether the given condition is true or false. Based on the outcome of the evaluation, Puppet selects the block of code to execute.

The if statement

If you have ever done programming or scripting, you are probably familiar with the if statement; this is used to evaluate whether given the condition is true or false. When the if condition is true, the program executes a block of code. Otherwise, this block of code is ignored.

The syntax of the if statement in Puppet is as follows:

```
if condition1 {
   statement1
}
```

The if statement is often combined with the else statement that defines what to do when condition is false or not true. Or, to evaluate multiple conditions, we can add an elsif block in between else and if blocks in the following way:

```
if condition1 {
   statement1
}
elsif condition2 {
   statement2
```

```
}
else {
  statement3
}
```

Let's see how we can utilize the `if` statement in the `bootstrap` module to conditionally apply a class based on the value of variable `role`. Open the file `bootstrap/manifests/init.pp` in the text editor and add the following content to it:

The file `init.pp` defines a class `bootstrap` that has three input parameters and conditional statements for checking the role of the node.

Let's look at the input parameters first on lines 2, 3, and 4.

- Line 2: The `$puppetmaster_ip` parameter defines the IP address of the Puppet Master node. This parameter is referenced on line 4 in the template file `bootstrap/templates/ifcfg-eth1.erb`, which we created a moment ago. If we don't provide this parameter at the time when applying, the class Puppet Master will be configured with the IP address 192.168.56.2.

- Line 3: The `$puppetmaster_netmask` parameter defines the subnet mask for Puppet Master node. This variable is referenced in the template file `ifcfg-eth1.erb` on line 5 and the default subnet mask value 255.255.255.0.

- Line 4: The `$role` variable defines the role of the Puppet node. The default value is *unquoted* false, which means that the value is a so-called *Boolean value*. The variable `$role` is referenced by the `if` statement on line 6, where Puppet evaluates whether the role is `master`.

The conditional statement that begins on line 6 and ends on line 11 has the following logic:

- Line 6: The `if $role == 'master'` statement checks whether the input parameter value is the master. This condition is true only if we provide this parameter at the time when the class is applied, if we don't, it defaults to false and the statement inside the `if` block is ignored.

  We can provide the variable value by applying the class using syntax `class { 'bootstrap': role => 'master' }`.

- Line 7: If the condition on line 6 is true, then Puppet includes the class `bootstrap::master`.

- Line 8: The `if` statement is closed with a closing curly bracket.

- Line 9: The `else` block (lines 9-11) is processed only if the `if` statement is false. In practice, this means that if we don't set the value `master` for the variable `$role`, the statement `class { 'bootstrap::agent': role => $role }` inside the `else` block is processed.

  This statement passes the parameter `role` into the class `bootstrap::agent`, and we can use the role parameter to configure the `certname` of the Puppet Agent.

- Line 12 closes the class `bootstrap`.

Next, we should try to apply the class on the Puppet Master node. Before we apply the class, I'd recommend that you revert Puppet Master virtual machine state to snapshot host-only-networking.

Here are the steps required to restore the snapshot:

1. Select the virtual machine **learn_puppet_centos-6.5** and click on the **Snapshots** button.

2. Select the snapshot **host-only-networking** and click on the Restore Snapshot button.

3. Uncheck the box that says **Create a snapshot of the current machine state**, and then click on the **Restore** button:

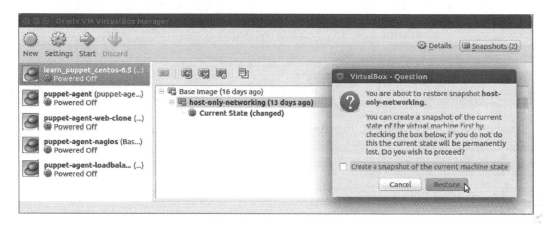

Creating site.pp file for node classification

We have already done node classification from the command line when applying Puppet manifests. In Puppet terminology, node classification means to associate a set of Puppet classes with the Puppet Agent node. Once Puppet Agent is linked with the Puppet Master, we no longer run Puppet from the command line, instead, we run Puppet Agent in so-called **daemon mode**. In the daemon mode, Puppet Agent connects to Puppet Master periodically to check whether Puppet Master has new manifests that should be applied on the agent.

The site.pp file defines what classes should be applied on the Puppet Agent node when it connects to the Puppet Master. This file is stored under the directory called manifests that lives in the root of the environment directory on the Puppet Master. We defined an environment directory called development inside the class bootstrap::master (line 7 to 9) that we created in the *Creating class bootstrap::master* section. In the same class, we also created the directory manifests as a link (line 12 to 15) and pointed the link to the directory /media/sf_learning/manifests in the shared folders, which doesn't exist yet.

Here you can find the example site.pp file that contains node classifications for three nodes.

Node classification begins with the keyword `node` followed by the `certname` of the node, which is wrapped in single quotation characters. After `certname`, there comes an opening curly brace { and a list of classes that should be applied on the Puppet Agent. Node classification ends with the closing curly brace character }, as shown in the following screenshot:

```
site.pp (~/learning/manifests) - gedit

site.pp ×

 1 node 'web.development.vm' {
 2   include nagios::client
 3   include webapp
 4 }
 5 node 'loadbalancer.development.vm' {
 6   include nagios::client
 7   include loadbalancer
 8 }
 9 node 'nagios.development.vm' {
10   include nagios::server
11   include nagios::client
12   include nagios::resources
13 }
```

Before you create the `site.pp` file in text editor, create a new directory called `manifests` under the `Shared Folders` directory (for example /home/jussi/ learning). Then, create `site.pp` with the preceding contents and save it inside the directory `manifests`.

Applying bootstrap class on Puppet Master

Now, we are ready to apply the bootstrap class with role master:

1. Start the Puppet Master virtual machine. Once it boots up, you can log on with the username `root` and password `puppet`.

2. Go to the directory /media/sf_learning:

    ```
    # cd /media/sf_learning
    ```

3. Apply the `bootstrap` class with the `role` parameter and value `master`:

```
# puppet apply --modulepath=./ -e 'class { 'bootstrap': role =>
'master' }'
```

![Terminal window titled "learn_puppet_centos-6.5 (host-only-networking) [Running] - Oracle VM VirtualBox" showing Puppet apply output]

```
[root@learning /]# cd /media/sf_learning/
[root@learning /media/sf_learning]# puppet apply --modulepath=./ -e 'class { 'bo
otstrap': role => 'master' }'
Notice: Compiled catalog for learning.puppetlabs.vm in environment production in
 0.51 seconds
Notice: /Stage[main]/Bootstrap::Master/User[pe-puppet]/groups: groups changed ''
 to 'vboxsf'
Notice: /Stage[main]/Bootstrap::Master/File[/etc/puppetlabs/puppet/environments/
development]/ensure: created
Notice: /Stage[main]/Bootstrap::Master/File[/etc/puppetlabs/puppet/environments/
development/manifests]/ensure: created
Notice: /Stage[main]/Bootstrap::Master/File[/etc/puppetlabs/puppet/environments/
development/modules]/ensure: created
Notice: /Stage[main]/Bootstrap::Master/File[/etc/sysconfig/network-scripts/ifcfg
-eth1]/content: content changed '{md5}f90d0b3852ba630aeb2b7d37f8c74b26' to '{md5
}baec138c9d1ec6678391791e865d690e'
Notice: /Stage[main]/Bootstrap::Master/Service[network]: Triggered 'refresh' fro
m 1 events
Notice: /Stage[main]/Bootstrap::Master/File[/etc/profile.d/puppetdb.sh]/ensure:
defined content as '{md5}bfba3a5f1a69f74ff30ca08437da576c'
Notice: Finished catalog run in 6.76 seconds
[root@learning /media/sf_learning]# hostname -I
10.0.2.15 192.168.56.2
[root@learning /media/sf_learning]# reboot_
[0] 0:*                                    Quest: Begin - Progress: No Tasks.
```

 Once Puppet has finished applying the class, you can check whether the IP address was changed by running the command `hostname -I`. The hostname command shows two IP addresses of which the second address belongs to host-only network interface eth1.

Once Puppet has successfully applied the `bootstrap` class on the Puppet Master, we must reboot the host so that Puppet Master services register the new IP address 192.168.56.2 and the new environment called `development`. You can reboot the system by running the command `reboot` on the command line. Alternatively, you can stop and start the virtual machine from the VirtualBox Manager.

A first look at the Puppet Enterprise Console

Puppet Enterprise Console is a web application that runs on the Puppet Master node. We will have a look at it more in detail in *Chapter 9*, *The Puppet Enterprise Console*, but in this chapter, we will use it to create a node group and sign certificates for Puppet Agent nodes.

Bypassing the certificate warning message

After rebooting the Puppet Master, you should be able to access Puppet Enterprise Console from `https://192.168.56.2`. When you open the Enterprise Console for the first time, you may see an SSL certificate warning message displayed in the browser. The warning message is caused by a self-signed SSL certificate used by Puppet Enterprise Console. Here is the certificate warning message that appears when you're using Chromium web browser. To proceed to the login screen, we need to first click the **Advanced** link, and then click the link that says **Proceed to 192.168.56.2(unsafe)**:

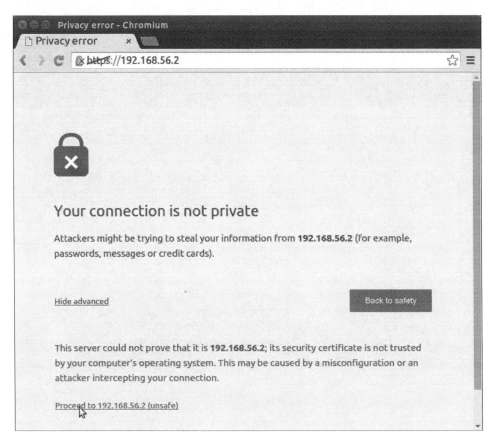

Logging on to the Puppet Enterprise Console

Once you have got past the certificate warning messages, you should see a login form in front of you. You can log on to the Puppet Enterprise Console using the username admin and password learningpuppet.

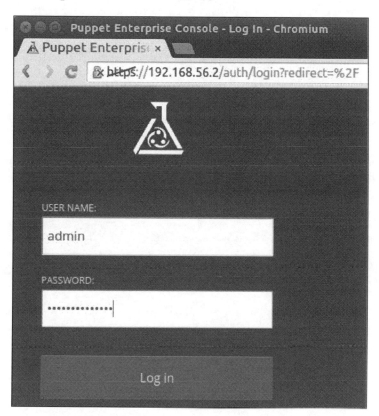

503 Service Temporarily Unavailable?

If you are seeing error **503 Service Temporarily Unavailable** instead of the logging screen, run the following commands on the Puppet Master node:

```
# service pe-console-services restart
# service pe-httpd restart
```

Then, refresh the browser window by pressing *F5* key, and now the login form should appear.

Creating a node group

Puppet node group is a method to group Puppet Agents and link the group with an environment. The class `bootstrap::master` (lines 7 to 9 in file `bootstrap/manifests/master.pp`) that we applied on the Puppet Master created an environment called `development`. Now, we need to add some Puppet Agents into this environment, and that can be done with a node group that we'll create next.

1. Log on to Puppet Enterprise Console with the username `admin` and password `learningpuppet`.

2. Click the **Classification** menu to open the node group list.

3. In the **Node group name** field, type in **development**. The parent name should be default.

4. From the **Environment** drop-down menu, select the environment called the **development**.

5. Click on the **Add group** button.

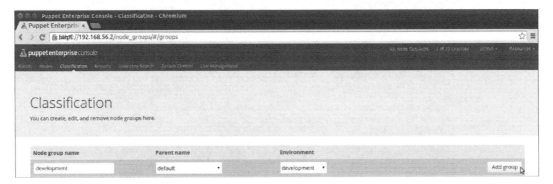

6. Find the **development** node group from the node group list and open it.

7. Click the **Edit node group metadata** link in the right-hand top corner of the node group view.

8. Tick the **Override all other environments** checkbox. This option ensures that the node group doesn't inherit any Puppet classes from the parent node group. Only classes listed in the node classification file `site.pp` are applied on the nodes in the development node group.

9. Click on the **Commit 1 change** button to save changes.

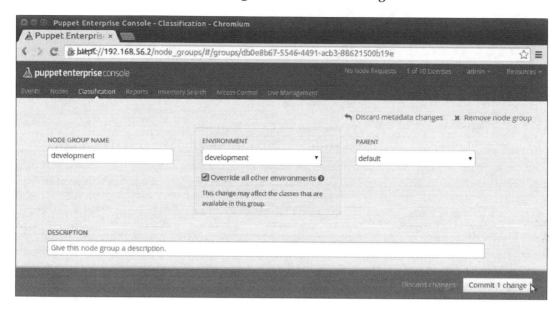

We now have a node group called development that doesn't contain any nodes yet. We can leave the Puppet Master node running while we bootstrap the Web Server node. Once Puppet Agent node is bootstrapped, we will return to Puppet Enterprise Console to sign the Agent's certificate and add it to the node group.

Bootstrapping Puppet Agent

The else block inside the class bootstrap (line 9 to 11) references the class bootstrap::agent, which we haven't yet created. The bootstrap process on the Agent should perform the following two tasks:

- Add a new Puppet Master IP address into the file /etc/hosts so that the agents can connect to Puppet Master using the preconfigured Puppet Master host name learning.puppetlabs.vm

- Configure a certname for the Puppet Agent based on the input parameter role

The `bootstrap::agent` class definition shown in the following screenshot will perform these tasks for us:

The class `bootstrap::agent` contains two Puppet resources and an `if` statement. Let's inspect the class line by line:

- Line 1 begins the class definition. This class accepts an input parameter called `role`, which is passed in from the class `bootstrap` (line 10 in the file `bootstrap/manifests/init.pp`).

- Line 2 defines a host resource for the host name `learning.puppetlabs.vm`.

- Line 3 adds a host alias called `puppetmaster` for the host resource.

- Line 4 sets the IP address for the host resources. Here we use an out of scope variable to reference the variable `puppetmaster_ip` defined in the class `bootstrap`.

- Line 5 closes the host resource definition.

- Line 6 has a `if` statement that checks whether input parameter `$role` was defined. The default value `false` is defined as an input parameter on line 1. Unless `$role` is defined at runtime, it defaults to `false` and the `if` block is not processed.

- Line 7 begins an `exec` resource statement, which sets the `certname` on the node based on the value of the parameter `$role`.

- Line 8 specifies the command that sets the `certname` value for the Puppet Agent. The value of the certname value is a combination of a variable `$role` (wrapped in curly braces) and a string `development.vm`.

- Line 9 is needed to make the `exec` resource idempotent, which means that the command on line 8 will be executed unless the command on line 9 returns a value 0. This command first prints out the current `certname` of the host and the output of the command is piped (`|`) into the `grep` command that matches the output to the pattern `${role}.development.vm`.

- Line 10 closes the `exec` resource.

- Line 11 closes the `if` statement.

- Line 12 finally closes the class `bootstrap::agent`.

That's everything we need to bootstrap Puppet Agent nodes. Now, it's your turn to create the file `bootstrap/manifests/agent.pp` with the preceding content. Once you are done with it, it's time to apply it on the Web Server node.

Applying the bootstrap::agent class via the bootstrap class

We will first apply the class `bootstrap::agent` on the Web Server node. The name of the Web Server virtual machine is puppet-agent and it contains a snapshot called puppet-agent-web, which we should restore prior to launching the virtual machine.

Here are the steps to bootstrap the Web Server node:

1. Restore the puppet-agent virtual machine to snapshot puppet-agent-web.

2. Launch the virtual machine.

3. Log on to virtual machine using the username `root` and password `puppet`.

4. Move to the shared folder directory `/media/sf_learning`:

   ```
   # cd /media/sf_learning
   ```

5. Apply the class `bootstrap` with the role `web`:

   ```
   # puppet apply --modulepath=./ -e 'class { 'bootstrap': role =>
   'web' }'
   ```

Please note that we don't call the class bootstrap::agent directly, but instead we use the bootstrap class as the entry point. If we called bootstrap::agent directly, the out-of-scope variable ${bootstrap::puppetmaster_ip} would not be visible to the bootstrap::agent class that references it.

Initiate a connection with the Puppet Master:

```
# puppet agent -t
```

When Puppet runs properly and you've run the puppet agent -t command, the following activity is printed on the screen:

```
puppet-agent (puppet-agent-web) [Running] - Oracle VM VirtualBox
[root@learning ~]# cd /media/sf_learning/
[root@learning /media/sf_learning]# puppet apply --modulepath . -e 'class { 'bo
tstrap': role => 'web' }'
Notice: Compiled catalog for web.development.vm in environment production in 0.
8 seconds
Notice: /Stage[main]/Bootstrap::Agent/Host[learning.puppetlabs.vm]/ip: ip chang
d '127.0.0.1' to '192.168.56.2'
Notice: /Stage[main]/Bootstrap::Agent/Host[learning.puppetlabs.vm]/host_aliases
 host_aliases changed 'localhost localhost.localdomain localhost4' to 'puppetma
ter'
Notice: Finished catalog run in 0.67 seconds
[root@learning /media/sf_learning]# puppet agent -t
Info: Caching certificate for ca
Info: csr_attributes file loading from /etc/puppetlabs/puppet/csr_attributes.ya
]
Info: Creating a new SSL certificate request for web.development.vm
Info: Certificate Request fingerprint (SHA256): 1F:6E:DB:1E:98:37:0D:DB:29:CA:2
:8A:3C:5B:99:06:D4:BF:95:82:45:4D:9C:D4:98:FC:EE:42:C9:CE:FC:98
Info: Caching certificate for ca
Exiting; no certificate found and waitforcert is disabled
[root@learning /media/sf_learning]# _
Right Ctrl
```

The command puppet agent -t that we executed as the last step of the bootstrapping process initiates a connection with the Puppet Master. This command creates a new certificate signing request, which the Agent sends to the Puppet Master. You will also see a message Exiting: no certificate found and waitforcert is disabled, which we will rectify by signing the Puppet Agent's certificate on the Puppet Master.

> Let the puppet-agent virtual machine keep running while we visit the Puppet Enterprise Console to sign the certificate. Once the certificate has been signed, we will rerun the puppet agent -t command on Puppet Agent.

Signing the certificate on the Puppet Enterprise Console

The command `puppet agent -t` that we just ran on the Puppet Agent node resulted in a certificate signing request the to the Puppet Master. Now, we can sign the Puppet Agent certificate on the Puppet Enterprise Console by following these steps:

1. Open the URL `https://192.168.56.2` in the web browser.

2. Log on with the username `admin` and password `learningpuppet`.

3. If you already were logged on to the Puppet Enterprise Console, refresh the window by pressing F5.

4. Click on the **1 Node Request** link in the right-hand top corner of the landing page.

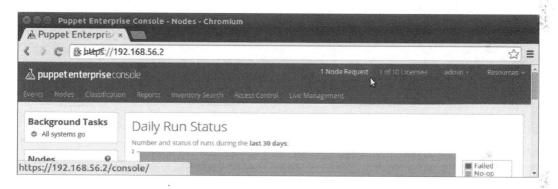

5. Click the **Accept** button to sign the certificate.

 If you happen to find more than one node in the node request view, only sign the certificate of the node `web.development.vm`.

6. After clicking the **Accept** button, you should see a message **Node request accepted** that confirms the certificate was signed successfully:

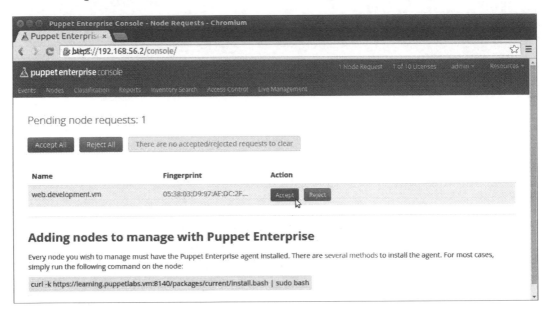

Next, we'll add the node `web.development.vm` into the `development` node group.

Adding nodes to the node group

Now that the certificate has been signed, we should add the Web Server node into the node group called `development`. As mentioned earlier, node group is a collection of nodes and each node group has an environment, which is also called `development`. Once the node has been added to the node group, we can rerun the command `puppet agent -t` on the node `web.development.vm` to trigger deployment.

Here are the steps on how to add the node `web.development.vm` to the node group `development`:

1. On the Puppet Enterprise Console, go to the **Classification** menu.
2. Open the node group **development**.
3. In the Rules view, click the **Certname** textbox at the bottom of the page to expose a list of Puppet Agent nodes.
4. Select the node **web.development.vm**.
5. Click on the **Pin node** button.
6. Click on the **Commit 1 change** button at the bottom of the page.

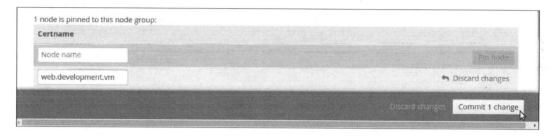

Deploying the Web Server node against Puppet Master

We have now signed the Puppet Agent certificate and added the node `web.development.vm` into the node group called development. Now, we can deploy the node using the command `puppet agent -t`. The option `-t` stands for `test` and it enables the Puppet Agent process to run on the foreground and to report Puppet Agent activity on screen.

> Running the `puppet agent` command without the `-t` option will start the Puppet Agent process on the background and the activity is logged into the file `/var/log/messages`.

Here are the steps the Puppet in the agent mode:

1. Log on to the Web Server node with the username `root` and password `puppet`.

2. Run Puppet Agent on the foreground:

   ```
   # puppet agent -t
   ```

During the Puppet Agent run, you will see the following messages, which you can safely ignore:

```
Warning: Local environment: "production" doesn't match server specified
node environment "development", switching agent to "development".
```

This message means that the default Puppet environment `production` is overridden by the environment `development` that we configured on the Puppet Master.

```
Warning: The package type's allow_virtual parameter will be changing its
default value from false to true in a future release. If you do not want
to allow virtual packages, please explicitly set allow_virtual to false.
    (at /opt/puppet/lib/ruby/site_ruby/1.9.1/puppet/type/package.rb:430:in
'block (3 levels) in <module:Puppet>')
```

This warning comes from the `puppetlabs-apache` module and it can be safely ignored.

When Puppet run finishes successfully, you should see the following lines at the end of the Puppet run:

```
Notice: /Stage[main]/Apache::Service/Service[httpd]/ensure: ensure
changed 'stopped' to 'running'
```

```
Finished catalog run in 96.83 seconds
```

```
Info: /Stage[main]/Apache::Service/Service[httpd]: Unscheduling refresh
on Service[httpd]
```

The best way to verify whether the Web Server deployment was successful is to open the Web Server URL `http://192.168.56.11`. Please note that Web Server IP address may be different from 192.168.56.11 in your environment. You can check the Web Server's IP address with commands `hostname -I` and `ifconfig eth1`.

Bootstrapping Load Balancer and Nagios Server nodes

Congratulations for successfully connecting your first node with the Puppet Master. Now, we should repeat the bootstrap process on the load balancer and the Nagios nodes.

I feel that I don't have to describe this process in detail as it is identical to bootstrapping process on the Web Server node. Just as a reminder: here is an overview of the process of bootstrapping the load balancer and Nagios Server nodes:

1. Restore the virtual machines to the previous snapshot state.

2. Boot up the virtual machines and run the bootstrap commands.

3. The bootstrap command for load balancer and Nagios Server nodes are as follows:

   ```
   # puppet apply --modulepath=./ -e 'class { 'bootstrap': role =>
   'loadbalancer' }'
   ```

   ```
   # puppet apply --modulepath=./ -e 'class { 'bootstrap': role =>
   'nagios' }'
   ```

4. Run the command `puppet agent -t` to generate the certificate signing request.

5. Sign certificates and add nodes to the `development` node group on the Puppet Enterprise Console.

If you don't see the nodes `loadbalancer.development.vm` and `nagios.development.vm` on the drop-down list when adding nodes to the node group, try typing in both names, and then click on the **Pin node** button.

6. Run the command `puppet agent -t` on Puppet Agent nodes to deploy them.

Summary

In this chapter, we discussed Puppet features that help manage Puppet environments at scale. By now, you should have a fairly good understanding on what Puppet Master is used for, how to link Puppet Agents with the Master, and how to manage the Agents' certificates. We discussed the concept of node classification and created a `site.pp` file that defines which classes to associate with Puppet Agents.

This chapter also introduced a couple of new Puppet language features. These features were out-of-scope variables that make variables accessible from one Puppet module to another and conditional statements to enable Puppet to apply decision-making logic to the manifest execution.

Next, in *Chapter 7, Making the Configuration Dynamic*, we'll learn how make use of stored configurations and PuppetDB to enable nodes to exchange configurations between them.

7
Making the Configuration Dynamic

Having a Puppet Master that distributes manifests across multiple nodes is convenient. However, getting Puppet agents linked up with the Puppet Master requires a fair amount of time to get the manifests in the right order. One can ask if this exercise really worth the effort. I'd say yes, but only if we utilize the additional Puppet Master capabilities.

In the previous chapter, we briefly discussed the topic of PuppetDB. In this chapter, we will learn how make use of it in practice to transform a static configuration into a dynamic one using PuppetDB and a feature called exported resources that sits on top of PuppetDB.

In this chapter, we'll cover the following topics:

- An introduction to PuppetDB and exported resources
- Exported resources versus PuppetDB
- Exporting and importing resources
- Tagging resources and using a tag as a filter when importing resources
- Creating a check on the Nagios client and exporting resources to the nagios server
- Purging Nagios resources
- Querying PuppetDB from the command line
- Using the query_nodes and query_facts functions in Puppet manifests
- Purging resources from PuppetDB

An introduction to PuppetDB and exported resources

PuppetDB is a database service that is used to store and query information of Puppet Agents. It typically runs on the Puppet Master node, but it can also be installed on a separate database server for performance and/or security reasons.

PuppetDB consists of two key components:

- A SQL database to store data
- An API to query and manipulate the data

The software that provides the SQL database is called PostgreSQL, which is a popular open source database project. The PostgreSQL process listens on the TCP port 5432 for the incoming connections from the API. Although the PostgreSQL database can be accessed directly from client software, it is not recommended. Instead, the connection to PuppetDB should always be done via the API. PuppetDB API exposes the information from the SQL database to the API clients via the HTTP protocol, and it is also used by Puppet to query and store the information in the database. PuppetDB API comes with a built-in web server called Jetty that listens on TCP ports 8080 (HTTP) and 8081 (HTTPS).

The connectivity from the PuppetDB Client to the PostgreSQL database via PuppetDB API can be illustrated with the following diagram:

Exported resources

One of the services that PuppetDB provides is called exported resources, also known as `storeconfigs`. Exported resources enable the Puppet Agent nodes to exchange resources between them by exporting a resource on one node and importing the resource to another node. We can export any type of a Puppet resource, including the custom types. In this chapter, we will learn how to export and import the built-in resource types, `nagios_host` and `nagios_service`.

Before we dive into this, let's briefly take a look at the benefits of using exported resources.

Exported resources are useful when configuring a cluster of nodes that share services between them, and the nodes need to be able to discover services from each other automatically. If the formation of the cluster is static (a fixed number of nodes in the cluster), its configuration can be managed without exported resources. However, clusters these days are not static but dynamic. Modern clusters are scaled up and down according to demand. To manage a configuration that can adjust to changes as they happen, we need tools such as exported resources that dynamically adjust the configuration of the cluster.

To demonstrate how exported resources enable you to turn a static configuration into a dynamic one, we will revisit the nagios module, which we created in *Chapter 4, Monitoring Your Web Server*, and modify it slightly.

Exporting and importing resources

Before we add logic to export and import resources, let's take a look at the nagios::resources class in its current form:

```
1 class nagios::resources {
2   nagios_host { 'web-server':
3     host_name        => 'web-server',
4     address          => '192.168.56.11',
5     use              => 'linux-server',
6     target           => '/etc/nagios/conf.d/hosts.cfg',
7     notify           => File['/etc/nagios/conf.d'],
8     require          => Package['nagios'],
9   }
10  nagios_service { 'HTTP':
11    host_name           => 'web-server',
12    service_description => 'HTTP',
13    check_command       => 'check_http',
14    use                 => 'local-service',
15    target              => '/etc/nagios/conf.d/services.cfg',
16    notify              => File['/etc/nagios/conf.d'],
17    require             => Package['nagios'],
18  }
19  file { '/etc/nagios/conf.d':
20    recurse  => true,
21    owner    => 'nagios',
22    require  => Package['nagios'],
23    notify   => Service['nagios'];
24  }
25 }
```

Lines 2 to 9 include the nagios_host definition of our web server. The nagios_service resource on lines 10 to 18 defines the HTTP monitoring check, which is associated with the web server node.

This configuration works fine as long as the web server node uses the IP address 192.168.56.11 (set by the address attribute on line 4). When the IP address of the web server changes, or we add another web server for monitoring, we are required to manually update the manifest to reflect the changes in the cluster.

A better way to do this is to make the nagios_host and nagios_service resources as exported resources, and let the nagios server node import them. This way, the resources get automatically updated when the IP address changes or when we add more nodes to the cluster, and we don't have to manually update the manifest every time the change happens.

To achieve this, we are going to move the nagios_host and nagios_service resources to a new class called nagios::check_http, and make the resources exported.

Exporting resources

Let's create a new file called check_http.pp under the nagios/manifests directory, and declare a nagios::check_http class with the following content:

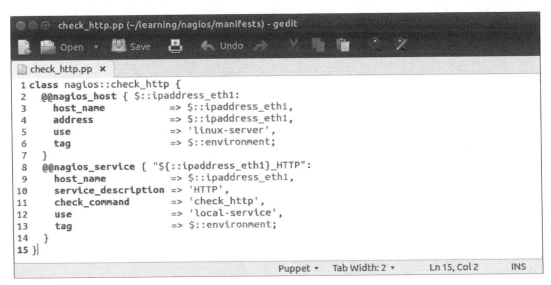

```
1 class nagios::check_http {
2   @@nagios_host { $::ipaddress_eth1:
3     host_name          => $::ipaddress_eth1,
4     address            => $::ipaddress_eth1,
5     use                => 'linux-server',
6     tag                => $::environment;
7   }
8   @@nagios_service { "${::ipaddress_eth1}_HTTP":
9     host_name          => $::ipaddress_eth1,
10    service_description => 'HTTP',
11    check_command      => 'check_http',
12    use                => 'local-service',
13    tag                => $::environment;
14  }
15 }
```

 You can cut lines 2 to 18 from the nagios::resources class, paste them into the nagios::check_http class, and remove the target, notify, and require attributes.

The nagios::check_http class declares the nagios_host and nagios_service resources that are exported. To export a resource, we prefix the type with a double at sign notation, as in @@nagios_host and @@nagios_service.

Let's take a look at the `nagios::check_http` class more in detail:

- Line 1 begins with the `nagios::check_http` class definition.
- Line 2 declares an exported resource `@@nagios_host`.

  The name of the resource is a reference to `facter ipaddress_eth1`. The reason why we use `facter` as the exported resource name is because the name of the resource must be unique for every resource that is exported. If we use a fixed string, for example, `web-server`, for the resource name, this would cause a `Duplicate declaration` error when the resources are collected from more than one node. Using `facter ipaddress_eth1` as the resource name, we can be sure that the resource name is unique when multiple nodes export the same resource.

- Lines 3 and 4 set the `host_name` and `address` attribute values based on `facter ipaddress_eth1`.

- Line 5 associates `nagios_host` with the host template called `linux-server`.

- Line 6 introduces a `tag` attribute, which is often used with exported resources.

  We tag the `nagios_host` resource with the name of the Puppet environment (the `${::environment}` variable reference) of the node that exports the resource. When the resource is imported, which we will do on the Nagios Server host shortly, we will use the tag as a filter to only collect the resources that are exported on hosts that belong to a specific environment.

- Line 7 closes the `nagios_host` resource definition.

- Line 8 declares another exported resource called `nagios_service`, which creates a Nagios HTTP check.

  As every Puppet resource name must be unique, we construct a unique name by joining the value of `facter ipaddress_eth1` and a string `_HTTP`. By creating a unique name this way, we can associate this check with multiple hosts and not have to worry about the resource name clashes.

- Line 9 associates the check with the `nagios_host` resource.

- Lines 10 to 12 define attributes that must be supplied with the `nagios_command` resource.

  Refer to *Chapter 4, Monitoring Your Web Server,* for a description of the attributes.

- Line 13 tags the `nagios_service` resources with the name of the environment.

- Line 14 closes the `nagios_service` definition.

- Line 15 closes the `nagios::check_http` class.

Once the `nagios::check_http` class has been created, save the file as `check_http.pp` under the manifests directory.

Then we need to associate the class with the web server node. You can choose whether you want to do it by adding an `include nagios::check_http` statement to the `webapp` class in the `learning/webapp/manifests/init.pp` file or by associating the `nagios::check_http` class via the node definition file `learning/manifests/site.pp`.

I would prefer to include the class in the node definition file `learning/manifests/site.pp`. This is how the definition of the `web.learning.vm` node will look like after I've associated the `nagios::check_http` class with the node on line 4:

```
site.pp (~/learning/manifests) - gedit

site.pp ×

1 node 'web.development.vm' {
2   include nagios::client
3   include webapp
4   include nagios::check_http
5 }
                                  Puppet ▾    Tab Width: 2 ▾    Ln 5, Col 2    INS
```

Importing resources

Before we can see how exported resources work, we must configure a resource collector that imports the `nagios_host` and `nagios_service` resources from PuppetDB to the nagios server host. Importing resources is done with the `Resource_type <<| tag == search_expression |>>` syntax.

For example, to collect all the `nagios_host` resources that belong to our environment, we do it with the following statement:

```
Nagios_host <<| tag == $::environment |>>
```

The statement begins with a reference to the type of the resource we wish to collect. When referencing a Puppet resource, the resource type must begin with a capital letter (`Nagios_host` instead of `nagios_host`). After the resource type declaration, we have the so-called `spaceship` notation `<<| |>>` with an optional `tag` parameter inside it. Although the `tag` parameter is optional, I recommend that you use it; otherwise, the collection is done for every `nagios_host` resource that is stored in PuppetDB.

We can collect the exported `nagios_host` and `nagios_service` resources by altering the `nagios::resources` class in the `file resources.pp` file, as shown in the following screenshot:

The `nagios::resources` class contains two file resources and a resource for importing the `nagios_host` and `nagios_service` resources.

File resources (on lines 2 to 9) create the so-called symbolic links that are needed when purging Nagios resources with Puppet. We will cover Nagios resource purging in detail later in this chapter, but here is some background on why these symbolic links are needed.

By default, Puppet stores the `nagios_host` resources in the `/etc/nagios/nagios_host.cfg` configuration file and the `nagios_service` resources in the `/etc/nagios/nagios_service.cfg` file. The issue with these file locations is that the nagios server does not process these files unless it is explicitly told to do so in the main nagios server configuration file, `/etc/nagios/nagios.cfg`. Symbolic links are created to workaround this problem.

By default, the nagios server processes all the files, including symbolic links, that have the `.cfg` file extension in the `/etc/nagios/conf.d` directory. To make Puppet play nicely with the default nagios server configuration, we create two links in the `/etc/nagios/conf.d` directory, which points to the `/etc/nagios/nagios_host.cfg` and `/etc/nagios/nagios_service.cfg` files.

Once the links are created, we declare the resource collection for the `nagios_host` and `nagios_service` resources.

Resource definitions for nagios_host and nagios_service that were previously present in this class have been replaced by the resource collectors for Nagios_host and Nagios_service.

There are two import statements:

- Lines 10 to 13 collect all the Nagios_host resources that are tagged with the name of our environment:

  ○ Using the require attribute, we tell Puppet that the nagios package must be installed prior to collecting the Nagios_host resources

  ○ The notify attribute sends a restart signal to the nagios service after the collection is finished

- Lines 14 to 17 repeat the same steps as lines 10 to 13 but for the Nagios_service resource

Testing exported resources

Now that we have created the nagios::check_http class for exporting resources and a nagios::resources class that collects resources, we can test how the resource collection works in practice.

Before we apply manifests, let's move the /etc/nagios/conf.d/hosts.cfg and /etc/nagios/conf.d/services.cfg files to the /etc/nagios/ directory and rename them. This can be done by running the following two commands on the command line on the nagios server:

```
mv /etc/nagios/conf.d/hosts.cfg /etc/nagios/nagios_host.cfg
```

```
mv /etc/nagios/conf.d/services.cfg /etc/nagios/nagios_service.cfg
```

Here is a screenshot that shows you the output of the mv commands followed by the ls command to list the files in a new location:

For testing, we need the following three virtual machines running:

- Puppet Master: It stores the exported resources in PuppetDB. This host is called `learn_puppet_centos-6.5` in the VirtualBox Manager.

- Web server: It exports the `nagios_host` and `nagios_service` resources. This host is called `puppet-agent` in the VirtualBox Manager.

- Nagios server: It imports resources from PuppetDB. This host is called `puppet-agent-nagios` in the VirtualBox Manager.

When working with exported resources, it is important to know in which order to run Puppet on nodes. For the nagios server node to successfully import resources from the web server node, the Puppet run that exports the resources must happen before the run that imports resources. As resources are exported on the web server node, we must run Puppet on it before we run Puppet on the nagios server node that imports resources.

Run the `puppet agent -t` command on nodes in the following sequence:

1. The web server (puppet-agent).
2. The nagios server (puppet-agent-nagios).

The Puppet run on the web server node doesn't show any nagios-related activity in the Puppet report but, when Puppet is run on the nagios server node, you will see the new `Nagios_host` and `Nagios_service` resources being imported on the server.

Here is a screenshot of the Puppet run that shows the resources that are imported on the nagios server:

After the Puppet run is complete on the nagios server, open the nagios web interface at http://192.168.56.12/nagios. Click on the **Services** link in the navigation pane, which is on the left-hand side of the page, to list all the hosts, and check whether they are currently configured on the nagios server as shown in the following screenshot:.

The list should contain the following three hosts:

- 192.168.56.11: This is the web server host that we just created with the exported resources

- localhost: This is the nagios server itself

- web-server: This is the original nagios_host record that was created in *Chapter 4, Monitoring Your Web Server*

 If nagios throws an error message Whoops! Error: Could not read host and service status information!, when you click on the **Services** link, rerun puppet agent -t to start the nagios server process.

Purging resources

As you probably noticed that the **Services** view in the nagios web interface contains two nagios host resources for the web server. There is a resource for the host 192.168.56.11 that we created on the web server using exported resources a moment ago. There is also a resource for the nagios host called web-server, which was created in *Chapter 4, Monitoring Your Web Server*. Although we just removed the nagios_host record from the nagios::resources class and reran Puppet, the resource didn't get removed. Why is that?

The reason for this is because Puppet does not automatically remove resources when resources are removed from the manifest file. Instead, we have to explicitly tell Puppet to purge resources of a certain type that are no longer present in the manifests. Puppet has a special resource type called resources that can be used to purge resources that are no longer needed. To purge old resources using type resources, we can use the following syntax:

```
resources { 'type_of_resource':
  purge => true;
}
```

To purge the old nagios_host and nagios_service resources from the nagios server, we will create a new class that contains all the purging-related logic, and associate this class with the nagios server.

Let's create a new class called nagios::purge with the following content:

```
1 class nagios::purge {
2   resources { ['nagios_host', 'nagios_service']:
3     purge => true;
4   }
5   ~>
6   # Nagios configuration reload after purging
7   exec { 'reload-nagios':
8     refreshonly => true,
9     command     => '/etc/init.d/nagios reload';
10  }
11 }
```

On lines 2 to 4, we declare a resource called resources that is applied to the nagios_host and nagios_service resource types. The resource contains a purge => true attribute that tells Puppet to delete all the nagios_host and nagios_service resources that have been removed from the manifests.

Once Puppet has purged resources, we tell it to reload the nagios process using the `exec` resource type that is defined on lines 7 to 10.

The notify arrow notation (tilde + greater-than) on line 5 means that only if the `nagios_host` and/or `nagios_service` resources are purged, then the notify signal is sent to the `exec` resource. Note the `refreshonly => true` attribute on line 8. This attribute is specific to the `exec` resource, and it means that the resource will only be processed if the notify signal is received.

In other words, the `reload-nagios exec` resource will only run the `/etc/init.d/nagios reload` command, in case the `nagios_host` or `nagios_service` resources were purged.

Once you have created the `nagios::purge` class, save the file as `nagios/manifests/purge.pp`.

Purging resources with the nagios::purge class

We are now ready to try resource purging on the nagios server. Before we do this, let's add the `nagios::purge` class to the catalog of the nagios server.

Open the node classification file, `manifests/site.pp`, and add an `include nagios::purge` statement to the `nagios.development.vm` node definition block, as shown on line 14 in the following screenshot:

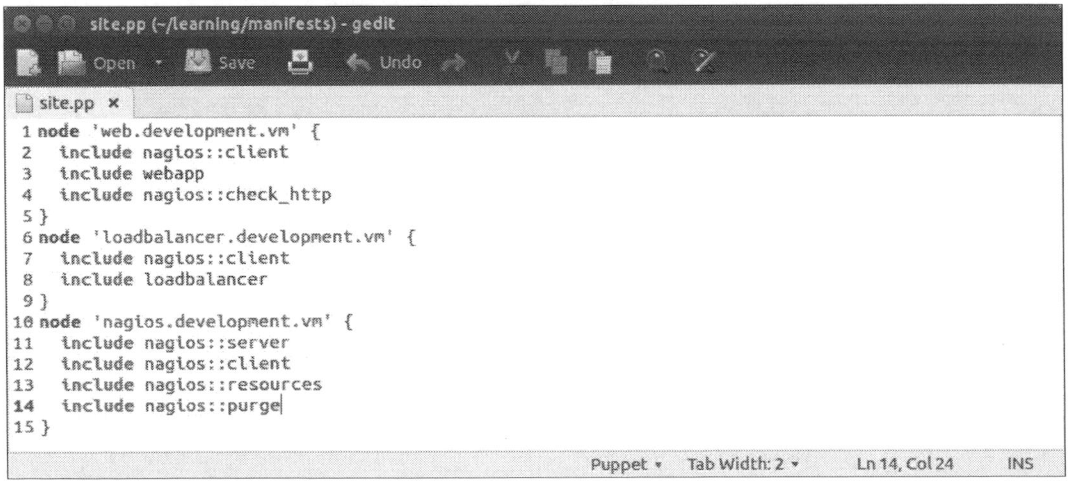

Once you've saved the file, go to the nagios server console and run the
puppet agent -t command. The following output confirms that the nagios_host
and nagios_service resources were removed successfully, and the nagios server
process got reloaded:

```
puppet-agent-nagios (agent-deployed) [Running] - Oracle VM VirtualBox
[root@learning ~]# puppet agent -
[root@learning ~]# puppet agent -t
Warning: Local environment: "production" doesn't match server specified node env
ironment "development", switching agent to "development".
Info: Retrieving pluginfacts
Info: Retrieving plugin
Info: Loading facts
Info: Caching catalog for nagios.development.vm
Warning: The package type's allow_virtual parameter will be changing its default
 value from false to true in a future release. If you do not want to allow virtu
al packages, please explicitly set allow_virtual to false.
   (at /opt/puppet/lib/ruby/site_ruby/1.9.1/puppet/type/package.rb:430:in `block
(3 levels) in <module:Puppet>')
Info: Applying configuration version '1431454184'
Notice: /Stage[main]/Nagios::Purge/Nagios_host[web-server]/ensure: removed
Info: Computing checksum on file /etc/nagios/nagios_host.cfg
Notice: /Stage[main]/Nagios::Purge/Nagios_service[HTTP]/ensure: removed
Info: Computing checksum on file /etc/nagios/nagios_service.cfg
Notice: /Stage[main]/Nagios::Purge/Exec[reload-nagios]/returns: executed success
fully
Notice: Finished catalog run in 1.72 seconds
[root@learning ~]# _

[0] 0:*                                    Quest: Begin - Progress: No Tasks.
                                                                     Right Ctrl
```

Now go to the nagios web interface at http://192.168.56.12/nagios, and refresh
the page by clicking on the **Services** link in the navigation pane on the left-hand side
of the page. Did the web server nagios host disappear from the list?

You should now have a fairly good understanding of how exported resources can be
used to exchange Puppet resources between nodes. Next, we will take a look at how
to query the node information from PuppetDB.

The PuppetDB query

Where exported resources are used to exchange Puppet resources between nodes,
the PuppetDB query is used to query information about the Puppet agent nodes.

For example, if we wish to find out the IP address that belongs to the nagios server
node, we can make a query that asks for the value of the ipaddress_eth1 facter on
the node that has the nagios::server class in its catalog.

Or if we want to know what `certnames` belong to Puppet agents in our environment, we can make a query that returns a list of `certnames` that belong to an environment called `development`.

There are a a couple of aspects to the PuppetDB query that some users may find a bit off-putting.

Firstly, the PuppetDB query syntax is quite complex, and the PuppetDB documentation available online (`http://docs.puppetlabs.com/puppetdb/`) signally fails to make it easier to learn. For example, to query the value of the `ipaddress_eth1` fact of the `nagios.development.vm` node, we use the following command on the Puppet Master node:

```
curl -G http://localhost:8080/v3/facts/ipaddress_eth1 --data-
urlencode 'query=["=", "certname", "nagios.development.vm"]'
```

Let's take a look at this command more in detail:

- The command that we use is called `curl`. Curl is a handy utility that enables you to make HTTP requests from the command line.

- The `http://localhost:8080/v3/facts/ipaddress_eth1` URL we connect to is the `PuppetDB API` endpoint for querying facts.

  In this instance, the fact we want to query is called `ipaddress_eth1`.

- The `--data-urlencode` option encodes the query parameters and appends parameters to the URL.

  The parameter we provided is `certname=nagios.development.vm`.

In English, this query can be described as "Please give me the value of `fact ipaddress_eth1` that belongs to the Puppet agent that has the `certname` value `nagios.development.vm`".

The query response is the following set of key-value pairs.

```
[ {
  "value" : "192.168.56.12",
  "name" : "ipaddress_eth1",
  "certname" : "nagios.development.vm"
} ]
```

With this query, we learned that the node with `certname nagios.development.vm` has an `ipaddress_eth1` facter with value `192.168.56.12`. That's nice, but how can the query results be integrated with the Puppet deployment when the only documented interface is from the command line using Curl?

This brings us to the second issue with PuppetDB. There is no built-in interface to the PuppetDB query from the Puppet manifest, which is similar to what we have for exported resources, that uses the @@ notation to export resources and the << | | >> notation to import resources in the Puppet manifest.

Don't give up hope yet as there is a simple solution that provides a remedy for both of the previously mentioned issues. This is the Puppet community add-on module, which we will take a look at next.

Installing the dalen-puppetdbquery module

The Puppetdbquery module, created by Mr. Erik Dalén (documentation is available at https://github.com/dalen/puppet-puppetdbquery), is a handy tool that provides a simple command-line interface to PuppetDB as well as the functions to access PuppetDB from the manifests.

The Puppetdbquery module is available in Puppet Forge, and it can be installed with the following command:

```
puppet module install dalen-puppetdbquery --
modulepath=/media/sf_learning/
```

The following screenshot shows the output of the preceding command:

Adding puppetdbquery into the RUBYLIB environment variable

We have installed the dalen-puppetdbquery module in the /media/sf_learning/puppetdbquery directory. Before we can start experimenting with it, we need to add the module to the command-line environment on Puppet Master.

We can achieve this by adding the /media/sf_learning/puppetdbquery/lib path to the RUBYLIB environment variable using the following command:

```
export RUBYLIB=/media/sf_learning/puppetdbquery/lib
```

To make this change permanent, we don't have to manually run the command every time we log on to the Puppet Master. We can configure the bootstrap::master class to create an /etc/profile.d/puppetdb.sh file, which contains the preceding command.

Open the /media/sf_learning/bootstrap/manifests/master.pp file and add lines 30 to 33, as shown in the following screenshot:

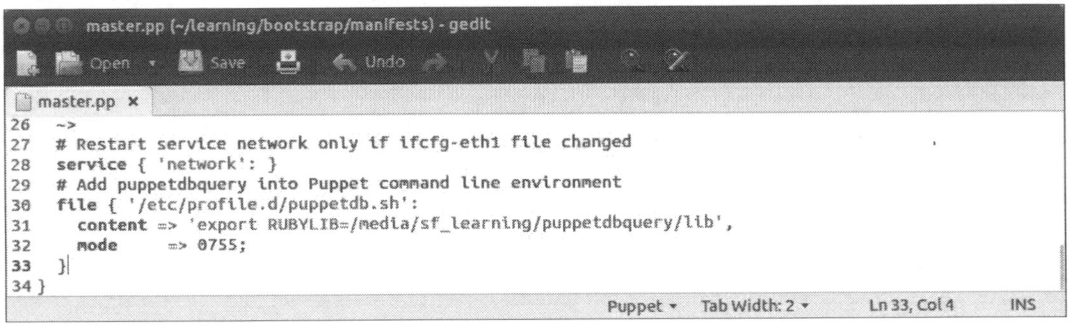

Once you have saved the file, reapply the bootstrap::master class on the Puppet Master node using the following two commands:

```
cd /media/sf_learning
```

```
puppet apply --modulepath=./ -e "class { 'bootstrap': role => 'master' }"
```

The puppet apply command produces the following report, confirming that the /etc/profile.d/puppetdb.sh file was created:

To make the change effective, you must log out and log in to the Puppet Master node. Once you are logged in again, you can verify that the `puppetdbquery` module is available by running the `puppet help query` command, which displays the `help` menu, as shown in the following screenshot:

```
learn_puppet_centos-6.5 (puppetmaster-and-3-agents-deployed) [Running] - Oracle VM
[root@learning ~]# puppet help query

USAGE: puppet query <action> [--puppetdb_host PUPPETDB] [--puppetdb_port PORT]

undocumented subcommand

OPTIONS:
  --render-as FORMAT          - The rendering format to use.
  --verbose                   - Whether to log verbosely.
  --debug                     - Whether to log debug information.
  --puppetdb_host PUPPETDB    - Host running PuppetDB.
  --puppetdb_port PORT        - Port PuppetDB is running on

ACTIONS:
  events    Serves as an interface to puppetdb allowing a user to query for a
            list of events
  facts     Serves as an interface to puppetdb allowing a user to query for a
            list of nodes
  nodes     Perform complex queries for nodes from PuppetDB

See 'puppet man query' or 'man puppet-query' for full help.
[root@learning ~]# _

[0] 0:*                                          Quest: Begin - Progress: No Tasks.
                                                           Right Ctrl
```

 An alternative to logging out and logging in again is that you can run the `source /etc/profile.d/puppetdb.sh` command source to update the `RUBYLIB` environment variable.

Examples of Puppet query commands on the command line

Now we are ready to start experimenting with the `puppet query` command. As seen in the preceding screenshot, `puppet query` has three actions: `events`, `facts`, and `nodes`.

Querying certname with action nodes

Let's first try the nodes action and make a PuppetDB query that returns the certname of the node that includes the nagios::server class in its catalog. We can do the query using the following command:

```
puppet query nodes 'Class["nagios::server"]'
```

A query returns the string nagios.development.vm, which is the certname of the nagios server node.

To expand the scope of the query, we need to also include the certname of the node that has the webapp class in its catalog. We can do this using the or operator to join two search patterns:

```
puppet query nodes 'Class["nagios::server"] or Class["webapp"]'
```

In addition to the string nagios.development.vm, the query returns a string web.development.vm, which is the certname of the web server node, as shown in the following screenshot:

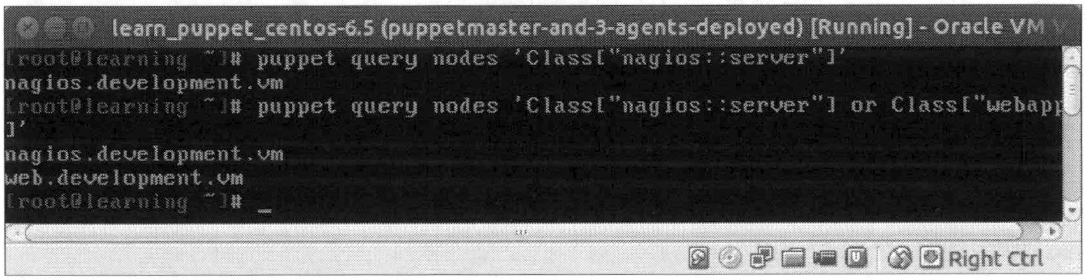

Querying facts with action facts

Querying facts works in a similar fashion to querying nodes. The syntax for querying facts is the puppet query facts 'search pattern'. This will print out all the facts from the nodes that match the search pattern. To filter the query results so that the command only returns the selected facts instead of all the facts, we can use the --facts parameter to specify a list of facts that the command should return.

Here is a sample command on how to query the `ipaddres_eth1` and uptime facts from the nagios server node:

```
puppet query facts 'Class["nagios::server"]' --facts
ipaddress_eth1,uptime
```

This command will return the following hash of facts from the node:

```
nagios.development.vm.
```

```
nagios.development.vm
{"ipaddress_eth1":"192.168.56.12","uptime":"2:30 hours"}
```

To choose a different output format, we can add the `-render-as yaml` parameter to make the query return the yaml document instead of the standard PuppetDB query hash:

```
puppet query facts 'Class["nagios::server"]' --facts
ipaddress_eth1,uptime -render-as yaml
```

Here are the query results in the yaml document format:

```
---

nagios.development.vm:

  uptime: "2:30 hours"

  ipaddress_eth1: "192.168.56.12"
```

Following is the screenshot of the preceding output:

Using the puppetdbquery functions

The Puppetdbquery module on the command line is a useful tool for testing query patterns and discovering information about nodes in PuppetDB. How can these queries be made part of the Puppet deployment?

The Puppetdbquery module comes with a couple of handy Puppet functions called query_nodes and query_facts that allow us to make the PuppetDB queries from the Puppet manifest. We can make use of these functions, for example, when configuring a load balancer node to balance the HTTP requests between the web server nodes. Instead of using static IP addresses for the load balancer configuration (like we currently do in the loadbalancer/manifests/create.pp file), we can use the query_nodes function to discover the IP addresses of all the web server nodes and configure the load balancer accordingly. Using this method, the load balancer configuration will automatically update if the web server node's IP address changes or if we add more web servers to the environment.

Before we dive into this, let's take a look at the syntax of the functions.

The query_nodes function

The query_nodes function accepts two arguments:

- A query pattern
- A fact name (optional)

If only the query pattern is provided, the query returns a list of certnames that match the pattern. If the fact name is provided, the response is a list of fact values from the nodes that match the query pattern.

To give you a better idea of the syntax, we can convert one of the command-line queries, as we did earlier in the query_nodes function call:

- The command line query:

```
puppet query nodes 'Class["nagios::server"] or
Class["webapp"]'
```

- The query_nodes function:

```
query_nodes('Class["nagios::server"] or Class["webapp"]')
```

When we call the function on the Puppet Master node, the query returns a list in the following format:

```
['nagios.development.vm', 'web.development.vm']
```

If we want the `query_nodes` function to return a list of facts instead of the `certnames`, we can specify the fact as the second argument in the query with the following syntax:

The `query_nodes` function returns a list of fact values:

```
query_nodes('Class["nagios::server"] or Class["webapp"]',
ipaddress_eth1)
```

This time, the query returns a list of IP addresses from the web server and nagios server nodes, [192.168.56.11, 192.168.56.12].

The query_facts function

The `query_facts` function returns a hash of hashes that contains facts from the nodes that match the query pattern.

To query the values of the `ipaddress_eth1` and uptime facts from the nagios server node, which we already tried on the command line, using the `query_facts` function.

On the command line, type the following command:

```
puppet query facts 'Class["nagios::server"]' --facts
ipaddress_eth1,uptime
```

Using the `query_facts` function in Puppet manifests, the syntax is slightly different:

```
query_facts('Class["nagios::server"]', [ipaddress_eth1,uptime])
```

This query returns a hash of hashes that contains the key-value pairs:

```
{ 'nagios.development.vm' =>
{"ipaddress_eth1":"192.168.56.12","uptime":"1:30 hours"} }
```

Creating a custom type for testing PuppetDB queries

Getting the PuppetDB query syntax right can often be tricky. When creating queries, it is important to test them properly to ensure that the queries return the desired results. To test PuppetDB queries, I usually create a short manifest that I run on the Puppet Master node, and examine the PuppetDB query results.

Create a new file in a text editor called `puppetdb.pp` with the following content:

```
puppetdb.pp (~/learning) - gedit

  Open      Save      Undo

puppetdb.pp  ×
1 define puppetdb_query {
2   notice("Value: ${name}")
3 }
4 $list = query_nodes('Class["nagios::server"] or Class["webapp"]')
5 $hash = query_facts('Class["nagios::server"]', [ipaddress_eth1,uptime])
6 $hash_to_string = join_keys_to_values($hash , " is ")
7 puppetdb_query { $list: }
8 puppetdb_query { $hash_to_string: }

                        Puppet ▼   Tab Width: 2 ▼      Ln 8, Col 36      INS
```

The preceding manifest contains a custom defined type (lines 1-3), three variables (lines 4-6), and two references to a defined type (lines 7-8). Let's take a look at the manifest in detail:

- Line 1 begins with a defined type called `puppetdb_query`.

  This type is used for printing out PuppetDB query results.

- Line 2 uses a Puppet function called `notice` (`https://docs.puppetlabs.com/references/latest/function.html#notice`) that outputs a string value `joined` with the value of the `${name}` variable, which is set at the time when the type is called (lines 7-8).

- Line 3 closes the custom defined type block.

- Line 4 creates a variable called `$list`, where we store the PuppetDB query results from the `query_nodes` function.

  The `query_nodes` function makes a PuppetDB query that returns a list of node names, such as a `certname`, that has the `nagios::server` or `webapp` class in its catalog.

- Line 5 creates a `$hash` variable, where we store the results from the `query_facts` function.

  The `$hash` variable name implies that the `query_facts` function returns a hash type of data (which means key-value pairs). The hash contains the values of facts `ipaddress_eth1` and the uptime.

- Line 6 defines the third and last variable that is used to store the hash content of the `$hash` variable in the format of a string, hence the name `$hash_to_string`.

The hash data type has to be converted to the string format so that we can use it when we call the type puppetdb_query (on line 8), which prints out the results of this query.

- Line 7 calls the puppetdb_query defined type with the $list variable as the name of the resource.

  Calling the defined type with a data type list as the name of the resource results in Puppet to call the type once per each element on the list.

  Assuming that the query_nodes function (line 4) returns a list of two node names, the type puppetdb_query is called twice.

- Line 8 makes another call to puppetdb_query, but this time using the $hash_to_string variable as the resource name.

  In this case, puppetdb_query is only called once, and the whole content of the hash produced by the query_facts function (line 5) is printed on the screen.

Once you have created the file, save it as puppetdb.pp under the Puppet module directory learning (on the virtual machine /media/sf_learning/puppetdb.pp).

Then, we can try to apply the manifest to the Puppet Master node. Log on to the Puppet Master and run the following two commands:

```
cd /media/sf_learning
puppet apply --modulepath=./ puppetdb.pp
```

On a successful Puppet run, you should see the following events being reported.

The output from the Puppet run may look a little bit messy, but when we take a look at it more closely, we can identify the following three Puppet events:

1. `nagios.development.vm`: This is the first record returned from PuppetDB by the `query_nodes` function, and it matches the query pattern `Class["nagios::server"]` (line 4 in `puppetdb.pp`).

2. `web.development.vm`: This is the second record returned from PuppetDB by the `query_nodes` function, and it matches the query pattern `Class["webapp"]` (line 4 in `puppetdb.pp`).

3. `nagios.development.vm is {"uptime"=>"0:30 hours", "ipaddress_eth1"=>"192.168.56.12"}`: This is the content of the hash returned from PuppetDB by the `query_facts` function (line 5 in `puppetdb.pp`).

Using the PuppetDB query to configure the load balancer

We now have a better understanding of how to interact with PuppetDB using the `query_nodes` and `query_facts` functions. Let's see how we can make use of these functions to configure the load balancer node.

In *Chapter 5, Load Balancing the Cluster*, we created the `loadbalancer` and `loadbalancer::create` classes. The `loadbalancer` class created an HTTP proxy that routes the requests to the nagios server as well as to web server nodes via a load balancer that was created by the `loadbalancer::create` class.

One problem with these classes is that they are currently using the static IP configuration for the nagios server and web server connectivity. The `loadbalancer` class assumes that the nagios server has an IP address `192.168.56.11`, and in the `loadbalancer::create` class, we assume that the web server nodes have the IP addresses `192.168.56.12` and `192.168.56.13`.

Since *Chapter 5, Load Balancing the Cluster*, I've been bouncing all the virtual machines a number of times, and VirtualBox has allocated different IP addresses to virtual machines. At this moment, my web server has an IP address `192.168.56.11`, and the nagios server's IP address is `192.168.56.12`. I guess in your environment, virtual machines have a different set of IP addresses.

You can check the host's IP address with the `hostname -I` and `ifconfig eth1` commands.

Unfortunately the virtual machine's IP addresses have changed, which means that the load balancer configuration in my environment is currently broken. The good news is that we can easily rectify the situation by making a couple of minor changes to the `loadbalancer` and `loadbalancer::create` classes.

Let's first tackle the `loadbalancer` class, and add a couple of PuppetDB queries to it. Here is a screenshot of the `loadbalancer` class in its current state:

```puppet
 1 class loadbalancer ($nagios_path = '/nagios',
 2                     $nagios_url  = 'http://192.168.56.11/nagios',
 3                     $webapp_path = '/webapp',
 4                     $webapp_url  = 'http://192.168.56.12/') {
 5   include apache
 6   $balancer_name = 'webapp'
 7   $balancer_url  = "balancer://${balancer_name}"
 8   include loadbalancer::create
 9   apache::vhost { 'loadbalancer':
10     ip        => $::ipaddress_eth1,
11     docroot   => '/var/www/html',
12     proxy_pass => [
13                   { 'path' => $nagios_path, 'url' => $nagios_url },
14                   { 'path' => $webapp_path, 'url' => $balancer_url} },
15                  ]
16   }
17 }
```

The `$nagios_url` variable on line 2 defines the nagios server address as `http://192.168.56.11/nagios`, and the variable is referenced on line 13 by the `proxy_pass` attribute.

Instead of using a predefined IP address in the `$nagios_url` variable, we can use the `query_nodes` function to extract the nagios server IP address from PuppetDB, and pass the IP address to the `$nagios_url` variable. We'll also add a similar PuppetDB query for web server nodes, which we can reference from the `loadbalancer::create` class.

Here is a redesigned `loadbalancer` class that introduces you to two new PuppetDB queries and constructs the `$nagios_url` variable value from the query results:

```
init.pp (~/learning/loadbalancer/manifests) - gedit

   Open    Save    Undo

init.pp  ×

 1 class loadbalancer ($nagios_path = '/nagios',
 2                     $webapp_path = '/webapp') {
 3   $nagios_server_ip = query_nodes('Class["nagios::server"]', ipaddress_eth1)
 4   $web_server_ips  = query_nodes('Class["webapp"]', ipaddress_eth1)
 5   $nagios_url      = "http://${nagios_server_ip}/nagios"
 6   include apache
 7   $balancer_name   = 'webapp'
 8   $balancer_url    = "balancer://${balancer_name}"
 9   include loadbalancer::create
10   apache::vhost { 'loadbalancer':
11     ip         => $::ipaddress_eth1,
12     docroot    => '/var/www/html',
13     proxy_pass => [
14                    { 'path' => $nagios_path, 'url' => $nagios_url },
15                    { 'path' => $webapp_path, 'url' => $balancer_url },
16     ]
17   }
18 }

                                    Puppet ▾   Tab Width: 2 ▾   Ln 13, Col 17   INS
```

Let's take a look at what has changed in the `loadbalancer` class:

- Line 2 that was used to define the `$nagios_url` variable has been moved to line 5.

- Line 4 was used to define the `$webapp_url` variable, but the variable is no longer needed, so this has been removed.

- Line 3 creates a new variable called `$nagios_server_ip`. We store the nagios server's IP address in this variable. The IP address is queried from PuppetDB using the `query_nodes` function.

- Line 4 creates a `$web_server_ips` variable. This variable stores a list of web server IP addresses, which are going to be referenced from the `loadbalancer::create` class.

- Line 5 constructs the value for the `$nagios_url` variable based on the `$nagios_server_ip` variable (on line 3).

Before we try running this manifest on a load balancer, let's make a couple of changes to the `loadbalancer::create` class, which currently has the following content:

```
create.pp.v1 (~/learning/loadbalancer/manifests) - gedit

create.pp.v1 ×

 1 class loadbalancer::create {
 2   apache::balancer { $::loadbalancer::balancer_name:
 3     collect_exported => false;
 4   }
 5   apache::balancermember { "web1":
 6       balancer_cluster => $::loadbalancer::balancer_name,
 7       url              => "http://192.168.56.12/",
 8   }
 9   apache::balancermember { "web2":
10       balancer_cluster => $::loadbalancer::balancer_name,
11       url              => "http://192.168.56.13/",
12   }
13 }
```

The `loadbalancer::create` class creates two `apache::balancermember` records, which we are going to substitute with a defined type that creates the `apache::balancermember` record for each web server IP address that the PuppetDB query returns (line 4 in the `loadbalancer/manifests/init.pp` file). Here is the screenshot of the newly designed `loadbalancer::create` class:

```
create.pp (~/learning/loadbalancer/manifests) - gedit

create.pp ×

 1 class loadbalancer::create {
 2   apache::balancer { $::loadbalancer::balancer_name:
 3     collect_exported => false;
 4   }
 5   define balancermember {
 6     apache::balancermember { $name:
 7         balancer_cluster => $::loadbalancer::balancer_name,
 8         url              => "http://${name}/",
 9     }
10   }
11   loadbalancer::create::balancermember { $::loadbalancer::web_server_ips: }
12 }
```

Let's take a look at what has changed in the `loadbalancer::create` class:

- Lines 5 to 12 in the previous version of `create.pp` have been replaced by the defined type `balancermember` (lines 5 to 10). The `balancermember` type contains a reference to another defined type called `apache::balancermember`, which creates a new load balancing endpoint based on the `${name}` variable. The endpoint URL is defined by the `url` attribute on line 8, which has a value `http://${name}/`. The `${name}` variable is a reference to the name of the defined type, which is specified at the time when a type is called (on line 11). For example, if the type is referenced with a name `192.168.56.11`, then the value of the `url` attribute will be `http://192.168.56.11/`.

- Line 11 references the `loadbalancer::create::balancermember` defined type (on lines 5 to 10). Here, we use the `$::loadbalancer::web_server_ips` variable as the name of the type, which is a reference to the `$web_server_ips` variable that is defined in the `loadbalancer` class (line 4 in the `loadbalancer/manifests/init.pp` file). The `$::loadbalancer::web_server_ips` variable stores the results of the PuppetDB query `query_nodes('Class["webapp"]', ipaddress_eth1)`. If the PuppetDB query returns a list of multiple IP addresses (this means that PuppetDB contains a record for more than one node matching the query pattern `Class["webapp"]`), the `loadbalancer::create::balancermember` defined type is called once per each entry in the list.

Once you are done with the changes made to the `init.pp` and `create.pp` files and have saved the files in the `loadbalancer/manifests` directory, we can move on to apply manifests on the load balancer node.

Testing the PuppetDB query manifests on the load balancer node

To test our manifest changes, you need to boot up the load balancer node and have Puppet Master running of course.

Once the load balancer node is running, log in with the username `root` and password `puppet`.

Then, execute the following two commands:

```
cd /media/sf_learning
puppet agent -t
```

When the Puppet run completes successfully, you will see the following events displayed on the screen:

If you have the nagios server and web server nodes running, you should be able to access both of them via the load balancer node at `http://<loadbalancer_ip>/nagios` and `http://<loadbalancer_ip>/webapp`.

You can find out the value of `<loadbalancer_ip >` by running the `hostname -I` or `ifconfig eth1` commands on the load balancer node.

Summary

In this chapter, we learned how to turn the Puppet configuration from static to dynamic through exported resources and PuppetDB queries. We saw how exported resources can help you dynamically create new monitoring checks, and how checks can be easily purged using the resource type resources. We also saw how we can interact with PuppetDB from the command line, and how to make PuppetDB queries an integral part of deployments using the PuppetDB function.

8

Extending Puppet

In the earlier chapters, we explored various facts and functions that Puppet provides out-of-the-box. You may recall that, in *Chapter 3, My First Puppet Module,* we created a variable called $fact_list (line 3 in the webapp class), and we used it to store values of facts $::ipaddress_eth1 and $::uptime. These two facts are built into Puppet. Once we declared the $fact_list variable, we created a file resource with the content attribute that used the template function (line 7 in the webapp class) to populate the content of the file. The template function is a commonly used function that comes bundled with Puppet.

When you start using Puppet on a regular basis, you soon realize that the built-in facts and functions may not be sufficient to build configurations you want to build. Luckily, custom facts and functions are quick and easy to write yourself.

This chapter will focus on how to extend Puppet beyond the built-in functionality. We will learn how to create your own facts and functions, and how these are distributed across the nodes in the environment.

In this chapter, we will cover the following topics:

- How functions work and how to distribute them
- Writing a simple function to distribute the SSH keys across all nodes in the environment
- Writing a simple custom fact and making it available everywhere
- Converting fact string values to arrays and hashes

Puppet functions

So what do we know about Puppet functions?

- We can reference functions from the Puppet manifests... check!

- Function calls use the `function_name(argument1, argument2)` syntax ... check!

- Puppet has built-in functions, such as `template()`... check!

- Puppet can use custom functions, such as `query_nodes()` and `query_facts()`, from the `puppetdbquery` module... check!

Let's talk about the last bullet point more in detail. How are custom functions created and distributed?

Functions are written in the Ruby programming language, which are stored in the `lib/puppet/parser/functions` directory in a Puppet module with a name that uses the `functionname.rb` syntax.

All the functions that are stored in Puppet modules that are available in the Puppet Agent's modulepath will be synchronized at the beginning of each Puppet run. Once the functions have been synchronized, they can be referenced from the Puppet manifests.

There is one important thing to remember about how functions are executed. When running Puppet in "master-less" mode (`puppet apply --modulepath ...`), functions are executed on the Puppet Agent node. When Puppet is run against the Puppet Master (`puppet agent -t`), functions are executed on the Puppet Master node.

The best way to demonstrate the difference in function execution is to create a simple Puppet function and try running it in both the modes.

Creating a Puppet module for custom functions

Although functions can be distributed from any Puppet module, I prefer to store functions (and facts) in a dedicated Puppet module, which I have included in the Puppet's modulepath, and I can then reference these functions from the other Puppet modules.

The name of the module is not that important, but I usually include the word `lib` in the name of the module, which indicates that the module contains a library of functions. A suitable name for our functions module can be, for example, `learning-flib`.

Let's create a new module for functions with the following set of commands:

```
# cd /media/learning
# puppet module generate learning-flib –skip-interview
```

This command creates an empty Puppet module. Then, we rename the directory from `learning-flib` to `flib`:

```
# mv learning-flib flib
```

Now we use the `mkdir` command to create a directory structure to store functions, facts, and tests:

```
# mkdir -p flib/lib/puppet/parser/functions flib/lib/facter flib/tests
```

Once all the preceding commands have been executed, we can view the folder structure with the `tree flib/` command, as shown in the following screenshot:

Writing a function

Now that we have created a module to store our custom functions, we can write our first function. Let's create a function called `cli_command`, which accepts a command-line command as an argument, executes the command, and returns the results.

Here is the content of the `cli_command` function:

```
cli_command.rb (~/learning/flib/lib/puppet/parser/functions) - gedit

cli_command.rb ×
1 Puppet::Parser::Functions::newfunction(:cli_command, :type => :rvalue, :doc => <<-'ENDHEREDOC') do |args|
2
3   Function cli_command executes the command specified as an argument and returns command output
4   Usage:
5     cli_command('/opt/puppet/bin/puppet config print certname')
6   Returns:
7     learning.puppetlabs.vm
8   ENDHEREDOC
9
10  # Check whether number of arguments is 1
11  raise Puppet::ParseError, ("cli_command(): Wrong number of arguments (#{args.length}; must be = 1)") unless args.length == 1
12
13  # Execute command and return results to Puppet
14  return %x[#{args[0]}]
15
16 end

                                    Ruby ▾   Tab Width: 2 ▾      Ln 16, Col 1      INS
```

The syntax of the `cli_command` function looks very different from the syntax that we have been using so far in Puppet manifests. This is because functions are written in the Ruby programming language instead of Puppet DSL. Let's take a look at the `flib/lib/puppet/parser/functions/cli_command.rb` file line by line:

- Line 1 references a `newfunction` method in the `Puppet::Parser::Functions` Ruby module. As the name suggests, this method is used to create new Puppet functions. The `newfunction` method has three arguments:
  - The first argument `:cli_command` is the name of the function prefixed with a colon character.
  - The second argument defines the type of the function. The type of the function is `rvalue`, which means that this function returns a value. If `rvalue` is not specified, the function is a statement type that does not return a value.
  - The third argument `:doc` is a placeholder for the documentation. The `<<-'ENDHEREDOC'` value indicates the end tag of the documentation block (see line 8).

- Lines 3 to 8 include the documentation for the function. It is not obligatory to include the documentation in your function, but it is good practice to add a short description of what the function does (line 3), how to use the function (lines 5-4), and a description of what the function returns (lines 6-7).

- Line 11 is an optional error handler that checks whether the number of arguments passed to the function is as expected.

  If the number of arguments passed to the function is not 1, then the user will receive a visible error message during the Puppet run.

- Line 14 executes the command that is passed to the function as an argument.

- Once you have created the function, save it as `flib/lib/puppet/parser/functions/cli_command.rb`.

Test-driving the Puppet function

As I mentioned earlier, Puppet functions are executed either on the Puppet Agent or on the Puppet Master, depending on whether the Agent is run against the Puppet Master.

Let's test our new `cli_command` function in standalone mode without the Puppet Master, before we try running it on the Puppet Master, and then compare the results from the function.

Testing a Puppet function on the Puppet Agent node

To decide whether we want the function to run on the Puppet Agent or on the Master, we must have a class that calls the function. Open `flib/manifests/init.pp`, and replace the content generated by the `puppet module generate` command with the following four lines:

```
1 class flib {
2   $output = cli_command('/opt/puppet/bin/puppet config print certname')
3   notify { "Function cli_command returns ${output}": }
4 }
```

- Line 1 begins with class `ftlib`.

- Line 2 calls the function `cli_command` with the `/opt/puppet/bin/puppet config print certname` command (Puppet Enterprise only), which returns the `certname` of the node, where the function is executed. The output of the command is stored in the `$output` variable. In Puppet open source, the command would be slightly different—for example, `/usr/bin/puppet config print certname`.

- Line 3 creates a `notify` resource that prints out the function's return value that is stored in the `${output}` variable.

- Line 4 closes the class `ftlib`.

Once the file has been saved, then we can try to apply the `flib` class to the web server node. Log on to the Web Server node (with the username `root` and password `puppet`), and run the following two commands:

```
# cd /media/learning
# puppet apply --modulepath=./  -e 'include flib'
```

On a successful run, Puppet will report a message saying `Notice: Function cli_command returns web.development.vm`, which is an evidence of the function being executed on the Puppet Agent node.

Testing a Puppet function against Puppet Master

Next, we can try to apply the `flib` class to the Puppet Agent against the Puppet Master. In order to apply the class, we must include it in the Agent's catalog, which is defined in the `manifests/site.pp` file.

Open the `manifests/site.pp` file and add a line `include flib` to the `'web.development.vm'` block. To make the Puppet report shorter, I've also commented out the `include` statements for the other classes associated with the `web.development.vm` node.

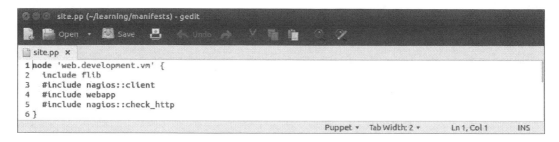

To run the function on the Puppet Master, we need to have both the web server and the Puppet Master nodes running. Once you have both the nodes running, you can apply the `flib` class by running the `puppet apply -t` command to the Web Server node. This produces the following Puppet report:

```
puppet-agent (agent-deployed) [Running] - Oracle VM VirtualBox
[root@learning ~]# puppet agent -t
Warning: Local environment: "production" doesn't match server specified node en
vironment "development", switching agent to "development".
Info: Retrieving pluginfacts
Info: Retrieving plugin
Info: Loading facts
Info: Caching catalog for web.development.vm
Info: Applying configuration version '1433785845'
Notice: Function cli_command returns learning.puppetlabs.vm

Notice: /Stage[main]/Flib/Notify[Function cli_command returns learning.puppetla
s.vm
]/message: defined 'message' as 'Function cli_command returns learning.puppetla
s.vm
'
Notice: Finished catalog run in 0.45 seconds
[root@learning ~]# _
```

When comparing the output of the commands, `puppet agent -t` and `puppet apply`, we can see that the function applied to the `puppet agent -t` command returns a certname `learning.puppetlabs.vm` that belongs to the Puppet Master. The `puppet apply` command returns a certname `web.development.vm`, which is the certname that belongs to the web server.

We now have enough evidence to show that the functions can be run on the Puppet Agent and on the Puppet Master nodes, depending on the mode the Puppet Agent runs on. Let's move on and write a function that distributes the file content across the environment.

Distributing SSH keys with a Puppet function

Secure Shell, or SSH, is a protocol that is widely used for remote connectivity between computers. It enables you to create a secure connection from one computer to another. SSH provides a variety of authentication methods, such as the username/password authentication but also password-less authentication based on the **public key infrastructure (PKI)**. Setting up the PKI authentication involves the following steps:

1. Generate a public and private key pair.

2. Distribute a public key to a remote host.

In the following example, we will create a public/private key pair on the Puppet Master, and then create a Puppet function that reads the public key on the Puppet Master, and finally output its content to a /root/.ssh/authorized_keys file on the Puppet Agent node.

Creating a public and private key pair

Creating public and private keys involves two commands, which we can Puppetize. As the key pair creation is just a one-off job, I think we can as well do it manually, and use Puppet for key distribution.

Here are the steps for creating a public and private key pair:

1. Start the Puppet Master node.

2. Log on to the Puppet Master with the following details:
   ○ username: root
   ○ password: puppet

3. Create a /root/.ssh directory for the keys:

   ```
   # mkdir /root/.ssh
   ```

4. Create keys with the ssh-keygen command:

   ```
   # ssh-keygen -N '' -f /root/.ssh/id_rsa
   ```

5. Finally, verify that the id_rsa (the private key) and id_rsa.pub (the public key) files were created in the /root/.ssh directory:

   ```
   # ls /root/.ssh
   ```

When the preceding three commands are successfully run, you will see the following events logged on the screen:

Writing a Puppet function to distribute a public key

Now we have the public and private key pair on the Puppet Master, and we want to distribute the public key to the Puppet Agent nodes. To achieve this, we'll write a function called `read_file` that reads a file and returns its content.

Create a new file called `read_file.rb` and save it in the `flib/lib/puppet/parser/functions` directory in the `flib` module. Here is the content of the `read_file.rb` file:

```ruby
1 Puppet::Parser::Functions::newfunction(:read_file, :type => :rvalue, :doc => <<-'ENDHEREDOC') do |args|
2
3   Function read_file accepts a file path as an argument and returns its content
4   Usage:
5     read_file('/root/.ssh/id_rsa.pub')
6   Returns:
7     ssh-rsa AAAA......
8   ENDHEREDOC
9
10  # Check whether number of arguments is 1
11  raise Puppet::ParseError, ("read_file(): Wrong number of arguments (#{args.length}; must be = 1)") unless args.length == 1
12
13  begin
14    File.read(args[0])
15  rescue
16    raise Puppet::ParseError, ("read_file(): Failed to read file #{args[0]}")
17  end
18 end
```

Let's take a look at the content more closely:

- Line 1 begins with a new Puppet function called read_line.

- Lines 3 to 8 provide the documentation for the function with examples on how to use it and what it returns.

- Line 11 validates the number of arguments passed to the function. If the number of arguments is 1, then the function will report an exception during the Puppet run.

- Line 13 has the begin keyword, which in the Ruby programming language is used to handle exceptions.

- Line 14 specifies the command that we want the function to execute.

  The File.read method in Ruby reads a file that is provided as an argument (args[0]) when the function is called.

  If the file read operation fails, an exception is handled by the rescue block on lines 15 and 16.

- Line 15 begins with the rescue block.

- Line 16 raises a Puppet::ParserError event in case the file read operation on line 14 fails.

- Line 17 closes the begin/rescue block.

- Line 18 ends the read_file function.

Now save the file as flib/lib/puppet/parser/functions/read_file.rb after which we'll take a look at how to create a file resource that calls the read_file function.

Calling the custom function from the file resource

To push the public key onto the Puppet Agent, we need to create a file resource that gets its content from the read_file function. By default, the public key is stored in a file called authorized_keys that is stored in the .ssh directory under the user's home directory. For example, if the root user's home directory is /root, then the public key is stored in the /root/.ssh/authorized_keys file.

Let's move on and create a class called flib::public_key that declares two file resources. Here is a screenshot of the class:

```
○ ● ○  public_key.pp (~/learning/flib/manifests) - gedit

  ▣  ▣ Open  ▾  ▣ Save  ▣  ↶ Undo  ↷  ∨  ▣  ▣  ⟲ ✕

▣ public_key.pp ×
1 class flib::public_key {
2   file {
3     '/root/.ssh':
4       ensure   => 'directory';
5     '/root/.ssh/authorized_keys':
6       require  => File['/root/.ssh'],
7       content  => read_file('/root/.ssh/id_rsa.pub');
8   }
9 }

                              Puppet ▾   Tab Width: 2 ▾      Ln 1, Col 23      INS
```

In the preceding `flib::public_key` class, we have one `file` block (lines 2 to 8) that declares two file resources:

- Lines 3 to 4 declare a file resource for a `/root/.ssh` directory, where we are going to store the `authorized_key` file.

- Lines 5 to 7 create the `/root/.ssh/authorized_keys` file.

  Using the `require` attribute (line 6), we ensure that the `/root/.ssh` resource must be processed prior to processing the `authorized_keys` file.

  The `content` attribute on line 7 calls the `read_file` function with a `/root/.ssh/id_rsa.pub` argument, which is the path to the public key file on the Puppet Master.

Let's add the `flib::public_key` class to the Puppet catalog and give it a test run. Open the node definition file, `manifests/site.pp`, and change the `include flib` statement to the `include flib::public_key` statement in the node definition block for `web.development.vm`, as shown in the following screenshot:

```
○ ● ○  site.pp (~/learning/manifests) - gedit

  ▣  ▣ Open  ▾  ▣ Save  ▣  ↶ Undo  ↷  ∨  ▣  ▣  ⟲ ✕

▣ site.pp ×
1 node 'web.development.vm' {
2   include flib::public_key
3   #include nagios::client
4   #include webapp
5   #include nagios::check_http
6 }
7 node 'loadbalancer.development.vm' {
8   include nagios::client
9   include loadbalancer
10 }

                              Puppet ▾   Tab Width: 2 ▾      Ln 2, Col 3      INS
```

Once you have saved the file, you can try running Puppet on the Web Server node. To apply the catalog, you must have the Puppet Master and Web Server nodes running in parallel. Once the Web Server is running, you can apply the catalog by performing the following steps:

1. Log on to Web Server node with the following credentials:

    ◦   Username: `root`

    ◦   Password: `puppet`

2. Go to the Puppet module directory:

    ```
    # cd /media/sf_learning
    ```

3. Run Puppet in agent mode:

    ```
    # puppet agent -t
    ```

 If you get a message `"Could not retrieve catalog from remote server: Error 400"` on the Puppet Agent node, try restarting the pe-`console-services` and pe-`httpd` processes on the Puppet Master with the following commands:

```
# service pe-console-services restart
# service pe-httpd restart
```

When the Puppet run completes successfully, you will see the following events reported on the screen:

```
puppet-agent (agent-deployed) [Running] - Oracle VM VirtualBox
Notice: /File[/var/opt/lib/pe-puppet/lib/puppetdb.rb]/ensure: defined content as
'{md5}8293627a0f388c92e3a98772eb00d19a'
Notice: /File[/var/opt/lib/pe-puppet/lib/puppetdb/astnode.rb]/ensure: defined co
ntent as '{md5}22004c25bfdff10e78e3d6b579dc6045'
Notice: /File[/var/opt/lib/pe-puppet/lib/puppetdb/connection.rb]/ensure: defined
 content as '{md5}d10aa996616878d8c0e740b4fde24b1a'
Notice: /File[/var/opt/lib/pe-puppet/lib/puppetdb/grammar.racc]/ensure: defined
content as '{md5}76cd28f9ea5b879aeb1c2039683df24d'
Notice: /File[/var/opt/lib/pe-puppet/lib/puppetdb/lexer.rb]/ensure: defined cont
ent as '{md5}6c29d8912fd05729a5166d142c91b79e'
Notice: /File[/var/opt/lib/pe-puppet/lib/puppetdb/lexer.rex]/ensure: defined con
tent as '{md5}e8a7722365726dcab5ed8489f4130477'
Notice: /File[/var/opt/lib/pe-puppet/lib/puppetdb/parser.rb]/ensure: defined con
tent as '{md5}20428aa77fb78f35f814e4c582607587'
Notice: /File[/var/opt/lib/pe-puppet/lib/puppetdb/util.rb]/ensure: defined conte
nt as '{md5}5618f606db5a476978ba180ba82503db'
Info: Loading facts
Info: Caching catalog for web.development.vm
Info: Applying configuration version '1434614117'
Notice: /Stage[main]/Flib::Public_key/File[/root/.ssh]/ensure: created
Notice: /Stage[main]/Flib::Public_key/File[/root/.ssh/authorized_keys]/ensure: d
efined content as '{md5}e54ebd2ee55198cd45cbc031c5ba308c'
Notice: Finished catalog run in 0.48 seconds
[root@learning /media/sf_learning]#
[0] 0:*                                        Quest: Begin - Progress: No Tasks.
                                         Right Ctrl
```

Testing the password-less SSH session

I trust that your Puppet run was successful. Let's verify it by doing a test to see whether we can establish the password-less login from the Puppet Master to the Web Server node. This can done by performing the following steps:

1. Log on to the Puppet Master node as a `root` using the password `puppet`.

2. Query the certname of the node we are currently on:

   ```
   # puppet config print certname
   ```

   This returns the Puppet Master's certname: `learning.puppetlabs.vm`.

3. Open the SSH session on the Web Server node:

   ```
   # ssh 192.168.56.11
   ```

4. Query the certname of the node we are currently on:

   ```
   # puppet config print certname
   ```

   The command returns the web server's certname `web.development.vm`.

5. Disconnect the SSH session with the `exit` command.

I hope the test worked well for you. Next, we will shift our focus from functions to custom facts.

Creating custom facts

So far, in this book, we have been using Puppet's built-in facts, such as the `ipaddress_eth1` and `uptime`. In comparison to functions, facts are much easier to use as they don't accept arguments. We just reference them like we reference any Puppet variable using the `$fact_name` or `$::fact_name` syntax. Personally, I like to use the `$::fact_name` syntax because it clearly defines the scope of the variable. This is also the syntax recommended in the Puppet Language Style Guide (`https://docs.puppetlabs.com/guides/style_guide.html`). The `$::` prefix in Puppet variables means that the variable scope is global (`$::fact_name`) as opposed to local (`$fact_name`). Although Puppet doesn't allow you to declare a local variable with the same name as a fact, it is a good practice to include the scope prefix (`$::`) when referencing facts. When someone is studying a manifest that I've written, they can easily see from the `$::` prefix that the variable is referencing the fact rather than the local variable.

There are a couple of ways to create your own facts. Let's first take a look at the most simple type of fact, which is called the external fact.

External facts

External facts are defined as key-value pairs in a text file that is stored in the `/etc/puppetlabs/facter/facts.d` directory on the Puppet Agent node (Puppet Enterprise only). In the Puppet open source, the path is `/etc/facter/facts.d/`.

External facts support three different types of document formats: text, **JSON (JavaScript Object Notation)**, and **YAML (YAML Ain't Markup Language)**. For example, to declare an external fact called `text_fact` in the text format that returns a value `Hello world`, we create an `/etc/puppetlabs/facter/facts.d/my_facts.txt` file with the following code:

```
text_fact=Hello world
```

In the preceding example, the string `text_fact` on the left-hand side of the `=` sign is the key, and the string `Hello world` is the value of the key. Let's see how the preceding example works in practice on the Web Server virtual machine. Start the Web Server node if it's not already running, and run the the following three commands:

```
# mkdir -p /etc/puppetlabs/facter/facts.d
```

This creates the required directory structure for the external fact.

```
# echo text_fact=Hello world > /etc/puppetlabs/facter/facts.d/my_facts.txt
```

This creates a `my_facts.txt` file that defines an external fact called `my_external_fact` that returns a value `Hello world`.

```
# cat /etc/puppetlabs/facter/facts.d/my_facts.txt
```

This prints out the content of the `my_facts.txt` file.

Here is a screenshot of the Web Server console after the preceding three commands have been executed:

Next, we need to create a Puppet manifest file that calls the fact `text_fact`. For testing purposes, we can create an `external_fact.pp` manifest file in the `flib` module under the `flib/manifests` directory. Here is the content of the file, which prints out the value of the fact when the manifest is applied by Puppet.

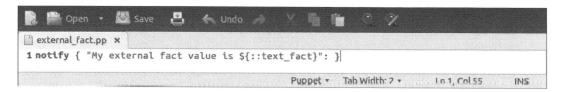

Then, apply the manifest to the Web Server node by running the following two commands:

```
# cd /media/sf_learning
# puppet apply flib/manifests/external_fact.pp
```

When the manifest is successfully applied, Puppet reports a message `Notice: My external fact value is Hello world`, as shown in the following screenshot:

```
puppet-agent (agent-deployed) [Running] - Oracle VM VirtualBox
root@learning /media/sf_learning # cd /media/sf_learning/
root@learning /media/sf_learning # puppet apply flib/manifests/external_fact.p
Notice: Compiled catalog for web.development.vm in environment production in 0.
3 seconds
Notice: My external fact value is Hello world
Notice: /Stage[main]/Main/Notify[My external fact value is Hello world]/message
 defined 'message' as 'My external fact value is Hello world'
Notice: Finished catalog run in 0.19 seconds
root@learning /media/sf_learning # _
```

Well done. You have just created your first custom fact!

What about the other two document formats, JSON and YAML, that I mentioned earlier? Why would we choose to use them instead of the text format?

Creating facts that return structured data

JSON and YAML are used for structured data types, such as a hash and a list. Facts defined in text format only return the string type of data. Let's take a look at how we can create a fact that returns an array of strings that are defined in the YAML format. Here is an example of the YAML document my_facts.yaml, which defines a fact called yaml_fact that returns a list of strings:

```
---                      # Begin YAML document
yaml_fact:               # Name of the list/fact
   - Hello world         # 1st list item
   - Hello Puppet        # 2nd list item
   - Hello handsome!  # 3rd list item
```

The preceding YAML document defines a fact called yaml_fact that contains a list of strings. For clarity, I've added comments (the # prefix) that describe what each line of the document means.

Once you have examined the preceding YAML document, create a /etc/puppetlabs/facter/facts.d/my_facts.yaml file on the Web Server node using the Nano editor. Just as a reminder, you can create the file in the Nano editor by running the following command on the Web Server host:

nano /etc/puppetlabs/facter/facts.d/my_facts.yaml

To save the file and exit from the Nano editor, press Control + X, and confirm the save operation by pressing Y and Enter.

> It is important to use the correct file extension for the external facts file. Facts defined in the YAML document will reside in the file that has the .yaml file extension. The external facts file for the text data has the extension .txt, and facts defined in the JSON format will reside in the file that has a .json file extension.

Now that we have the YAML document ready, we need to write more Puppet code that will consume the content of the document. We can do this by extending the flib/manifests/external_fact.pp file. Open the file in the text editor, and add lines 3 to 6 to it, as shown in the following screenshot:

```
external_fact.pp  ✕
1 notify { "My external fact value is ${::text_fact}": }
2
3 define yaml_fact_processor {
4   notify { "YAML list item: ${name}": }
5 }
6
7 yaml_fact_processor { $::yaml_fact: }
```

Puppet ▾   Tab Width: 2 ▾   Ln 7, Col 38   INS

Let's take a look at the `external_fact.pp` file more closely, starting from line 3.

- Line 3 begins with the defined type `yaml_fact_processor`.

- Line 4 creates a notify resource, which prints one screen text **YAML** list item: `$name`. The `$name` variable is a reference to the Puppet resource name.

- Line 5 closes the defined type.

- Line 7 calls the custom **defined type** named `yaml_fact_processor`. The name of the type is a reference to the `yaml_fact` list, which we just specified in the YAML document.

  Using the list as a name of the defined type results in a type to be called once per each list item.

  As our `yaml_fact` list has three list items, we can expect that type to be called three times.

Once you have added lines 3 to 6 to the `external_fact.pp` file, save it, and then apply the manifest to the following commands:

```
# cd /media/sf_learning
# puppet apply flib/manifests/external_fact.pp
```

After Puppet has applied the manifest, you will see the following events reported on the screen:

When analyzing the output in detail, we can see that the `yaml_fact` list got processed by the defined type `yaml_facts_processor` that produced the following messages:

Notice: YAML list item: Hello world

Notice: YAML list item: Hello Puppet

Notice: YAML list item: Hello handsome!

We now should have a fairly good understanding of how to create external facts that return a string as well as more advanced data types, such as a list. Next, we will take a look at how to write custom facts in the Ruby programming language.

Writing custom facts in Ruby

External facts are easy to create, but they are difficult to distribute. To make custom facts available for all the nodes in the cluster, it is better to bundle them with Puppet modules. In order to do this, custom facts must be written in the Ruby programming language.

Custom facts in the modules reside in the `lib/facter` directory, and the filename must contain the name of the fact followed by the `.rb` file extension. For example, if we create a custom fact called `certname`, we will store the implementation in the `lib/facter/certname.rb` file.

Custom facts written in Ruby always include the following two statements:

```
Facter.add('fact_name') do
```

This is a method that adds a new custom fact to the inventory.

```
setcode do
```

This begins with a block of code that defines the action to be executed when a fact is called.

Creating a custom fact to extract certname

Every Puppet Agent that connects to the Puppet Master must have a unique **certname**. At the moment, there is no good visibility on what certnames have been configured on the nodes in our cluster. Let's write a fact that extracts the certname from the `/etc/puppetlabs/puppet/puppet.conf` file.

We already know how the certname can be queried using the `puppet config print certname` command. This is a good starting point as we now only have to work on how to create a fact that executes this command.

Here is an example of `certname.rb` that executes the command:

```
1 # Fact: certname
2 #
3 # Purpose: extract node's certname from file /etc/puppetlabs/puppet/puppet.conf
4 #
5 Facter.add('certname') do
6   setcode do
7     %x[/usr/local/bin/puppet config print certname].chomp
8   end
9 end
```

Let's take a look at the preceding code snippet in detail:

- Lines 1 to 4 are the comment lines that provide information on what fact does.

- Line 5 calls the add method from the Facter module. The add method creates a new fact called certname.

- Line 6 defines the setcode statement that marks the beginning of the code block that contains the implementation of the fact.

- Line 7 defines the command that we want the facter to execute.

  To make Ruby execute a command-line command, we simply wrap it inside the statement that begins with %x[and the statement is terminated with the] character.

  To remove special characters from the command output, such as a new line character \n, we will add the .chomp method at the end of the execute statement.

- Line 8 closes the setcode block.

- Line 9 closes the Facter.add block.

So that's how the certname fact is created. Let's test it by creating a new class called flib::certname that calls the certname fact and prints out the value. Here's the content of the class:

- Line 1 begins with the ftlib::certname class
- Line 2 creates a notify resource that prints out the value returned by the certname fact
- Line 3 closes the class

Then, we can test-drive the result by executing the following two commands on the Web Server node:

```
# cd /media/sf_learning/
# puppet apply --modulepath= . -e 'include flib::certname'
```

On a successful Puppet run, the following events are reported:

To demonstrate how custom facts are easy to distribute, we can try running the same command on the Nagios Server host (virtual machine name: puppet-agent-nagios).

Launch the Nagios Server virtual machine, and log in with the username `root` and password `puppet`. Then, run the preceding two commands on the host, and this time, you will see the message `My certname is nagios.development.vm` appears in the Puppet report.

Distributing certname records across the cluster

We now have a certname fact that prints out the certname of the node that calls the fact. It's nice but not very useful in terms of functionality. Let's build a practical application that populates the `certname` fact as a Puppet's `host` resource from one node to another.

Host resources are stored in the `/etc/hosts` file. Currently, the file contains two records: the first host record is for the Puppet Master that was created by the `bootstrap::agent` class. The second record is a default record that points to the local host.

Here is a screenshot showing the current content of the `/etc/hosts` file on the Nagios Server. The output is produced by the `cat /etc/hosts` command.

We begin the process by extending the `flib::certname` class, and add a host resource that is exported (with the @@ -prefix) and a line that imports host resources from PuppetDB. Here is an example of how the class will look like once we have added host resource statements:

```puppet
1 class flib::certname {
2   notify { "My certname is ${::certname}": }
3
4   @@host { $::certname:
5     tag => $::environment,
6     ip  => $::ipaddress_eth1;
7   }
8   Host <<| tag == $::environment |>>
9 }
```

The newly added content is found on lines 4 to 8. Let me explain what each added line does:

- Line 4 creates the exported host resource that uses the `$::certname` fact as the resource name.
- Line 5 tags the exported resource with our environment name.

- Line 6 specifies the IP address that is going to be associated with the host resources. The IP address gets its value from the built-in `ipaddress_eth1` fact.

- Line 7 closes the exported host resources.

- Line 8 specifies an import statement for the host resources. The import statement uses the `${::environment}` variable as a filter, which means that we want Puppet to collect all the exported host resources that belong to our environment.

Before we can apply the class, we need to include `class flib::certname` in the node's catalog. This can be done by editing the node definition file `manifests/site.pp`. In the following example, I've added the statement that includes `flib::certname` in each node definition block (lines 6, 11, and 18).

```
site.pp (~/learning/manifests) - gedit

   Open    ▼    Save

site.pp  ✕

 1 node /web.*\.development\.vm/ {
 2    include flib::public_key
 3    include nagios::client
 4    include webapp
 5    include nagios::check_http
 6    include flib::certname
 7 }
 8 node 'loadbalancer.development.vm' {
 9    include nagios::client
10    include loadbalancer
11    include flib::certname
12 }
13 node 'nagios.development.vm' {
14    include nagios::server
15    include nagios::client
16    include nagios::resources
17    include nagios::purge
18    include flib::certname
19 }

                          Puppet ▼   Tab Width: 2 ▼      Ln 18, Col 25      INS
```

Now we are ready to apply the `flib::certname` class starting from the Nagios Server node, after which we can apply it to the Web Server node.

On the Nagios Server, run the following two commands:

```
# cd /media/sf_learning/
# puppet agent -t
```

When the Puppet run is successful, you will see the following lines appear on the screen:

```
● ● ●    puppet-agent-nagios (agent-deployed) [Running] - Oracle VM VirtualBox
[root@learning /media/sf_learning]# puppet agent -t
Warning: Local environment: "production" doesn't match server specified node env
ironment "development", switching agent to "development".
Info: Retrieving pluginfacts
Info: Retrieving plugin
Info: Loading facts
Info: Caching catalog for nagios.development.vm
Warning: The package type's allow_virtual parameter will be changing its default
 value from false to true in a future release. If you do not want to allow virtu
al packages, please explicitly set allow_virtual to false.
   (at /opt/puppet/lib/ruby/site_ruby/1.9.1/puppet/type/package.rb:430:in `block
 (3 levels) in <module:Puppet>')
Info: Applying configuration version '1436110206'
Notice: /Stage[main]/Nagios::Purge/Exec[reload-nagios]/returns: executed success
fully
Notice: My certname is nagios.development.vm
Notice: /Stage[main]/Flib::Certname/Notify[My certname is nagios.development.vm]
/message: defined 'message' as 'My certname is nagios.development.vm'
Notice: /Stage[main]/Flib::Certname/Host[nagios.development.vm]/ensure: created
Info: Computing checksum on file /etc/hosts
Notice: Finished catalog run in 1.90 seconds
[root@learning /media/sf_learning]# _



[0] 0:*                                    Quest: Begin - Progress: No Tasks.
```

Then, we can proceed to run the same two commands on the Web Server node. The command output on the Web Server will show you two new host records created: one for certname `web.learning.vm` and another one for `nagios.learning.vm`.

If the host record creation is not visible in the Puppet report, this may be due to a vast amount of changes happening during the Puppet run. To verify that the host records got created, we can run the `cat /etc/hosts` command, and this will show you two new records in the file. To verify that the records are effective, we can run a Ping command against certname `nagios.learning.vm`, and this will show that the Nagios Server replies to the ping. Here is the ping command:

```
# ping -c 1 nagios.learning.vm
```

The following screenshot shows the content of the /etc/hosts file and the results of the ping command:

```
puppet-agent (agent-deployed) [Running] - Oracle VM VirtualBox
[root@learning /media/sf_learning]# cat /etc/hosts
# HEADER: This file was autogenerated at 2015-07-05 15:34:11 +0000
# HEADER: by puppet.  While it can still be managed manually, it
# HEADER: is definitely not recommended.
192.168.56.2     learning.puppetlabs.vm  puppetmaster
::1       localhost       localhost.localdomain localhost6 localhost6.localdomain
192.168.56.11   web.development.vm
192.168.56.12   nagios.development.vm
[root@learning /media/sf_learning]# ping -c 1 nagios.development.vm
PING nagios.development.vm (192.168.56.12) 56(84) bytes of data.
64 bytes from nagios.development.vm (192.168.56.12): icmp_seq=1 ttl=64 time=0.2
4 ms

--- nagios.development.vm ping statistics ---
1 packets transmitted, 1 received, 0% packet loss, time 0ms
rtt min/avg/max/mdev = 0.234/0.234/0.234/0.000 ms
[root@learning /media/sf_learning]# _
```

Summary

We have come to the end of this chapter in which we learned how we can extend Puppet beyond the built-in functionality. The first half of the chapter was dedicated to custom functions, and we discussed how to use create a custom function called read_file that we used to distribute the public SSH key from the Puppet Master to the Web Server node.

The latter half of the chapter focused on external facts and custom facts. We learned how easy it is to create external facts and make them return structured data types. We also experimented with custom facts that are written in Ruby and used this fact to populate the certname from one host to another.

I hope you found the topics that we covered very useful. In the next chapter, we'll take a look at the features and functionality of the Puppet Enterprise Console.

9
The Puppet Enterprise Console

So far, our journey has been quite focused on how to manage Puppet from the command line. However, I do acknowledge that not everybody is a great fan of the command-line interfaces. I regularly have encounters with people who find the command-line interfaces confusing and difficult to grasp. The Puppet Enterprise Console aims to solve this problem by offering a sleek and easy-to-use web interface to fully manage the Puppet environments and nodes, without having to log on to the Puppet agent nodes to trigger the Puppet runs.

The Puppet Enterprise Console is a web-based management console that runs on the Puppet Master node. It comes bundled with the Puppet Enterprise edition, which is the version this book is based on.

In this chapter, we'll focus on the following topics:

- Role-based Access Control
- Creating a user account
- Assigning roles to a user account
- Creating a node group
- Adding a node to a node group
- Using the External Node Classifier
- Trigger the Puppet runs using Live Management
- Viewing the Puppet reports
- Discovering nodes using Inventory Search

Role-based Access Control

A role defines what permissions a user account inherits. A role can be applied to a single user or a group of users. A user cannot do anything in the Puppet Enterprise Console until a role has been assigned to it.

Creating a user and assigning a role

I've a colleague called Terry who is a tester. To us colleagues, he is known as Terry the Tester. He is a genuinely nice bloke and an excellent colleague to work with. Let's imagine a scenario where Terry needs access to the Puppet Enterprise Console so that he can manage nodes in his test environment. He is not interested in managing the **Puppet Enterprise (PE)** user accounts. He just needs the ability to add nodes to the node group, trigger the Puppet runs, and access the Puppet reports via the Puppet Enterprise Console.

Creating a user account

To give Terry the appropriate level of access, we first have to create a user account for Terry and then assign it an `Operators` role .

> In case you are unable to access the PE console due to an error `Service Temporarily Unavailable`, run the following two commands on the Puppet Master to restart the PE console processes and reload the login page:
>
> **`service pe-console-services restart`**
>
> **`service pe-httpd restart`**

Let's take it step by step and create the user account now. These are the hoops to jump through:

1. Open the PE console at `https://192.168.56.2`. If the web browser warns you about the SSL certificate you can ignore the warning and continue to load the login page.

2. Log in with the username as `admin` and password as `learningpuppet`.

3. Click on the **Access Control** link and go to the **Users** page.

4. On the **Users** page, type in the name of the user in the **Full name** field. I'll call my user `Terry the Tester`, but you are free to pick which ever name you fancy.

5. Then, enter the login name in the **Login** textbox. I choose the login name `terry` (all in lowercase).

6. Finally, create the user account by clicking on the **Add local user** button on right-hand side of the page, as shown in the following screenshot:

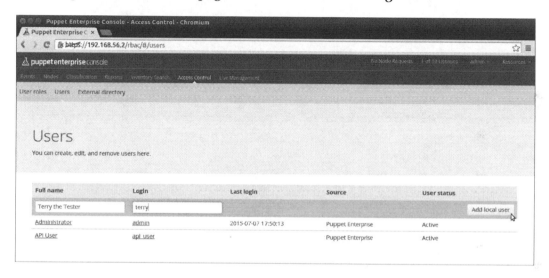

Enabling login for a user account

Terry now has an account, but he is unable to log in to the Puppet Enterprise Console because we haven't provided him with the login details. What we should do next is enable Terry's login by providing him with a link to the page where he can set his own password using the following steps:

1. On the **Users** page, click on the account that you just created.

2. Click on the **Generate password reset** link in the top right-hand corner of the page.

3. In the **Password reset link** dialog box, copy the the address by pressing *Ctrl + C* as shown in the following screenshot:

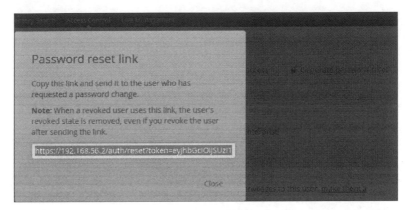

4. Open a new browser window, and paste the address into the address bar by pressing *Ctrl + V*, then hit *Enter* to open the **Reset Password** page.

5. Enter the account password (minimum 6 characters) twice, and then click on the **Reset Password** button as shown in the following screenshot.

   For Terry, I set a password `tester`, all in lowercase:

Terry's login has now been enabled, but he cannot do anything in the Puppet Enterprise Console until we grant him rights by assigning a role to the account.

Assigning a role to the account

The Puppet Enterprise Console has three built-in roles for the user accounts:

- Administrators: A role that allows full access to the Puppet Enterprise console
- Operators: A role that enables the management of node groups and signs the Puppet Agent certificates
- Viewers: A role that provides read-only access to the Puppet Enterprise console

As Terry requires access that enables him to manage the nodes in the test environment, the most appropriate role for his account is the **Operator** role. Perform the following steps to assign an **Operator** role for Terry's account:

1. Open the **Access Control** tab, and click on the **Operator** role.
2. Click on the **Select a user to add to the role** option, and select the account `Terry the Tester` from the drop-down list.
3. Click on the **Add user** button.
4. Click on the **Commit 1 change** button in the bottom right-hand corner of the page as shown in the following screenshot:

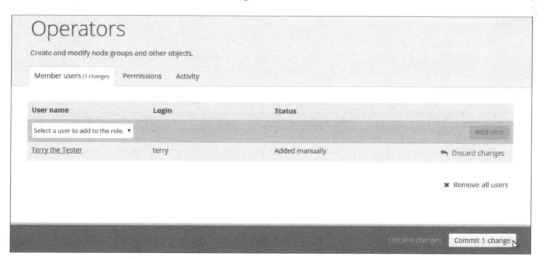

Now we can try logging in as `Terry the Tester`. We first have to terminate our current admin session by clicking on the **admin** link in the top right-hand corner of the page and choosing **Log out** as shown in the following screenshot:

When the **Log in** form loads up, log on using the username `terry` and the password `tester`.

Creating a node group

`Terry the tester` needs a test environment for testing the Puppet modules that we developed in the `development` environment. A logical name for the test environment is `test`. You may recall that in *Chapter 6, Scaling Up the Puppet Environment*, we created a node group called `development` and associated it with the environment named `development`. We'll repeat this process and create a `test` node group, which we'll also associate with the `development` environment.

Why would we associate a `test` node group with the `development` environment? Shouldn't the `test` node group have its own environment called `test`?

Yes, we can do that, but then we will have to modify the `bootstrap::master` class, and add a `file` resource to it that creates an `/etc/puppetlabs/puppet/environments/test` directory for the new environment. This will give us a new environment with no Puppet modules in it.

As Terry's goal is to test the Puppet modules that we developed in the `development` environment, the best option is to create a new node group and associate the node group with the `development` environment. This way the nodes in Terry's node group will automatically get access to all the modules that are stored in the `/etc/puppetlabs/puppet/environments/development` directory on the Puppet Master.

You can think of the Puppet environment as a repository for Puppet modules. An environment can be shared by one or more node groups, but a node group can belong to only one environment at the time.

Perform the following steps to create a node group called `test`:

1. Click on the **Classification** link to open the list of node groups.
2. In the **Node group name** field, type in **test**.
3. In the **Parent name** field, select `default` from the drop-down menu.
4. In the **Environment** field, select `development` as the environment of the node group.
5. Then, click on the **Add group** button to create a node group **test** as shown in the following screenshot:

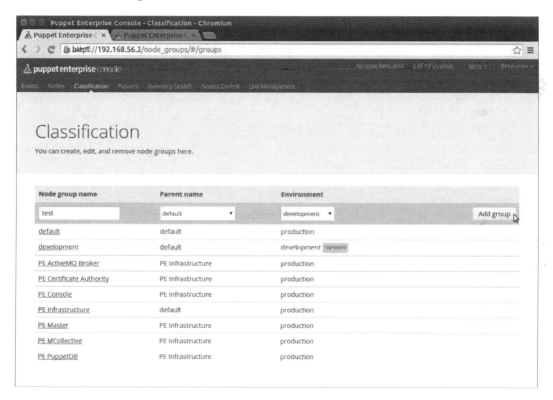

Signing the Puppet agent's certificate

We now have the `test` node group, but the node group doesn't have any nodes in it yet. We'll add a web server to this node group, but before we can do this, we must bootstrap the node and sign its certificate.

In the list of virtual machines in the VirtualBox Manager, you can find a machine called puppet-agent-web-clone. Select the virtual machine, and restore it back to the snapshot called Base Image. By restoring the snapshot, we ensure that all the configurations that have been applied to the node get deleted. We discussed the snapshot restore in *Chapter 3*, *My First Puppet Module* in detail. Perform the following steps to restore a snapshot:

1. Select the puppet-agent-web-clone virtual machine in the VirtualBox Manager.

2. Click on the **Snapshots** button.

3. Select the Base Image snapshot.

4. Click on the **Restore Snapshot** button.

Start this virtual machine, and log on using the username root and password puppet. Then, run the following commands to bootstrap the machine:

```
# cd /media/sf_learning
# puppet apply --modulepath . -e 'class { 'bootstrap': role => 'webclone' }'
# puppet agent -t
```

When the commands complete successfully, you will see the following events reported on the console:

When we return to the Puppet Enterprise Console and refresh the page, we can see one new node request waiting in for certificate signing.

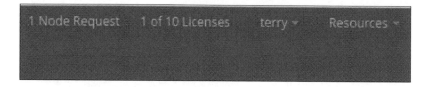

Click on the **1 Node Request** link, and then click on the **Accept** button to sign the certificate for the `web-clone.development.vm` agent as shown in the following screenshot:

A message node request accepted will be displayed once the certificate is successfully signed.

Adding a node to the node group

So the certificate of the `web-clone.development.vm` agent has been signed, and now we can add this node to the `test` node group. In the Puppet Enterprise Console, click on the **Classification** link in the navigation bar, and open the `test` node group, which you can find at the bottom of the node group list:

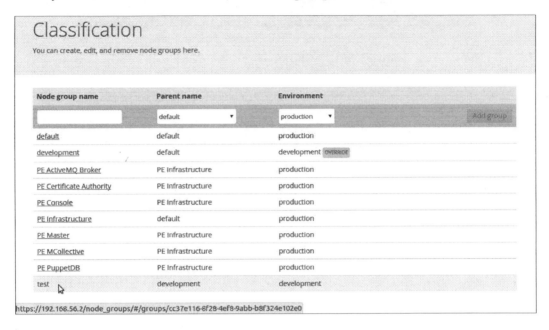

Once inside the `test` node group view, we need to tweak the node group's metadata. Click on the link that says `Edit node group metadata` at the top of the node group view. Then, check the `Override all other environments` checkbox under the **Environment** section. Lastly, confirm the change by clicking on the **Commit 1 change** button as shown in the following screenshot:

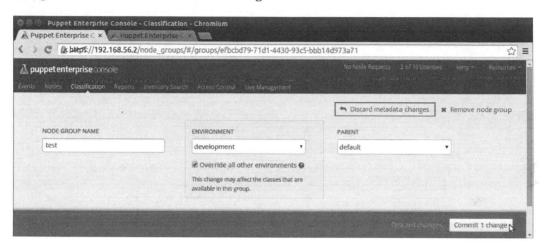

Once the metadata has been saved, and we are back in the node group view, find a text box with the title **Certname** and type in the `certname`, `web-clone.development.vm`. When we start typing the `certname`, a drop-down menu will appear, and you can select the `web-clone.development.vm` `certname` by clicking on it.

Then, click on the **Pin node** button and commit changes by clicking on the button that says **Commit 1 change**:

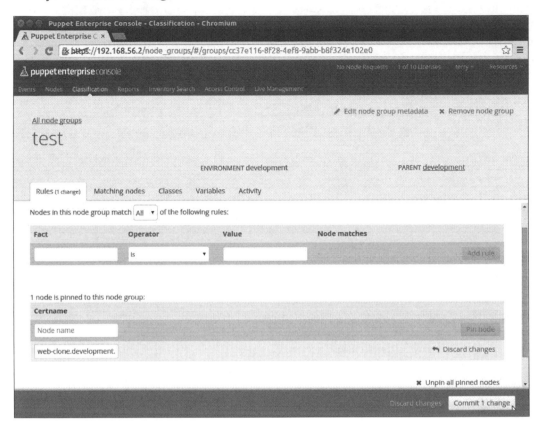

Well done! The `web-clone.development.vm` node has now been successfully added to the `test` node group. Next, we'll take a look how to classify nodes in the Puppet Enterprise Console.

Classifying nodes in the Puppet Enterprise Console

In *Chapter 6, Scaling Up the Puppet Environment*, we discussed node classification. We associated the Puppet classes with the Puppet agents in the `manifests/site.pp` file, which resides in the root of the Puppet modules directory `/media/sf_learning` on the Puppet Master node.

Puppet Enterprise offers an alternative way to classify nodes. Instead of creating the site.pp file that contains the **node** definitions, we can associate classes with the Puppet agents via the Puppet Enterprise Console.

In the Puppet terminology, this is called an **External Node Classifier (ENC)** for short. For users like Terry the Tester who likes to manage nodes via the Puppet Enterprise Console instead of editing the site.pp file, the External Node Classifier is a very useful feature. Let's take a look at how we can associate the webapp class with the test node group:

1. In the test node group view, click on the **Classes** link.
2. In the **Add new class** textbox, type in webapp.
3. A drop-down menu will appear, which confirms that the webapp class is available for the nodes in the test node group.
4. Click on the **Add class** button to add the webapp class in the catalogue.
5. Then, click on the **Commit 1 change** button to confirm the action, as shown in the following screenshot:

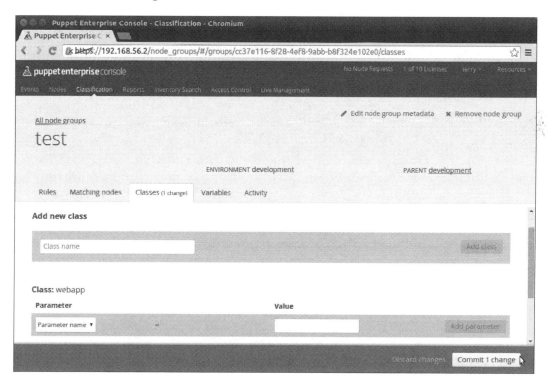

Moving the site.pp file temporarily out of the modulepath

In Puppet Enterprise, the `manifests/site.pp` node definition file takes priority over the ENC. This means that when the `manifests/site.pp` file is found in the environment directory (`/media/sf_learning/development`), the Puppet Master will classify the nodes against the file instead of ENC. If the file is moved outside the environment directory on the Puppet Master, the nodes are classified against ENC.

To allow the `webapp` class to be applied to the newly added `web-clone.development.vm` node, the `site.pp` file has to be temporarily moved to a location outside the environment directory.

The easiest way to move the file is to move it on the host computer using the preferred file manager program. The environment directory on my computer is `/home/jussi/learning`, mapped as a `/media/sf_learning` shared folder on the Puppet Master. Inside the `/home/jussi/learning` directory, I've a `manifests` subdirectory that contains the `site.pp` file. To move the file, right-click on the `site.pp` file and select **Cut**. Then, go back to root of the `/home/jussi` home directory and right-click again and choose **Paste**.

After the **Cut** and **Paste** operations are completed, the `site.pp` file will appear under `/home/jussi`, and the `/home/jussi/learning/manifests` directory is left empty. Then, we are ready to try out the classification against ENC.

Using Live Management

Live Management is a powerful Puppet Enterprise component that enables you to send commands to the Puppet Agent nodes. Perhaps the most useful feature of Live Management is called runonce, which enables you to trigger the Puppet run on a group of Puppet agents without having to log on to nodes and initiating the `puppet agent -t` command from the command line. Let's take a look at how to access **Live Management** and trigger the Puppet run on the `web-clone.development.vm` node.

The link to **Live Management** is located in the navigation menu at the top of the Puppet Enterprise Console view as shown in the following screenshot:

When you click on the **Live Management** menu, Puppet Enterprise automatically runs a node discovery task, and displays the results in the **Node Filter Results** view on the left-hand side of the page. On my machine, Puppet Enterprise discovered two nodes: `learning.puppetlabs.vm` and `web-clone.development.vm`.

> If the Puppet Enterprise discovers more nodes, such as the `loadbalancer.development.vm`, `web.development.vm`, and `nagios.development.vm` nodes, this means that Puppet remembers these nodes from earlier deployments. Because I've had to revert Puppet Enterprise to older snapshots a few times during the course of the writing, as a result, Puppet has lost knowledge of the other nodes.

The following screenshot shows the **Node Filter Results** view that contains two nodes. By default, Puppet marks all the nodes as selected. Puppet will perform the Live Management action on all the nodes in the selected state. To deselect a node, simply click on the node name. If we want to perform an action on the `web-clone.development.vm` node only, then we must deselect all the other nodes, such as the `learning.puppetlabs.vm` node, which is the `certname` of the Puppet Master node as shown in the following screenshot:

![Screenshot of the Live Management panel. Node filter with 'Wildcards allowed' text, an empty input box, an 'Advanced search' toggle, 'Filter' and 'Reset filter' buttons. Node Filter Results shows "1 of 2 nodes selected (50.0%)", "Select all · Select none", and two node entries: learning.puppetlabs.vm and web-clone.development.vm (highlighted).]

Next, we will trigger a Puppet run on the `web-clone.development.vm` node using the **runonce** function. **runonce** is found under the **Control Puppet** menu in the **Live Management** view as shown in the following screenshot:

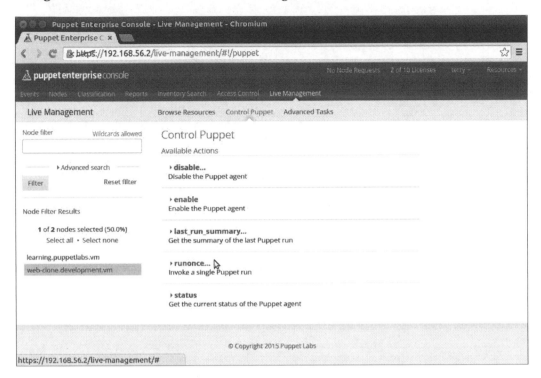

When you click on the **runonce** option, an empty form opens up. This form can be used to narrow down the scope of the nodes, where the Puppet run is performed. For example, we can set the **Environment** as `development` to run Puppet only on nodes that belong to that environment.

As we have already selected the `web-clone.development.vm` node in the **Node Filter Results** view, we can leave all the form fields empty. Simply click on the **Run** button at the bottom of the form, and this will trigger a Puppet run on the **web-clone.development.vm** node as shown in the following screenshot:.

▾ runonce...
Invoke a single Puppet run

Force   Will force a run immediately else subject to default splay time

Puppet Master Address and port of the Puppet Master in server:port format

Tags   Restrict the Puppet run to a comma list of tags

No-op   Do a Puppet dry run

Splay   Sleep for a period before initiating the run

Splay Limit   Maximum amount of time to sleep before run

Environment   Which Puppet environment to run

Run   Cancel

* denotes a required field.

Once you click on **Run**, the message **Signalled the running Puppet Daemon** is displayed as shown in the following screenshot:

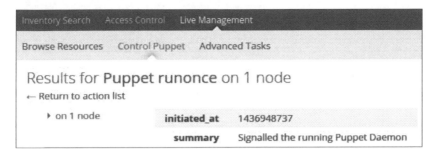

That's awesome, isn't it?

How does Terry the Tester know that the Puppet run was in fact triggered on the web-clone.development.vm node, and more importantly, what were the results of the Puppet run? We will find this out in reports, which we will take a look at in the next section.

Accessing reports via the Puppet Enterprise Console

Our Puppet deployments in the earlier chapters were triggered by executing the puppet agent -t command on the command line. The output of the command gave us a break down of the events that happened during the Puppet run in detail. The **runonce** task that we just performed on the web-clone.development.vm node didn't provide us any feedback on whether the Puppet run was a success or a failure. That's because the Puppet run triggered by **Live Management** is done using the component called Mcollective (we briefly discussed Mcollective in *Chapter 6, Scaling Up the Puppet Environment*). Mcollective is a message queue application. Although it is very good at passing messages from the Puppet Master to a large number of Puppet agents, it is not very good at reporting back on the activities that happen on the Puppet agent after the message has been processed from the message queue.

Puppet Enterprise provides a solution for this issue by exposing the Puppet reports in the Puppet Enterprise Console. At the end of every Puppet run, the Puppet agent sends a report to the Puppet Master, and the Puppet Master stores the report in PuppetDB. We can access these reports from the **Reports** menu.

When you click on the **Reports** link in the main navigation menu, the following view opens up, showing a list of reports from the various Puppet agents:

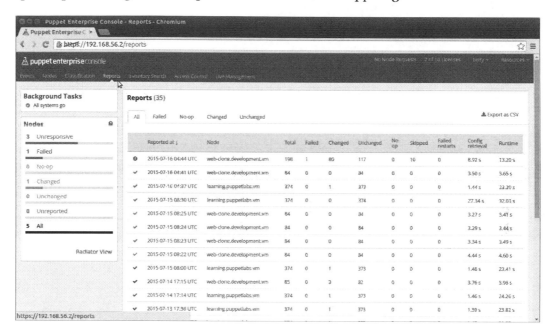

The first report, the one at top of the list, is from the `web-clone.development.vm` node. As you can see from the preceding screenshot, the most recent Puppet run on the `web-clone.development.vm` node has not been successful. The Puppet run failure is indicated by a round red symbol. We will take a look at the reason behind the failure in a moment, but let's quickly check what other useful information is available in the **Reports** overview:

- The first column (that doesn't have a heading) shows the status of the Puppet run:

  ○ The round red symbol with an exclamation mark inside it indicates a failure during the Puppet run

  ○ The green tick means that the Puppet run was successful, and Puppet made no changes to the node during the run

  ○ The blue tick also symbolizes a successful run, but during the run Puppet made a configuration change to the node

- The **Reported at** column shows the date and time of the Puppet run.

- The **Node** column shows the `certname` of the node that the report was produced on.

- The **Total** column shows the number of resources that Puppet manages on the node.

- The **Failed** column tells the number of failures that occurred during the Puppet run. In the preceding list, the `web-clone.development.vm` node had one failure during the latest Puppet run.

- The **Changed** column indicates how many resources were changed during the Puppet run. The most recent Puppet run on the `web-clone.development.vm` node changed 80 resources on the system.

- The **Unchanged** column shows how many resources were processed on the node but not changed during the Puppet run.

- The **No-op** column typically contains a zero value unless Puppet was run in dry run mode using the `--noop` flag.

- The **Skipped** column is useful as it tells you the number of resources that Puppet didn't change because of a failure in a resource that other resources depend on.

- The **Failed restarts** column indicates the number `Service` resources that Puppet failed to manage.

- The **Config retrieval** column shows you the time it took to compile the catalogue for the Puppet agent from the Puppet Master.

- The **Runtime** columns tells you the duration of the Puppet run on the agent.

We can access the report by clicking on the timestamp link, which is found in the **Reported at** column. If you click on the `certname` link in the **Node** column instead, (by accident, which happens to me very often) then that takes us to the **Nodes** view. Now click on the timestamp link, and a new page will open up that contains three tabs: **Metrics**, **Log**, and **Events** as shown in the following screenshot:

I personally don't find the **Metrics** tab very useful. It just shows the performance-related data. Unless we have hundreds of nodes in our environment, performance should not become an issue.

What I'm more interested in at the moment is to find out the cause of the failure during the Puppet run. This information is available in the **Log** view. When I click on the **Log** link, a familiar looking information shows up. The **Log** view contains events similar to what Puppet reports when we run the `puppet agent -t` command on the command line. There is one difference in how the information is displayed in the **Log** view compared to the command-line view; the **Log** view conveniently displays the log entries in the order of **errors**, **warnings**, and **notices**. On the command line, log entries are displayed in real time so that the resources get processed. This sometimes leads to a situation, where an error goes unnoticed if it occurs at an early stage of the Puppet run, and the Puppet report is too long to fit on the screen. In the **Log** view, this doesn't easily happen, as errors are always reported at the top of the view.

The following screenshot shows the **Log** view for the `web-clone.development.vm` node. All 81 events (80 changes + 1 failure) in the report are too many to fit nicely in to a single screenshot, therefore I've cropped the image to show the top three events only:

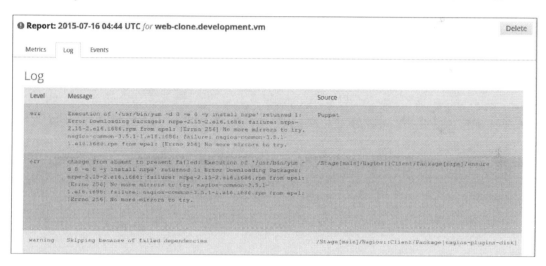

Although Puppet reported one failure, we can see two error messages. This is because the errors were reported from two different sources: `Puppet` and `/Stage[main]/Nagios::Client/Package[nrpe]/ensure`.

Anyways the error messages are related as they have common fingerprints. Puppet failed to install the `nagios-common-3.5.1-1.el6.i686.rpm` package, which is the so-called **RPM (Red Hat Package Manager)** dependency for the `nrpe` package. We've declared the `nrpe` package in the `nagios::client` class. Errors like these typically occur when the RPM dependency package, such as `nagios-common-3.5.1-1.el6.i686.rpm`, is removed from the third-party RPM package repository, which our deployment depends on.

The third message that is reported at the **warning** level is related to Puppet's failure to install the `nrpe` package. A warning is given because the `nagios-plugins-disk` package, which is also declared in the `nagios::client` class, requires the `nrpe` package that failed to install due to errors at the top of the **Log** view.

Although Terry's test failed, it should be considered a success because he has identified a problem in the deployment process.

So what information should be included in Terry's test report? Terry should definitely include the preceding error messages in the report. He can either copy and paste the errors into his report, or perhaps even better, copy the URL (`https://192.168.56.2/reports/35#!events-tab`) from the address bar and include the URL in the report. When a developer studies the report and clicks on the URL, it takes him directly to the Puppet Enterprise Console's **Reports** view.

 Please note that the URL specified previously may be different in your development environment.

Another valuable piece of information that should be included in the report is found on the **Events** tab. When you click on the **Events** link, the following information is shown:

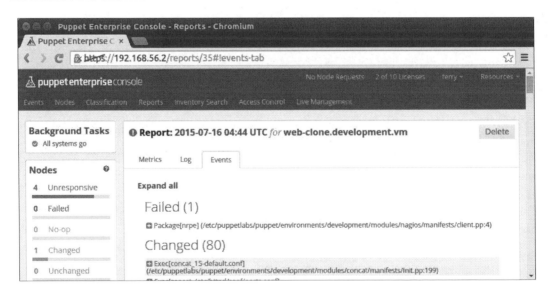

The **Events** view displays a list of Puppet manifest files and resources that were processed during the Puppet run. At the top of the view, in the **Failed** category, we can see that the file that caused the failure during the Puppet run was `/etc/puppetlabs/puppet/environments/development/modules/nagios/manifests/client.pp`. This is the file path of the Puppet Master. The four notation at the end of the filename indicates the line number in the `client.pp` file that caused the failure.

This information should also be included in Terry's test report as it clearly indicates which manifest file developers should take a look at first before they start to analyze the issue.

`Terry the Tester` has once again demonstrated how to add business value by uncovering a bug in the deployment process. Well done, Terry! As a reward, I'll buy you a bag of crisps on pay day.

Searching nodes with Inventory Search

In large Puppet environments, it may become difficult to find reports for a particular node. Puppet Enterprise provides a handy feature that enables you to find nodes quickly by searching nodes based on their fact values. This feature is called **Inventory Search**.

We can access **Inventory Search** from the main navigation menu. When you click on the **Inventory Search** link, a new form is loaded that contains two text fields and a drop-down menu. The first text field defines the **Fact Name**, and the second text field defines the **Fact Value**. In between the text fields, there is a drop-down menu for comparison operator.

To search for a node that has a fact `certname` of value `web-clone.development.vm`, we can do it with the following query:

- Fact name: `certname`
- Comparison operator: **is**
- Fact value: `web-clone.development.vm`

Once you have set the query parameters, click on the **Search** button to begin the query.

When a node or nodes matching the search pattern is found, the details are displayed below the **Search** button.

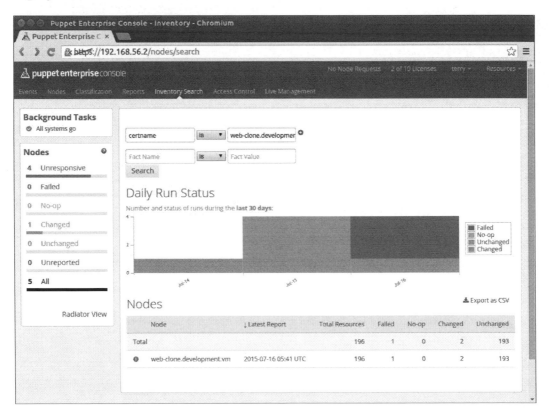

Once we have searched for one fact value, another set of text fields appear that enable us to narrow down our search by defining another fact value to include or exclude from the search.

When you click on the `web-clone.development.vm` node at the bottom of the page, this takes you to the node details view that shows a variety of information about the node. For example, in the **Member Groups** category, we can see the **node groups** node belong to and which classes are associated with the node as shown in the following screenshot:

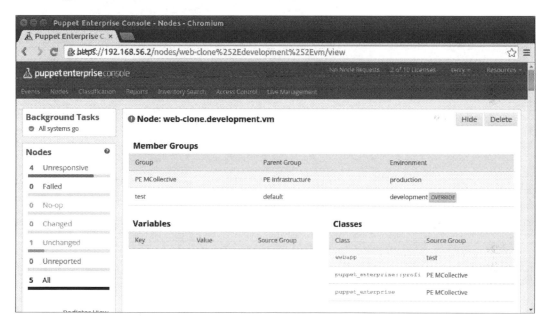

When you scroll down the page, we can find the **Daily Run Status** chart, showing the Puppet run statistics during the past 30 days accompanied by the performance chart that reveals the time elapsed for each of the last 30 Puppet runs:

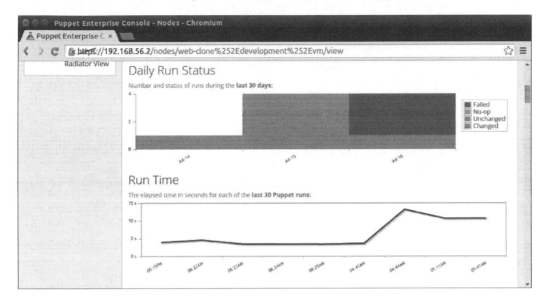

At the bottom of the page, we'll find a section called **Inventory** that lists all the facts and fact values that belong to the node:

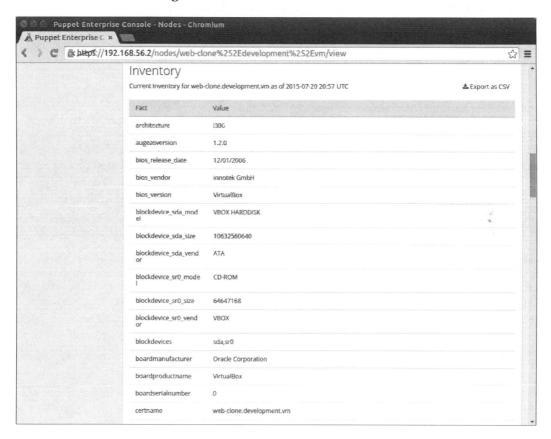

Summary

In this chapter, we covered the most important parts of the Puppet Enterprise Console. We discussed Role-based Access Control, which effectively means creating a user account and assigning a role to it. We learned how to create a user account for `Terry the Tester` and assign it an `Operator` role.

Following the Role-based Access Control, we discussed how to create a node group and add a node to it. Once the node was added to the node group, we learned how to use the External Node Classifier to associate the classes with the node group.

We also experimented with Live Management, which allows us to initiate the Puppet runs on the Puppet agent nodes via the Puppet Enterprise Console, without having to log on to the agent node and run Puppet from the command line.

The results of the Puppet run are validated in the **Reports** view, which provides us with a break down of resources that were changed by Puppet in detail.

Finally, we looked at how to use Inventory Search to discover nodes based on fact values.

I hope you enjoyed our exploration of the Puppet Enterprise Console. In the next (and final) chapter, we will take a step back to the basics and learn how to troubleshoot and overcome issues that most commonly occur with Puppet.

10
Troubleshooting Puppet

Over a period of time, Puppet environments tend to expand in terms of the size of nodes as well as in the number of Puppet manifests and modules. When environments grow, so does their complexity. Although Puppet is a tool that is designed to manage large environments, it does occasionally get its pants in twist for various reasons. I'd say most issues are caused by us, humans. A small number of issues are caused by the weird *behavior by design* that some people refer to as *bugs*. Issues often relate to the recent changes in the Puppet code or changes in the environment configuration. When problems arise, it is important to be able to identify the source of the problem before we can try to fix it.

In this final chapter, we'll take a look at how to identify the common issues in Puppet and how we to tackle them.

In this chapter, we will cover the following topics:

- Node definition issues
- Diagnosing duplicate declaration errors
- Getting around dependency cycle errors
- Troubleshooting missing resources
- How to rectify certificate errors
- Finding help online

Prerequisites

Before we start looking at particular error situations, I'll switch over to use the GNOME Terminal program and connect to the virtual machines via SSH instead of connecting using the VirtualBox console. The Terminal program enables me to adjust the background color to white, which makes error messages more visible and easier to read.

In this chapter, you can continue using the VirtualBox console, but in case you wish to make the same adjustments, then here is a breakdown of the changes that I'm going to do before we continue:

1. Open the **GNOME Terminal**.
2. Click on the **Edit** menu, and select **Profile Preferences**.
3. In the **Profile Preferences** menu, go to the **Colours** tab.
4. Uncheck the box that says **Use colours from system theme**.
5. Click on the **Background Colour** tab, and select the white color.
6. Click on the **Select** button to apply the changes:

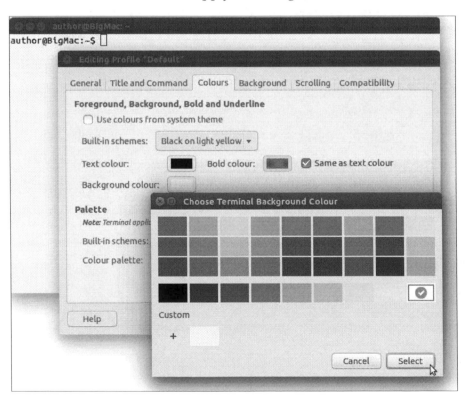

To log on to the virtual machine via SSH, we have to look up the IP address of the virtual machine. The IP address can be found by running the `hostname-I` command on the host. This command returns two IP addresses from which we choose the second IP address. On the `web-clone.development.vm` host, the second IP address is `192.168.56.11`.

Once the IP address is known to us, we can initiate the SSH session by running the `ssh root@192.168.56.11` command, where the address `192.168.56.11` is the IP address of the `web-clone.development.vm` host.

```
author@BigMac: ~
author@BigMac:~$ ssh root@192.168.56.11
root@192.168.56.11's password: █
```

When prompted, type in the password `puppet`, and press *Enter* to open the SSH session on the virtual machine.

To confirm that the SSH session was successfully established to the correct virtual machine, in this case, `web-clone.development.vm`, run the `facter -p certname` command (the option `-p` to load custom facts). The command returns the certname of the Puppet agent, as shown in the following screenshot:

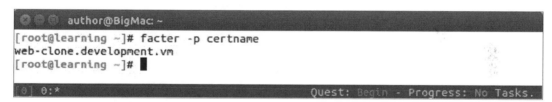

```
author@BigMac: ~
[root@learning ~]# facter -p certname
web-clone.development.vm
[root@learning ~]# █
0:*                                    Quest: Begin - Progress: No Tasks.
```

Now we have done all the necessary adjustments to the Terminal, and we can start troubleshooting Puppet.

Troubleshooting node definition issues

When we add new nodes to the Puppet environment, it is likely that the node definition file `manifests/site.pp` does not contain any records that match the certname of the new node that connects to the Puppet Master.

This results in an error `'Could not find default node or by name with` `'web-clone.development.vm,...'` during the Puppet run, as shown in the following screenshot:

```
author@BigMac: ~
[root@learning ~]# puppet agent -t
Warning: Local environment: "production" doesn't match server specified node env
ironment "development", switching agent to "development".
Info: Retrieving pluginfacts
Info: Retrieving plugin
Info: Loading facts
Error: Could not retrieve catalog from remote server: Error 400 on SERVER: Could
 not find default node or by name with 'web-clone.development.vm, web-clone.deve
lopment, web-clone, learning.puppetlabs.vm, learning.puppetlabs, learning' on no
de web-clone.development.vm
Warning: Not using cache on failed catalog
Error: Could not retrieve catalog; skipping run
[root@learning ~]# 
[0] 0:*                                          Quest: Begin - Progress: No Tasks.
```

The preceding error scenario can be easily reproduced. You may recall that, in *Chapter 9*, *The Puppet Enterprise Console*, we moved the `manifests/site.pp` file outside the modulepath directory to enable node classification against the External Node Classifier.

When we copy the `site.pp` file from the root of the home directory back to the `manifests` directory in the modulepath directory (on my machine, the modulepath directory is `/home/jussi/learning`), we effectively disable look-ups against the External Node Classifier, and the nodes are classified against `manifests/site.pp` instead.

Using **Cut** and **Paste** in the File Manager program, move the `site.pp` file back to the `learning/manifests` directory. Then, run `puppet agent -t` on the `web-clone.development.vm` host, and the preceding error message will be displayed on the screen.

 To successfully reproduce this node definition error, the Puppet Master virtual machine must be up and running.

The preceding error message tells us that the Puppet Master could not find the node definition for the certname, `web-clone.development.vm`. This is because the `learning/manifests/site.pp` file does not contain a record of the host.

There are a couple of ways to workaround this problem. The first and the most obvious option is to add a node definition to `web-clone.development.vm` in `learning/manifests/site.pp` using the following:

```
node 'web-clone.development.vm' {
}
```

Making the node definition file and ENC work concurrently

The second (and a better) option is to add a node definition to the `default` node in `site.pp`. The node definition of the `default` node works as a fallback option for every host that doesn't have an explicit node definition block in the `site.pp` file. The good news is that the `default` node definition enables the `site.pp` file and the External Node Classifier to work in parallel. We can have certain classes defined in `site.pp` and other classes defined in the External Node Classifier.

Let's try this out by creating two new classes called `flib::site` and `flib::enc`, which are stored in the `flib` module. The classes are very simple. They include only one `notify` resource each. Here is the content of the `flib::site` class that is stored in the `flib/manifests/site.pp` file:

When you apply the class to the node, Puppet will output a `Hello from site.pp` string.

The second `flib::enc` class looks very similar to the `flib::site` class, except that it outputs a `Hello from ENC` string. Add the following content to the `flib/manifests/enc.pp` file and save it:

Next, we need to add the node definition to the `default` node in the `manifests/site.pp` file and include the `flib::site` class in it. It doesn't matter where the node definition block is added to, at the top or at the bottom of the file. I'll add it to the top of the `manifests/init.pp` file just to make the screenshot look a bit more compact. This is how the first three lines of the `site.pp` file will look after adding the default node definition that includes the `flib::site` class:

Next, we will change the node classification in the ENC by removing the `webapp` class that is currently associated with the **test** node group, and replacing it with the `flib::enc` class.

We covered node classification in *Chapter 9, The Puppet Enterprise Console*, but as a reminder, here is a quick break-down of steps on how to replace the `webapp` class with the `flib::enc` class in the Puppet Enterprise Console:

1. Log on to `https://192.168.56.2` using the username `terry` and password `tester`.

2. Click on the **Classification** menu, and open the **test** node group, which is found at the bottom of the node group list.

3. Go to the **Classes** tab.

4. In the **Add new class** section, type in the class name `flib::enc`, and then click on the **Add class** button.

5. Do not click on **Commit 2 changes** yet.

6. In the **Class: webapp** section, click on the **Remove this class** link to remove the `webapp` class from the ENC.

7. Now commit both the changes by clicking on the **Commit 2 changes** button at the bottom of the page:

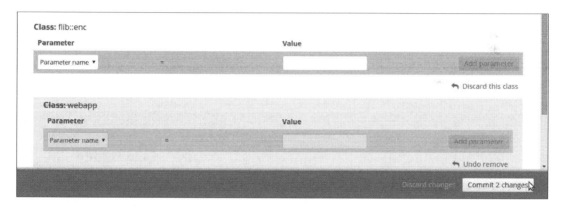

Voilà! We are now ready to test the node classification against the **ENC** and `manifests/site.pp`:

1. Log on to the `web-clone.development.vm` node as the user `root` using the password `puppet`.

2. Run the `puppet agent -t` command.

On a successful Puppet run, the classification error `'Could not find default node or by name with 'web-clone.development.vm,...'` is no longer reported. Instead, two notify events are reported. One notify event says `'Hello from site.pp'` and the other event says `'Hello from ENC'`.

```
author@BigMac: ~
[root@learning ~]# puppet agent -t
Warning: Local environment: "production" doesn't match server specified node env
ironment "development", switching agent to "development".
Info: Retrieving pluginfacts
Info: Retrieving plugin
Info: Loading facts
Info: Caching catalog for web-clone.development.vm
Info: Applying configuration version '1437830799'
Notice: Hello from site.pp
Notice: /Stage[main]/Flib::Site/Notify[Hello from site.pp]/message: defined 'mes
sage' as 'Hello from site.pp'
Notice: Hello from ENC
Notice: /Stage[main]/Flib::Enc/Notify[Hello from ENC]/message: defined 'message'
 as 'Hello from ENC'
Notice: Finished catalog run in 0.50 seconds
[root@learning ~]#
[0] 0:*                                    Quest: Begin - Progress: No Tasks.
```

Very good! We managed to rectify the node classification error; and, during the process, we improved the classification by introducing the `default` node classification that enables you to classify the node against `site.pp` and ENC.

Diagnosing duplicate declaration errors

Every Puppet resource must have a unique resource name. If a resource is declared twice in the catalog, Puppet displays the following error: `'Error: Could not retrieve catalog from remote server: Error 400 on SERVER: Duplicate declaration: Resource[name]...'`.

Duplicate declaration errors are very common and sometimes quite difficult to rectify. If it is a simple case, where a resource is declared twice with the same name, Puppet rightfully reports which files, and the line numbers in files, are clashing. Here is an example of a scenario when a `notify` resource has been declared twice with the same name:

```
author@BigMac: ~
[root@learning ~]# puppet agent -t
Warning: Local environment: "production" doesn't match server specified node en
vironment "development", switching agent to "development".
Info: Retrieving pluginfacts
Info: Retrieving plugin
Info: Loading facts
Error: Could not retrieve catalog from remote server: Error 400 on SERVER: Dupl
icate declaration: Notify[Hello from ENC] is already declared in file /etc/pupp
etlabs/puppet/environments/development/modules/flib/manifests/site.pp:2; cannot
 redeclare at /etc/puppetlabs/puppet/environments/development/modules/flib/mani
fests/enc.pp:2 on node web-clone.development.vm
Warning: Not using cache on failed catalog
Error: Could not retrieve catalog; skipping run
[root@learning ~]# █
```

Let's take a look at the preceding error message in detail, and see what information we can find from it so that it helps us troubleshoot the problem.

There are three important elements squeezed into one very long error message. The first piece of information that is relevant to us is `Error 400 on SERVER: Duplicate declaration: Notify[Hello from ENC] is already declared.....`

Here, Puppet specifies the name of the resource that is declared twice with the same name. The clashing resource in this case is a type of notify, and the name of the resource is `Hello from ENC`. You can probably guess which file is involved, as we just declared this resource in the previous paragraph. However, let's take a look at the other two important pieces of information that will help us troubleshoot the problem.

The following two messages are embedded in the error message that shows you the files (and the line numbers in the files) that are causing the clash:

`...in file /etc/puppetlabs/puppet/environments/development/modules/flib/manifests/site.pp:2`

`cannot redeclare at /etc/puppetlabs/puppet/environments/development/modules/flib/manifests/enc.pp:2`

So, according to Puppet, line 2 in the `flib/manifests/site.pp` file clashes with line 2 in the `flib/manifests/enc.pp` file. This is indicated by Puppet with `filename:linenumber` in the `enc.pp:2` syntax.

Let's open these files in a text editor and compare the file content:

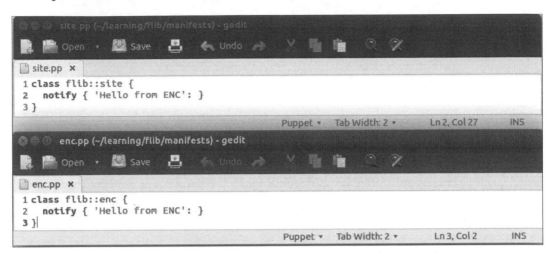

Oh dear! What have I done? For "quality and training" purposes, I've copied the notify resource from `flib/manifests/enc.pp` and pasted it into `flib/manifests/site.pp`, and this is causing the error. To eliminate the error, we need to change the name of the notify resource in `flib/manifests/site.pp` by making the name unique, such as `Hello from site.pp`.

In this instance, Puppet was very clear with its error reporting, and this helped us identify the issue quickly. However, there are scenarios when the duplicate declaration error message is not very helpful. Here is an example of an error message when a duplicate declaration error occurs in the custom defined type:

```
author@BigMac: ~
[root@learning ~]# puppet agent -t
Warning: Local environment: "production" doesn't match server specified node en
vironment "development", switching agent to "development".
Info: Retrieving pluginfacts
Info: Retrieving plugin
Info: Loading facts
Error: Could not retrieve catalog from remote server: Error 400 on SERVER: Dupl
icate declaration: Notify[message-of-day] is already declared in file /etc/pupp
etlabs/puppet/environments/development/modules/flib/manifests/hello.pp:4; canno
t redeclare at /etc/puppetlabs/puppet/environments/development/modules/flib/man
ifests/hello.pp:4 on node web-clone.development.vm
Warning: Not using cache on failed catalog
Error: Could not retrieve catalog; skipping run
[root@learning ~]# ▓
  0:*                                    Quest: Begin - Progress: No Tasks.
```

The preceding error message tells us that we have a duplicate declaration of the `Notify[message-of-day]` resource on line 4 in the `flib/manifests/hello.pp` file. Note that the error message contains the same filename and line number twice.

```
hello.pp  ×
1 define flib::hello ($message) {
2   notify { 'message-of-day':
3     message => $message;
4   }
5 }
```

Let's examine the `hello.pp` file and see what resources it contains.

- Line 1 declares a custom defined type called `flib::hello`. `flib::hello` accepts an input parameter called `$message`.

- Line 2 creates a `notify` resource called `'message-of-day'`.

- Line 3 defines the `message` attribute for the `notify` resource. The `message` attribute gets its value from the `$message` input parameter.

- Line 4 closes the `notify` resource. This is the line that the Puppet error message complained about.

- Line 5 terminates the custom define type block.

We can clearly see that the `flib::hello` type contains only one `notify` resource. So why is Puppet reporting a duplicate declaration error in this file? The answer is found in the file that calls the `flib::hello` type. The type is called in the `flib/manifests/site.pp` file. This is how the file looks since it was last edited.

```
site.pp (~/learning/flib/manifests) - gedit
hello.pp  ×   site.pp  ×
1 class flib::site {
2   flib::hello { 'message1': message => 'Defined types are great' }
3   flib::hello { 'message2': message => 'Duplicate declaration messages are not nice' }
4 }
```

The `flib/manifests/site.pp` file looks very different since the last time we had a look at it. The `notify` resource that used to be in the file has been replaced with two calls to the custom defined type `flib::hello`. The names of the `message1` and `message2` types are unique and also both of them have unique `message` attribute values. So why is Puppet not liking this? The reason is that we call the `flib::hello` type twice, but the type includes a `notify` resource that has a static name `message-of-day` (see line 2 in `flib/manifests/hello.pp`). If we call the `flib::hello` type just once, Puppet will not complain, but because it's called twice, we effectively declare the notify resource `message-of-day` twice, and this is what Puppet is trying to tell us. It just doesn't say it very clearly.

So what's the remedy? Let's take a look at a couple of available options.

Using the defined() function to avoid duplicate declarations

The `defined()` function is a handy way to prevent Puppet from declaring the same resource twice. Typically, the `defined()` function is used in conjunction with the **if** clause. The `if` clause and other conditional statements were discussed in *Chapter 6, Scaling Up the Puppet Environment*.

To check whether the `notify` resource `["message-of-day"]` has already been declared, we can do it using the following syntax:

```
if ! defined(Notify["message-of-day"]) {
# declare the the notify resource if not already declared
}
```

The exclamation mark (!) between the `if` and `defined` keywords negates the `if` statement. To express this in a natural language, instead of saying `if defined`, we can use `defined`.

Here is a new version of the `flib::hello` type that uses the `defined()` function:

```
1 define flib::hello ($message) {
2   if ! defined(Notify["message-of-day"]) {
3     notify { "message-of-day":
4       message => $message;
5     }
6   }
7 }|
```

The content of the `flib/manifests/hello.pp` file is the same as before, except that it now includes the `if ! defined(Notify["message-of-day"]) {` statement on line 2, and the `if` statement is terminated with closing curly braces (`}`) on line 6.

Now we can try running Puppet on `web-clone.development.vm`, and see how the new `flib::hello` type behaves:

```
author@BigMac: ~
[root@learning ~]# puppet agent -t
Warning: Local environment: "production" doesn't match server specified node en
vironment "development", switching agent to "development".
Info: Retrieving pluginfacts
Info: Retrieving plugin
Info: Loading facts
Info: Caching catalog for web-clone.development.vm
Info: Applying configuration version '1437842061'
Notice: Defined types are great
Notice: /Stage[main]/Flib::Site/Flib::Hello[message1]/Notify[message-of-day]/me
ssage: defined 'message' as 'Defined types are great'
Notice: Hello from ENC
Notice: /Stage[main]/Flib::Enc/Notify[Hello from ENC]/message: defined 'message
' as 'Hello from ENC'
Notice: Finished catalog run in 0.49 seconds
[root@learning ~]#
0:*                                          Quest: Begin - Progress: No Tasks.
```

As you can see, the `defined()` function helped us eliminate the duplicate declaration error, and we can see that `message1` prints out `'Defined types are great'`. Ideally, we want `flib::hello` to print out the messages of every call that we make to the type. At the moment, it only prints out one message and all the consecutive calls are ignored.

Using the $name variable in custom types

Puppet has its so-called reserved variables, which are built-in to Puppet. One of these reserved variables is called `$name`. This variable is a reference to the name of the resource, which we will define at the time when a resource is declared.

For example, in `flib/manifests/site.pp`, we have declared a resource `flib::hello` with the `message1` name. Here is how the resource is declared:

```
flib::hello { 'message1': message => 'Defined types are great' }
```

In the `flib::hello` type, any reference to the `$name` variable will resolve a value of `message1`. This variable is extremely useful when we want to ensure that each and every resource in the custom defined type has a unique name.

To ensure that each `notify` resource in the `flib::hello` type has a unique name, we simply add the `$name` variable to the name of the `notify` resource. Instead of using the static string `message-of-day` as the name of the `notify` resource, we include the `$name` variable as part of the name.

Here is an example of the `flib::hello` type after the `$name` variable has been added to two places. The notify resource in the `defined()` function on line 2 has the `$name` variable added to the name of the resource. Also, the `$name` variable has been added to the name of the notify resource on line 3:

```puppet
1 define flib::hello ($message) {
2   if ! defined(Notify["message-of-day-${name}"]) {
3     notify { "message-of-day-${name}":
4       message => $message;
5     }
6   }
7 }
```

Now we can rerun Puppet on `web-clone.development.vm`. The expected outcome is to see both the messages, `'Defined types are great'` and `'Duplicate declaration messages are not nice'`, appear in the Puppet report:

```
[root@learning ~]# puppet agent -t
Warning: Local environment: "production" doesn't match server specified node en
vironment "development", switching agent to "development".
Info: Retrieving pluginfacts
Info: Retrieving plugin
Info: Loading facts
Info: Caching catalog for web-clone.development.vm
Info: Applying configuration version '1437843417'
Notice: Defined types are great
Notice: /Stage[main]/Flib::Site/Flib::Hello[message1]/Notify[message-of-day-mes
sage1]/message: defined 'message' as 'Defined types are great'
Notice: Duplicate declaration messages are not nice
Notice: /Stage[main]/Flib::Site/Flib::Hello[message2]/Notify[message-of-day-mes
sage2]/message: defined 'message' as 'Duplicate declaration messages are not ni
ce'
Notice: Hello from ENC
Notice: /Stage[main]/Flib::Enc/Notify[Hello from ENC]/message: defined 'message
' as 'Hello from ENC'
Notice: Finished catalog run in 0.47 seconds
[root@learning ~]#
```

Getting around dependency cycle errors

Resource ordering is a very handy feature of Puppet, but it can sometimes cause so much grey hair. A resource order can be set in the resource with attributes, such as `before`, `require`, `notify`, and `subscribe`. Or to set the order outside the resource, we can use the arrow notations such as `->` (a hyphen and a greater than sign for `before`) or `~>` (a tilde and a greater than sign for `notify`).

When a resource ordering chain grows long, and we have dependencies between resources that are declared in various different manifest files and modules, the chance of a dependency cycle error increases.

Here is an example of an error message that is caused by the dependency cycle error:

```
author@BigMac: ~
[root@learning ~]# puppet agent -t
Warning: Local environment: "production" doesn't match server specified node environment "
development", switching agent to "development".
Info: Retrieving pluginfacts
Info: Retrieving plugin
Info: Loading facts
Info: Caching catalog for web-clone.development.vm
Info: Applying configuration version '1437915950'
Error: Could not apply complete catalog: Found 1 dependency cycle:
(Exec[/tmp/script1.sh] => Exec[/tmp/script2.sh] => Exec[/tmp/script1.sh])
Cycle graph written to /var/opt/lib/pe-puppet/state/graphs/cycles.dot.
Notice: Finished catalog run in 0.20 seconds
[root@learning ~]#
[0] 0:*                                          Quest: Begin - Progress: No Tasks.
```

The preceding error message shows a list of dependent resources separated by `=>` sign. The message shows that the `Exec['/tmp/script1.sh']` resource depends on the `Exec['/tmp/script2.sh']` resource, which has a dependency back to the `Exec['/tmp/script1.sh']` resource.

Let's take a look at the `flib/manifests/site.pp` manifest that is causing the dependency cycle error:

```
site.pp ×
1 class flib::site {
2    $script='#!/bin/bash
3            /bin/echo $0 says hello'
4
5    file { ['/tmp/script1.sh', '/tmp/script2.sh']:
6    |    content => $script,
7      mode    => '0755',
8    }
9    ->
10   exec { '/tmp/script1.sh':
11     logoutput => true,
12   }
13   ->
14   exec { '/tmp/script2.sh':
15     logoutput => true,
16     before    => Exec['/tmp/script1.sh'],
17   }
18 }
```

The contents of the `flib/manifests/site.pp` file have been replaced once again. It currently contains a variable named `$script`, a `file` resource, and two `exec` resources. Resources are ordered with an arrow notation.

Let's examine the file line by line, and see if we can find the reason for the dependency cycle error:

- Line 1 begins with the `flib::site` class.
- Line 2 defines a $script variable, which is a multiline variable that extends to line 3:

  The first line of the variable defines the `/bin/bash` program that is used as an interpreter to the script.

  The second line defines the `/bin/echo $0 says hello` command, which is executed when the script is run.

  The `$0` is a Bash (Bourne Again Shell) variable that refers to the name of the script itself. For example, if the script is saved in `/tmp/script1.sh`, the resulting output of the `/bin/echo $0 says hello` command is `/tmp/script1.sh says hello`.

- Line 5 defines the two `file` resources: `/tmp/script1.sh` and `/tmp/script2.sh`.

- Line 6 sets the content of the file based on the value of the $script variable, which is the multiline variable defined on lines 2 and 3.

  Line 7 defines the mode attribute, which is used to set the file access rights. Value 0755 makes the files executable, which is required for the scripts to work.

- Line 8 closes the file resources.

- Line 9 contains the arrow notation -> that sets the order, where the file resource must be processed before the exec resource on line 9.

- Line 10 creates an exec resource that executes the /tmp/script1.sh script, which the file resource creates on lines 5 to 8. The exec resource contains the logoutput => true attribute, which enables the output of the script to be visible in the Puppet report.

- Line 13 contains another arrow sign ->, and it sets the order so that the first exec resource (line 10) is processed before the second exec resource (line 11).

- Line 14 creates another exec resource, which is similar to the first one. This exec resource runs the /tmp/script2.sh script.

  In addition to the logoutput => true attribute, this resource contains a before => Exec['/tmp/script1.sh'] attribute.

  The before attribute causes the dependency cycle error because it conflicts with the arrow chain sign on line 13.

Now we can try removing the before => Exec['/tmp/script1.sh'] attribute from line 1, and then save the flib/manifests/site.pp file. Now the file should have the following content:

```
site.pp  x
1 class flib::site {
2   $script='#!/bin/bash
3         /bin/echo $0 says hello'
4
5   file { ['/tmp/script1.sh', '/tmp/script2.sh']:
6       content => $script,
7     mode    => '0755',
8   }
9   ->
10  exec { '/tmp/script1.sh':
11    logoutput => true,
12  }
13  ->
14  exec { '/tmp/script2.sh':
15    logoutput => true,
16  }
17 }
```

Puppet ▾   Tab Width: 2 ▾   Ln 15, Col 23   INS

Then, rerun Puppet, and the dependency cycle error will no longer appear. The following screenshot shows the resource ordering in action. In the beginning of the Puppet run, it creates two script files, and then executes scripts in the order of /tmp/script1.sh and /tmp/script2.sh:

```
author@BigMac: ~
[root@learning ~]# puppet agent -t
Warning: Local environment: "production" doesn't match server specified node environment "
development", switching agent to "development".
Info: Retrieving pluginfacts
Info: Retrieving plugin
Info: Loading facts
Info: Caching catalog for web-clone.development.vm
Info: Applying configuration version '1437920685'
Notice: /Stage[main]/Flib::Site/File[/tmp/script1.sh]/ensure: defined content as '{md5}527
ea37c11bec1e3fdcad3a394c4d083'
Notice: /Stage[main]/Flib::Site/File[/tmp/script2.sh]/ensure: defined content as '{md5}527
ea37c11bec1e3fdcad3a394c4d083'
Notice: /Stage[main]/Flib::Site/Exec[/tmp/script1.sh]/returns: /tmp/script1.sh says hello
Notice: /Stage[main]/Flib::Site/Exec[/tmp/script1.sh]/returns: executed successfully
Notice: /Stage[main]/Flib::Site/Exec[/tmp/script2.sh]/returns: /tmp/script2.sh says hello
Notice: /Stage[main]/Flib::Site/Exec[/tmp/script2.sh]/returns: executed successfully
Notice: Hello from ENC
Notice: /Stage[main]/Flib::Enc/Notify[Hello from ENC]/message: defined 'message' as 'Hello
 from ENC'
Notice: Finished catalog run in 0.66 seconds
[root@learning ~]#
 0:*                                              Quest: Begin - Progress: No Tasks.
```

So what type of ordering should we use, an arrow notation or the ordering attributes? In my opinion, both are useful. An arrow notation is shorter and simpler, and I typically use it to set the processing order for the resources that are created in the manifest. Just like we did in the flib/manifests/site.pp manifest.

Ordering with attributes (before, require, and so on) is useful when we want to depend on resources that are defined in other modules. Although an arrow notation can be used to order resources across modules, I prefer to use ordering attributes for cross-module dependency. For example, the Apache module defines a service resource for the httpd service. My local module defines a file resource, /etc/httpd/conf/httpd.conf. If I want the httpd service from the Apache module to restart every time the /etc/httpd/conf/httpd.conf file changes, I'd simply set the dependency with the notify attribute in the following way:

```
file { '/etc/httpd/conf/httpd.conf':
  content => '1.2.3',
  notify  => Service['httpd'];
}
```

Troubleshooting missing resources

When dealing with files and templates in Puppet modules, it sometimes happens that the reference to a file or a template in the manifest is not correct. Despite many years of puppeteering, I am still struggling to remember whether to use the `content` or `source` attribute. If I have to use the `source` attribute, what is the format of the URL that I must use when pointing to the file in a module? Did it have two or three forward slashes? I give up and use copy and paste instead!

Diagnosing template errors

The problem with copy and paste is that it often contains references to different Puppet modules. This results in Puppet reporting errors saying that Puppet cannot find a particular resource. Here is an example of the error when Puppet fails to find a template that is referenced in the `flib/manifests/site.pp` file:

```
author@BigMac: ~
[root@learning ~]# puppet agent -t
Warning: Local environment: "production" doesn't match server specified node environment "
development", switching agent to "development".
Info: Retrieving pluginfacts
Info: Retrieving plugin
Info: Loading facts
Error: Could not retrieve catalog from remote server: Error 400 on SERVER: Could not find
template 'webapp/timestamp.erb' at /etc/puppetlabs/puppet/environments/development/modules
/flib/manifests/site.pp:4 on node web-clone.development.vm
Warning: Not using cache on failed catalog
Error: Could not retrieve catalog; skipping run
[root@learning ~]#
 0:*                                            Quest: Begin - Progress: No Tasks.
```

The message `Error 400 on SERVER: Could not find template 'webapp/ timestamp.erb' at /etc/puppetlabs/puppet/environments/development/ modules/flib/manifests/site.pp:4` is quite self-explanatory. Puppet cannot find a `timestamp.erb` template in the `webapp` module.

Let's take a look at the content of the `flib/manifests/site.pp` file:

```
site.pp  ×
1 class flib::site {
2   file { '/tmp/timestamp':
3     content => template("webapp/timestamp.erb"),
4   }
5 }
                              Puppet ▾   Tab Width: 2 ▾   Ln 5, Col 2   INS
```

The `template` function used in the `content` attribute on line 4 contains a reference to the `webapp` module. This is because I copied the attribute from line 7 to the `webapp/manifests/init.pp` file. To fix the problem, I can either replace the string `webapp` with the string `flib`. Or a better solution is to replace the string `webapp` with the `${module_name}` variable. The `${module_name}` variable is one of the reserved Puppet variables, which refers to the name of the module that references the variable.

To workaround the problem, I'll replace the string `webapp` with the `${module_name}` variable. After making these changes, the `flib/manifests/site.pp` file has the following content. Only line 4 has changes since we last looked at the file:

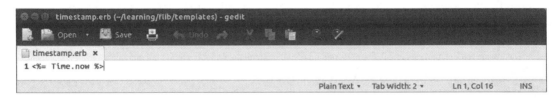

```
1 class flib::site {
2   file { '/tmp/timestamp':
3     content => template("${module_name}/timestamp.erb"),
4   }
5 }
```

Before we attempt to run Puppet again, we should also make sure that the `timestamp.erb` file is present in the `flib` module under the `templates` directory. As the templates directory doesn't exist yet, we must first create it. This can be done on the virtual machine by running the following command:

```
# mkdir -p /media/sf_learning/flib/templates
```

Then, we must create the `flib/templates/timestamp.erb` file. The content of the template is not very meaningful for the purpose of the exercise. Here is a simple template that generates the current timestamp in the Ruby programming language:

```
1 <%= Time.now %>
```

Once the file is saved as `flib/templates/timestamp.erb`, we can try running Puppet on the `web-clone.development.vm` node:

```
author@BigMac: ~
[root@learning ~]# puppet agent -t
Warning: Local environment: "production" doesn't match server specified node environment "
development", switching agent to "development".
Info: Retrieving pluginfacts
Info: Retrieving plugin
Info: Loading facts
Info: Caching catalog for web-clone.development.vm
Info: Applying configuration version '1437927333'
Notice: /Stage[main]/Flib::Site/File[/tmp/timestamp]/ensure: defined content as '{md5}03e5
c57251bbcf9771bf6d0210ba6190'
Notice: Hello from ENC
Notice: /Stage[main]/Flib::Enc/Notify[Hello from ENC]/message: defined 'message' as 'Hello
 from ENC'
Notice: Finished catalog run in 0.50 seconds
[root@learning ~]#
0:*                                          Quest: Begin - Progress: No Tasks.
```

Diagnosing missing source file errors

The error message related to the missing template was fairly clear. However, when dealing with static files that are stored in the files directory, the error that Puppet throws when a file is not found is slightly more confusing.

Here is an example when Puppet fails to find a `flib/files/static_file` file:

```
author@BigMac: ~
[root@learning ~]# puppet agent -t
Warning: Local environment: "production" doesn't match server specified node environment "development", swi
tching agent to "development".
Info: Retrieving pluginfacts
Info: Retrieving plugin
Info: Loading facts
Info: Caching catalog for web-clone.development.vm
Info: Applying configuration version '1437929350'
Error: /Stage[main]/Flib::Site/File[/tmp/static_file]: Could not evaluate: Could not retrieve information f
rom environment development source(s) puppet:///modules/flib/static_file
Notice: Hello from ENC
Notice: /Stage[main]/Flib::Enc/Notify[Hello from ENC]/message: defined 'message' as 'Hello from ENC'
Notice: Finished catalog run in 0.47 seconds
[root@learning ~]#
0:*                                          Quest: Begin - Progress: No Tasks.
```

When you see the error message `Could not evaluate: Could not retrieve information from environment...` for the first time, it is not obvious that the error is caused by the missing `flib/files/static_file` file. The best clue is that `puppet:///modules/flib/static_file` is at the end of the error message. This indicates that Puppet is trying to retrieve a `static_file` file from the `flib` module. The same URL is referenced by the `source` attribute on line 4 in the `flib/manifests/site.pp` file:

```
1 class flib::site {
2   file { '/tmp/static_file':
3     source => "puppet:///modules/${module_name}/static_file",
4   }
5 }
```

To fix this genuine problem, we first need to create a `flib/files` directory, and add the `static_file` file to it. This can be done by running the following two commands on the `web-clone.development.vm` node:

```
# mkdir -p /media/sf_learning/flib/files
```

```
# touch /media/sf_learning/flib/files/static_file
```

Here is a screenshot that shows when the commands are run in the **Terminal**, and Puppet is run after the command:

```
[root@learning ~]# mkdir -p /media/sf_learning/flib/files
[root@learning ~]# touch /media/sf_learning/flib/files/static_file
[root@learning ~]# puppet agent -t
Warning: Local environment: "production" doesn't match server specified node environment "development", swi
tching agent to "development".
Info: Retrieving pluginfacts
Info: Retrieving plugin
Info: Loading facts
Info: Caching catalog for web-clone.development.vm
Info: Applying configuration version '1437930784'
Notice: /Stage[main]/Flib::Site/File[/tmp/static_file]/ensure: defined content as '{md5}d41d8cd98f00b204e98
00998ecf8427e'
Notice: Hello from ENC
Notice: /Stage[main]/Flib::Enc/Notify[Hello from ENC]/message: defined 'message' as 'Hello from ENC'
Notice: Finished catalog run in 0.52 seconds
[root@learning ~]#
```

Rectifying certificate errors

Every Puppet Agent has its own unique certificate. In *Chapter 9*, *The Puppet Enterprise Console*, we learned how to sign a certificate for the `web-clone.development.vm` node. Certificates are the lifelines for the Puppet agent, which means that, without a working certificate, the Puppet agent can't get any service from the Puppet Master. Certificates do sometimes stop working and this causes problems with deployments. Certificates may stop working, for example, if a node is deleted on the Puppet Master. Let's take a look at certificate errors and how to fix them.

Listing certificates on the Puppet Master

Certificates are stored on the Puppet Master. Certificates can be listed on the command line by running the following command on the Puppet Master node:

```
# puppet cert list --all
```

The command outputs a list of certificates that are currently active:

The second certificate from the bottom belongs to the `web-clone.development.vm` node. Let's delete the certificate on the Puppet Master, and see how this affects the Agent's functionality.

Removing Puppet certificate on Puppet Master

A Puppet certificate can be deleted by running the `puppet cert clean <certname>` command on the Puppet Master. To remove the certificate of the `web-clone.development.vm` node, we run the following command:

```
# puppet cert clean web-clone.development.vm
```

This command will produce the following output:

```
author@BigMac: ~
[root@learning ~]# puppet cert clean web-clone.development.vm
Notice: Revoked certificate with serial 11
Notice: Removing file Puppet::SSL::Certificate web-clone.development.vm at '/etc/puppetlabs/puppet/ssl/ca/
signed/web-clone.development.vm.pem'
Notice: Removing file Puppet::SSL::Certificate web-clone.development.vm at '/etc/puppetlabs/puppet/ssl/cer
ts/web-clone.development.vm.pem'
[root@learning ~]#
0:*                                                          Quest: Begin - Progress: No Tasks.
```

If you rerun the `puppet cert list --all` command, you will notice that the certificate for the `web-clone.development.vm` node has disappeared from the certificate list.

Before we jump on to the Puppet Agent node, we have one more command to be run on the Puppet Master that makes the certificate removal effective. In Puppet Enterprise 3.7, the certificate removal doesn't become effective until we restart the `pe-puppetserver` process.

Here is the command to restart the `pe-puppetserver` process Puppet Enterprise 3.7:

```
# service pe-puppetserver restart
```

When the process is successfully restarted, the following events are reported on the console:

```
author@BigMac: ~
[root@learning ~]# service pe-puppetserver restart
Stopping pe-puppetserver:                            [  OK  ]
Starting pe-puppetserver:                            [  OK  ]
[root@learning ~]#
0:*                                                          Quest: Begin - Progress: No Tasks.
```

Now let's take a look at what impact the certificate removal had on the
`web-clone.development.vm` node. When you log on to the node and run the
`puppet agent -t` command, the following stack of errors is displayed:

```
author@BigMac: ~
[root@learning ~]# puppet agent -t
Warning: Unable to fetch my node definition, but the agent run will continue:
Warning: SSL_connect SYSCALL returned=5 errno=0 state=unknown state
Info: Retrieving pluginfacts
Error: /File[/var/opt/lib/pe-puppet/facts.d]: Failed to generate additional resources using 'eval_generate'
: SSL_connect SYSCALL returned=5 errno=0 state=unknown state
Error: /File[/var/opt/lib/pe-puppet/facts.d]: Could not evaluate: Could not retrieve file metadata for pupp
et://learning.puppetlabs.vm/pluginfacts: SSL_connect SYSCALL returned=5 errno=0 state=unknown state
Wrapped exception:
SSL_connect SYSCALL returned=5 errno=0 state=unknown state
Info: Retrieving plugin
Error: /File[/var/opt/lib/pe-puppet/lib]: Failed to generate additional resources using 'eval_generate': SS
L_connect SYSCALL returned=5 errno=0 state=unknown state
Error: /File[/var/opt/lib/pe-puppet/lib]: Could not evaluate: Could not retrieve file metadata for puppet:/
/learning.puppetlabs.vm/plugins: SSL_connect SYSCALL returned=5 errno=0 state=unknown state
Wrapped exception:
SSL_connect SYSCALL returned=5 errno=0 state=unknown state
Info: Loading facts
Error: Could not retrieve catalog from remote server: SSL_connect SYSCALL returned=5 errno=0 state=unknown
state
Warning: Not using cache on failed catalog
Error: Could not retrieve catalog; skipping run
Error: Could not send report: SSL_connect SYSCALL returned=5 errno=0 state=unknown state
[root@learning ~]#
[0] 0:*                                                        Quest: Begin · Progress: No Tasks
```

The errors are not very clear, but on several lines, we can see messages mentioning
SSL (Secure Socket Layer). SSL is the protocol that forms the basis of the Puppet
certificate management.

Regenerating Certificate Signing Request

Right now, we are in situation where the `web-clone.development.vm` node is
unable to connect to the Puppet Master. The Puppet Agent has a certificate stored
in the node, which has been removed from the Puppet Master.

To reestablish connectivity with the Puppet Master, we need to remove the old
certificate from the Puppet Agent and regenerate the Certificate Signing Request,
which we will then sign on the Puppet Master.

To delete the old certificate from the Puppet Agent, run the following command on
the `web-clone.development.vm` node:

```
# rm -rf $(puppet agent --configprint ssldir)
```

Once the old certificate has been removed, we need to establish a connection to the Puppet Master to regenerate the Certificate Signing Request. This can be done with the usual `puppet agent -t` command, which produces the following output:

```
author@BigMac: ~
[root@learning ~]# rm -rf $(puppet agent --configprint ssldir)
[root@learning ~]# puppet agent -t
Info: Creating a new SSL key for web-clone.development.vm
Info: Caching certificate for ca
Info: csr_attributes file loading from /etc/puppetlabs/puppet/csr_attributes.yaml
Info: Creating a new SSL certificate request for web-clone.development.vm
Info: Certificate Request fingerprint (SHA256): FA:74:BC:A4:87:1B:1A:43:B4:0A:22:A1:F9:16:A8:65:13:CA:88:7D
:82:49:65:89:15:03:99:69:FD:8C:F4:80
Info: Caching certificate for ca
Exiting; no certificate found and waitforcert is disabled
[root@learning ~]#
0:*                                                         Quest: Begin - Progress: No Tasks.
```

Signing a certificate on the command line

Unlike before, when we signed the certificate in the Puppet Enterprise Console, we can sign a certificate from the command line. Let's first confirm that the signing request has been received by the Puppet Master. Here is the command to do this:

```
# puppet cert list
```

The command output shows that we have one certificate from the `web-clone.development.vm` node that is waiting to be signed:

```
author@BigMac: ~
[root@learning ~]# puppet cert --list
  "web-clone.development.vm" (SHA256) FA:74:BC:A4:87:1B:1A:43:B4:0A:22:A1:F9:16:A8:65:13:CA:88:7D:82:49:65
:89:15:03:99:69:FD:8C:F4:80
[root@learning ~]#
0:*                                                         Quest: Begin - Progress: No Tasks.
```

> The `puppet cert list --all` command show all the certificates, signed or unsigned, on the Puppet Master.
>
> The `puppet cert list` command without the `--all` argument only shows the certificates that are unsigned.

Then, we can sign the certificate for the `web-clone.development.vm` node. Signing the certificate from the command line is done with the following command:

```
# puppet cert sign web-clone.development.vm
```

The output of the command confirms that the certificate was signed successfully.

```
author@BigMac: ~
[root@learning ~]# puppet cert sign web-clone.development.vm
Notice: Signed certificate request for web-clone.development.vm
Notice: Removing file Puppet::SSL::CertificateRequest web-clone.development.vm at '/etc/puppetlabs/puppet/
ssl/ca/requests/web-clone.development.vm.pem'
[root@learning ~]#
0:*                                                          Quest: Begin - Progress: No Tasks.
```

Once the certificate has been signed, we can test the connectivity between the `web-clone.development.vm` node and the Puppet Master. Testing is as simple as running the `puppet agent -t` command on the agent.

The following screenshot shows you that the Puppet Agent is able to connect to the Puppet Master, and the Agent is processing the `flib::enc` class, which is the class that has been associated with the test node group, which: is a member of.

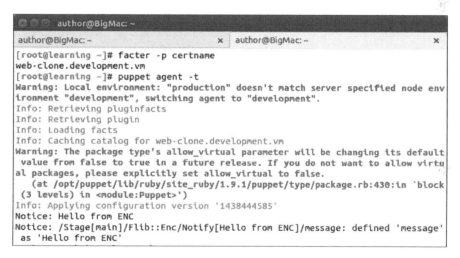

```
author@BigMac: ~
author@BigMac: ~          ×    author@BigMac: ~          ×
[root@learning ~]# facter -p certname
web-clone.development.vm
[root@learning ~]# puppet agent -t
Warning: Local environment: "production" doesn't match server specified node env
ironment "development", switching agent to "development".
Info: Retrieving pluginfacts
Info: Retrieving plugin
Info: Loading facts
Info: Caching catalog for web-clone.development.vm
Warning: The package type's allow_virtual parameter will be changing its default
 value from false to true in a future release. If you do not want to allow virtu
al packages, please explicitly set allow_virtual to false.
   (at /opt/puppet/lib/ruby/site_ruby/1.9.1/puppet/type/package.rb:430:in `block
 (3 levels) in <module:Puppet>')
Info: Applying configuration version '1438444585'
Notice: Hello from ENC
Notice: /Stage[main]/Flib::Enc/Notify[Hello from ENC]/message: defined 'message'
 as 'Hello from ENC'
```

Finding help online

We have now covered the most common issues that users have to deal with when working with Puppet. However, there are only a handful of issues that can be squeezed into a single chapter. Thankfully, we have the Internet provides us with various services, such as user groups, that enable collaboration between users.

To extend the coverage of the book beyond the printed pages, I've set up a user group in Google called **Learning Puppet - [PACKT]**, which you can find at `https://groups.google.com/forum/?hl=en#!forum/learning-puppet---packt`.

I'm hoping that this group becomes a forum for all those who read this book, and Puppet users in general, to help each other out with issues that they may encounter. In addition to this, I'd love to see some feedback signed posted on this group that will help me improve the content, in case there are any requests to make another edition of the Learning Puppet book.

At the time of writing, the group is open for public to view the posts. Creating a post is only available for group members. To become a member, send me a request via a group, and I'll approve it. Later, when there are enough members, we can vote whether to allow the public to post to this group.

Summary

We have just completed the tenth and final chapter of this book. This chapter focused on the most common issues that I, and the people I work with, regularly encounter with Puppet. We learned how to identify and rectify the node definition issues. We also looked at how to work around duplicate declaration and dependency cycle errors as well as what to do when Puppet reports resources are not found. Finally, we created a Puppet Agent certificate problem and learned how to fix it by regenerating the certificate signing request.

I hope you enjoyed this final chapter as well as the overall book.

Thanks!

Index

O

Oracle VirtualBox
downloading 4

P

packages
managing, in Puppet 35
parameterized class
about 108
calling, with parameters 108
creating 109
parameters
adding, to loadbalancer class 122-125
public key infrastructure (PKI) 200
Puppet
running, as user root 20, 21
troubleshooting 247
using, for examining current state
of resources 18, 19
**Puppet Agent, connecting with Puppet
Master**
about 137
bootstrap::agent class, applying via
bootstrap class 155, 156
bootstrap class, applying on
Puppet Master 148, 149
bootstrap::master, creating 140-142
bootstrap module, creating 137
certificate, signing on Puppet Enterprise
Console 157, 158
conditional statements 144
if statement 144-146
load balancer, bootstrapping 161
Nagios Server nodes, bootstrapping 161
node group, creating 152, 153
nodes, adding to node group 158, 159
out-of-scope variable, referencing from
Puppet template 142, 143
Puppet Agent, bootstrapping 153-155
Puppet Enterprise Console 150
Puppet Enterprise Console, logging on 151
resource processing, defining over arrow
notation 139

site.pp file, creating for node
classification 147, 148
static IP address, configuring on Puppet
Master 138
Web Server node, deploying against
Puppet Master 159-161
puppet-agent node
creating 45
package resources, purging 49, 50
snapshot of virtual machine, taking 46
virtual machine clone, creating 46-49
puppet apply command 60
Puppet class
about 57
applying 59, 60
module directory, renaming 59
resources 58
Puppet command line
versus Puppet manifests 27
Puppet configuration 31-34
PuppetDB
about 164
for exported resources 136
queries 136
reporting 136
URL, for documentation 176
PuppetDB query
about 175-177
manifests, testing on load balancer 190, 191
used, for configuring load balancer 186-190
puppetdbquery functions
custom type, creating for testing PuppetDB
queries 183-185
query_facts function 183
query_nodes function 182
using 182
**Puppet Domain Specific
Language (DSL) 21, 22**
Puppet dry run 17
Puppet Enterprise Console
503 Service Temporarily Unavailable
error 151
about 150
certificate warning message, bypassing 150
logging on 151

Thank you for buying
Learning Puppet

About Packt Publishing

Packt, pronounced 'packed', published its first book, *Mastering phpMyAdmin for Effective MySQL Management*, in April 2004, and subsequently continued to specialize in publishing highly focused books on specific technologies and solutions.

Our books and publications share the experiences of your fellow IT professionals in adapting and customizing today's systems, applications, and frameworks. Our solution-based books give you the knowledge and power to customize the software and technologies you're using to get the job done. Packt books are more specific and less general than the IT books you have seen in the past. Our unique business model allows us to bring you more focused information, giving you more of what you need to know, and less of what you don't.

Packt is a modern yet unique publishing company that focuses on producing quality, cutting-edge books for communities of developers, administrators, and newbies alike. For more information, please visit our website at www.packtpub.com.

About Packt Open Source

In 2010, Packt launched two new brands, Packt Open Source and Packt Enterprise, in order to continue its focus on specialization. This book is part of the Packt Open Source brand, home to books published on software built around open source licenses, and offering information to anybody from advanced developers to budding web designers. The Open Source brand also runs Packt's Open Source Royalty Scheme, by which Packt gives a royalty to each open source project about whose software a book is sold.

Writing for Packt

We welcome all inquiries from people who are interested in authoring. Book proposals should be sent to author@packtpub.com. If your book idea is still at an early stage and you would like to discuss it first before writing a formal book proposal, then please contact us; one of our commissioning editors will get in touch with you.

We're not just looking for published authors; if you have strong technical skills but no writing experience, our experienced editors can help you develop a writing career, or simply get some additional reward for your expertise.

Instant Puppet 3 Starter

ISBN: 978-1-78216-174-5   Paperback: 50 pages

Gain complete consistency from your systems with minimal effort using Instant Puppet 3 Starter

1. Learn something new in an Instant! A short, fast, focused guide delivering immediate results.

2. Learn how deterministic results can vastly reduce your workload.

3. Deploy Puppet Server as a Ruby-on-Rails application to handle thousands of clients.

4. Design your own module for complex configurations.

Mastering Puppet

ISBN: 978-1-78398-218-9   Paperback: 280 pages

Pull the strings of Puppet to configure enterprise-grade environments for performance optimization

1. Implement puppet in a medium to large installation.

2. Deal with issues found in larger deployments, such as scaling, and improving performance.

3. Step by step tutorial to utilize Puppet efficiently to have a fully functioning Puppet infrastructure in an enterprise- level environment.

Please check **www.PacktPub.com** for information on our titles

Made in the USA
San Bernardino, CA
03 September 2015